For Jodie Keep on desk
I hope you learn
a great deal about
the wide, wide world
from this book
        from
            Mama Ruth

HAMMOND

Family Reference

WORLD ATLAS

DOUBLEDAY & COMPANY, INC.

GARDEN CITY   NEW YORK

Contents

GAZETTEER-INDEX OF THE WORLD

ABBREVIATIONS

Aust.	—Australian	I.	—Island	Prot.	—Protectorate
Br.	—British	Is.	—Islands	Rep.	—Republic
Cond.	—Condominium	It.	—Italian or Italy	S.	—South
Den.	—Danish or Denmark	N.	—North	S. Afr.	—South Africa
E.	—East	Neth.	—Netherlands	Sp.	—Spain or Spanish
Eq. Guin.	—Equatorial Guinea	N.Z.	—New Zealand	sq. mi.	—square miles
Fr.	—France or French	pen.	—peninsula	S.S.R.	—Soviet Socialist Republic
Fr. Poly.	—French Polynesia	Port.	—Portugal or Portuguese	Trust.	—Trust Territory

U.A.R. —United Arab Republic
U.K. —United Kingdom
U.S.A. —United States of America
U.S. Adm. —U.S. Administration
U.S.S.R. —Union of Soviet Socialist Republics
W. —West

Country	Area (Square Miles)	Population	Index Ref.	Plate No.
Afars and Issas, Terr. of....	8,498	125,050	P 9	63
Afghanistan	250,000	15,751,000	A 2	48
Africa	11,682,000	311,000,000		62–65
Alabama, U.S.A.	51,609	3,462,000		104–105
Alaska, U.S.A.	586,400	253,000		106–107
Albania	11,100	1,965,000	E 5	35
Alberta, Canada	255,285	1,463,203		96–97
Algeria	919,591	12,540,000	G 5	62
American Samoa	76	29,000	K 7	56
Andaman & Nicobar Is., India	3,215	63,548	G6–7	49
Andorra	175	14,000	G 1	27
Angola (Port.)	481,351	5,293,000	K14	64
Antarctica	5,500,000			11
Antigua and Dependencies (Br.)	171	60,000	G 3	77
Antilles, Greater and Lesser	91,122	22,948,000	D 3	76
Arabia	1,200,000	14,310,000	D 5	44
Argentina	1,072,068	23,031,000		70
Arizona, U.S.A.	113,909	1,608,000		108–109
Arkansas, U.S.A.	53,104	1,960,000		110–111
Armenian S.S.R., U.S.S.R.	11,506	2,194,000	F 6	37
Ascension, I., St. Helena..	34	476	D13	64
Asia	17,032,000	1,884,695,000		42–43
Australia	2,974,581	12,000,000		58–59
Australian Capital Terr.	939	103,573	H 7	59
Austria	32,374	7,322,700	B 3	32
Azerbaidzhan S.S.R., U.S.S.R.	33,436	4,660,000	G 6	37
Azores, Portugal	893	327,480	B 4	62
Bahama Islands (Br.)	4,404	144,000	C 1	76
Bahrein	231	195,000	F 4	44
Balearic Islands, Spain	1,936	443,327	H 3	27
Barbados	166	244,962	G 4	77
Belgium	11,779	9,606,000	C 6	20
Bermuda (Br.)	21	51,000	G 2	77
Bismarck Arch., Terr. New Guinea	18,770	224,964	E 6	56
Bolivia	424,163	3,801,000	G 7	68
Botswana	219,815	593,000	L16	65
Brazil	3,286,473	85,655,000		69,71
British Columbia, Canada....	366,255	1,873,674		98–99
British Honduras	8,867	113,000	B 1	78
British Indian Ocean Terr.	58.3	2,000	L10	43
Brunei	2,226	104,000	E 4	54
Bulgaria	42,829	8,309,000	G 4	34
Burma	261,789	25,811,000	A 2	53
Burundi	10,747	3,340,000	N12	65
California, U.S.A.	158,693	18,602,000		112–113
Cambodia	69,898	6,415,000	D 4	53
Cameroon	183,568	5,493,000	J10	62
Canada	3,851,809	20,700,000		84–85
Canal Zone (U.S.A.)	553	55,600	E 3	79
Canary Islands, Spain	2,808	944,448	B 4	26
Cape of Good Hope, S. Afr.	262,079	3,936,306	L18	65

Country	Area (Square Miles)	Population	Index Ref.	Plate No.
Cape Verde Is. (Port.)	1,557	228,000	N 5	9
Caroline Is., Terr. Pacific Is.	367	52,166	E 5	56
Cayman Is. (Br.)	100	9,000	B 3	76
Celebes, Indonesia	72,986	6,288,043	G 6	55
Central African Republic ..	240,534	1,459,000	K10	63
Central America	196,928	14,628,000		78–79
Ceylon	25,332	11,741,000	E 7	49
Chad	495,753	3,500,000	K 8	63
Channel Is. (Br.)	75	115,000	E 6	17
Chatham Is., N.Z.	372	520	J10	56
Chile	292,257	8,780,000		70
China (mainland)	3,691,506	732,000,000		50–51
China (Taiwan)	13,948	13,700,000	K 7	51
Christmas I., Aust.	52	3,381	O11	43
Cocos Is., Aust.	5.4	684	N11	43
Colombia	439,513	19,215,000	F 3	68
Colorado, U.S.A.	104,247	1,969,000		114–115
Comoro Is. (Fr.)	838	244,000	P14	65
Congo, Democratic Republic of the	905,536	16,210,000	L12	65
Congo, Rep. of	132,046	1,000,000	J12	64
Connecticut, U.S.A.	5,009	2,832,000		116–117
Cook Is. (N. Z.)	93	19,251	K 7	56
Corsica, France	3,368	275,465	A 6	25
Costa Rica	19,575	1,610,000	E 5	79
Crete, Greece	3,218	483,075	G 8	35
Cuba	44,206	8,074,000	B 2	76
Curaçao, Neth. Antilles	182	134,250	E 4	77
Cyprus	3,473	614,000	E 5	46
Czechoslovakia	49,370	14,305,000	D 2	32
Dahomey	44,290	2,514,000	G10	62
Daito Is., Ryukyu Is.	17	3,896	M 6	51
Delaware, U.S.A.	2,057	505,000		139
Denmark	16,614	4,900,000	E 9	19
District of Columbia, U.S.A.	69	803,000	B 5	138
Dominica (Br.)	290	69,000	G 4	77
Dominican Republic	18,704	3,889,000	D 3	77
Ecuador .... approx.	109,483	5,508,000	E 4	68
Egypt (U.A.R.)	386,100	30,907,000	M 6	63
El Salvador	8,260	3,151,000	C 4	78
England, U.K.	50,327	45,680,870		17
Equatorial Guinea, Spain....	10,832	277,000	H11	62,64
Estonian S.S.R., U.S.S.R. ..	17,413	1,285,000	C 3	36
Ethiopia	471,776	24,581,027	O 9	63
Europe	4,063,000	620,890,000		14–15
Faerøe Is., Den.	540	38,000	D 2	14
Falkland Is. (Br.)	4,618	2,000	H14	71
Fernando Po, Eq. Guin.	786	76,000	H11	62
Fiji (Br.)	7,015	490,000	H 7	56
Finland	130,128	4,700,000	O 5	18
Florida, U.S.A.	58,560	5,805,000		118–119
France	212,841	50,000,000		24–25
French Guiana	35,135	37,000	K 3	69
French Polynesia	1,544	98,400	M 7	56

Country	Area (Square Miles)	Population	Index Ref.	Plate No.
Gabon	103,346	473,000	J12	64
Gambia	4,003	343,000	C 9	62
Georgia, U.S.A.	58,876	4,357,000	......	120–121
Georgian S.S.R., U.S.S.R.	26,911	4,548,000	F 6	37
Germany, East (German Democratic Republic)	41,814	17,067,000	......	22–23
Germany, West (Federal Republic of)	95,959	59,948,500	......	22–23
Ghana	91,843	8,400,000	F10	62
Gibraltar (Br.)	2	25,000	D 4	26
Gilbert & Ellice Is. (Br.)...	369	55,000	H 6	56
Great Britain & Northern Ireland (United Kingdom)	94,214	55,068,000	......	16–17
Greece	50,548	8,716,000	F 6	35
Greenland (Den.)	840,000	43,000	B12	10
Grenada (Br.)	133	97,000	G 6	77
Guadeloupe and Dependencies (Fr.)	687	320,000	F 3	77
Guam (U.S.A.)	212	94,000	E 4	56
Guatemala	42,042	4,717,000	B 3	78
Guinea	94,925	3,702,000	D 9	62
Guyana	83,000	645,098	J 2	69
Haiti	10,694	4,674,000	D 3	76
Hawaii, U.S.A.	6,424	711,000	......	122
Holland (Netherlands)	13,958	12,668,000	E 4	20
Honduras	43,277	2,445,440	D 3	78
Hong Kong (Br.)	398	3,900,000	J 7	51
Hungary	35,915	10,241,000	E 3	33
Iceland	39,768	200,000	C 2	14
Idaho, U.S.A.	83,557	692,000	......	123
Ifni, Spain	579	53,000	D 6	62
Illinois, U.S.A.	56,400	10,644,000	......	124–125
India	1,283,166	515,777,000	......	48–49
Indiana, U.S.A.	36,291	4,885,000	......	126–127
Indonesia	575,893	112,311,000	......	54–55
Iowa, U.S.A.	56,290	2,760,000	......	128–129
Iran	636,293	26,315,000	F 3	45
Iraq	167,924	8,380,000	D 3	44
Ireland	26,600	2,884,002	B 4	17
Israel	7,993	2,716,000	......	47
Italy	116,303	53,700,000	......	28–29
Ivory Coast	124,503	4,000,000	E10	62
Jamaica	4,411	1,880,000	C 3	76
Japan	142,734	100,300,000	......	52
Java, Indonesia	48,842	60,909,381	K 2	55
Jordan	37,737	2,123,000	......	47
Kansas, U.S.A.	82,264	2,234,000	......	130–131
Kazakh S.S.R., U.S.S.R.	1,048,301	12,129,000	G 5	38
Kentucky, U.S.A.	40,395	3,179,000	......	132–133
Kenya	224,960	10,300,000	O11	65
Kirghiz S.S.R., U.S.S.R. ..	76,641	2,652,000	H 5	38
Korea, North	46,540	12,400,000	C 2	52
Korea, South	38,452	30,067,000	C 3	52
Kuwait	6,177	491,000	E 4	44
Laccadive, Minicoy & Amindivi Is., India	746	24,108	C6,7	49
Laos	91,459	2,800,000	D 3	53
Latvian S.S.R., U.S.S.R. ..	24,595	2,263,000	B 3	36
Lebanon	4,015	2,460,000	F 6	46
Lesotho	11,716	877,000	M17	65
Liberia	43,000	1,115,000	E10	62
Libya	679,359	1,800,000	K 6	62–63
Liechtenstein	61	20,000	J 3	31
Lithuanian S.S.R., U.S.S.R.	25,174	2,986,000	B 3	36
Louisiana, U.S.A.	48,523	3,534,000	......	134–135
Luxembourg	999	335,000	H 8	20
Macao (Port.)	6.2	280,000	H 7	51
Madeira Is., Portugal	308	268,937	A 2	26
Maine, U.S.A.	33,215	993,000	......	136–137
Malagasy Republic	226,657	6,400,000	R15	65
Malawi	45,483	4,042,412	N14	65
Malaya, Malaysia	50,670	8,415,000	C 7	53
Malaysia	128,308	9,906,000	C–F 4	54
Maldive Islands	115	100,883	L 9	43
Mali	463,948	4,745,000	E 9	62
Malta	122	315,765	E 7	29
Man, Isle of (Br.)	227	50,423	D 3	17
Manitoba, Canada	251,000	963,066	......	92–93
Mariana Is., Terr. Pac. Is.	184	10,743	E 4	56
Marquesas Is., Fr. Poly.	492	4,837	N 6	56
Marshall Is., Terr. Pac. Is.	70	18,239	H 4	56
Martinique (Fr.)	425	330,000	G 4	77
Maryland, U.S.A.	10,577	3,519,000	......	138–139
Massachusetts, U.S.A.	8,257	5,348,000	......	140–141
Mauritania	397,954	1,100,000	D 8	62
Mauritius	709	790,000	S19	65
Mexico	761,601	45,671,000	......	80–81
Michigan, U.S.A.	58,216	8,218,000	......	142–143
Midway Is. (U.S.A.)	2	2,355	H 3	56
Minnesota, U.S.A.	84,068	3,554,000	......	144–145
Mississippi, U.S.A.	47,716	2,321,000	......	146–147
Missouri, U.S.A.	69,686	4,497,000	......	148–149
Moldavian S.S.R., U.S.S.R.	13,012	3,368,000	C 5	37
Monaco	368 acres	23,000	G 6	25
Mongolia	604,247	1,140,000	E–H 2	50–51
Montana, U.S.A.	147,138	706,000	......	150–151
Montserrat (Br.)	38	14,000	G 3	77
Morocco	171,834	14,140,000	E 5	62
Mozambique (Port.)	302,328	7,124,000	O15	65
Muscat and Oman	82,000	565,000	G 5	26
Natal, S. Afr.	33,578	2,979,920	N17	65
Nauru	8.2	6,056	G 6	56
Nebraska, U.S.A.	77,227	1,477,000	......	152–153
Nepal	54,362	10,294,000	E–F 3	49
Netherlands	13,958	12,668,000	E 4	20
Netherlands Antilles	394	212,000	E 4	77
Nevada, U.S.A.	110,540	440,000	......	154
New Britain, Terr. New Guinea	14,098	154,188	F 6	56
New Brunswick, Canada	28,354	616,788	C 3	86
New Caledonia (Fr.)	7,335	92,000	G 8	56
Newfoundland, Canada	156,185	493,396	J 4	86
New Guinea, Terr. of (Aust. Trust.)	92,160	1,582,439	E–F 6	56
New Hampshire, U.S.A.	9,304	669,000	......	155
New Hebrides (Br.-Fr. Cond.)	5,700	78,000	G 7	56
New Jersey, U.S.A.	7,836	6,774,000	......	156–157
New Mexico, U.S.A.	121,666	1,029,000	......	158–159
New South Wales, Aust.	309,433	4,300,083	H 6	59
New York, U.S.A.	49,576	18,073,000	......	160–161
New Zealand	103,736	2,747,093	M 7	59
Nicaragua	45,698	1,783,000	E 4	78
Niger	489,189	3,546,000	H 8	62
Nigeria	356,669	61,450,000	H10	62
Niue (N. Z.)	100	5,194	K 7	56
Norfolk I., Aust.	13.3	1,152	G 8	56
North America	9,363,000	294,000,000	......	74–75
North Carolina, U.S.A.	52,712	4,914,000	......	162–163
North Dakota, U.S.A.	70,665	652,000	......	164–165
Northern Ireland, U.K.	5,459	1,491,000	G 3	17
Northern Territory, Aust. ..	520,280	39,556	E 3	58
Northwest Territories, Canada	1,304,903	28,738	E–J 3	84–85
Norway	125,181	3,800,000	F 6	18
Nova Scotia, Canada	21,425	756,039	......	86–87
Ohio, U.S.A.	41,222	10,245,000	......	166–167
Oklahoma, U.S.A.	69,919	2,482,000	......	168–169
Ontario, Canada	412,582	6,960,870	......	90–91
Orange Free State, S. Afr.	49,866	1,386,547	M17	65
Oregon, U.S.A.	96,981	1,899,000	......	170–171
Orkney Is., Scotland	376	18,424	E 1	16
Pacific Is., Terr. of the (U.S. Trust.)	700	93,000	D–G 5	56
Pakistan	365,527	107,258,000	B3,C4	48
Palau Is., Terr. Pac. Is.	179	11,225	D 5	56
Panama	29,209	1,372,200	G 6	79
Papua (Aust.)	86,100	600,587	B 7	54
Paraguay	157,047	2,161,000	J 8	69,71
Pennsylvania, U.S.A.	45,333	11,520,000	......	172–173
Persia (Iran)	636,293	26,315,000	F 3	45
Peru	496,222	12,385,000	E 5	68
Philippines, Rep. of the	115,707	35,576,000	H 4	55
Pitcairn Is. (Br.)	1.8	96	O 8	56
Poland	120,664	31,944,000	......	21
Portugal	35,510	9,381,000	B 3	26
Portuguese Guinea	13,948	528,000	C 9	62
Portuguese Timor	5,762	560,000	H 7	55
Prince Edward I., Canada..	2,184	108,535	F 3	87
Puerto Rico	3,435	2,727,000	G 2	77
Qatar	8,500	75,000	F 4	45
Québec, Canada	594,860	5,780,845	......	88–89
Queensland, Aust.	667,000	1,688,529	G 4	59

Country	Area (Square Miles)	Population	Index Ref.	Plate No.
Réunion (Fr.)	969	418,000	R20	65
Rhode Island, U.S.A.	1,214	920,000	.....	141
Rhodesia	150,332	4,530,000	M15	65
Río Muni, Eq. Guin.	10,046	201,000	J11	64
Rumania	91,699	19,287,000	G 3	34
Russian S.F.S.R., U.S.S.R.	6,592,819	126,561,000	D–R 4	38–39
Rwanda	10,691	3,306,000	N12	65
Ryukyu Is. (U.S. Adm.)....	848	952,000	G 4	52
Sabah, Malaysia	29,388	588,000	F 4–5	54–55
St. Christopher-Nevis-Anguilla (Br.)	138	58,000	F 3	77
St. Croix, Virgin Is. (U.S.A.)	80	14,973	H 2	77
St. Helena (Br.)	47	5,125	E15	64
St. John, Virgin Is. (U.S.A.)	20	925	H 1	77
St. Lucia (Br.)	238	99,000	G 4	77
St-Pierre & Miquelon (Fr.)	93.5	5,000	H 6	87
St. Thomas, Virgin Is. (U.S.A.)	32	16,201	G 1	77
St. Vincent (Br.)	150	90,000	G 4	77
Sakhalin, U.S.S.R.	28,215	618,000	P 4	39
San Marino	23.4	18,000	D 2	28
São Tomé e Príncipe (Port.)	372	60,000	H11	64
Sarawak, Malaysia	48,250	903,000	E 5	54
Sardinia, Italy	9,301	1,400,103	B 4	29
Saskatchewan, Canada	251,700	955,344	.....	94–95
Saudi Arabia	920,000	6,870,000	D 4	44
Scotland, U.K.	30,411	5,187,000	D 2	16
Senegal	75,750	3,580,000	D 9	62
Seychelles (Br.)	109	48,000	T 6	9
Shetland Is., Scotland	551	17,719	G 1	16
Siam (Thailand)	198,456	34,800,000	C 3	53
Sicily, Italy	9,926	4,683,076	D 6	29
Sierra Leone	27,925	2,439,000	D10	62
Singapore	225	1,955,600	E 6	53
Society Is., Fr. Poly.	646	68,245	L 7	56
Solomon Is., Terr. New Guinea	4,080	56,000	F 6	56
Solomon Is. Prot. (Br.)	11,500	141,000	G 6	56
Somali Republic	246,200	2,700,000	R11	63,65
South Africa	471,663	18,733,000	L18	65
South America	6,875,000	166,000,000	.....	68–71
South Australia, Aust.	380,070	1,107,178	E 5	58
South Carolina, U.S.A.	31,055	2,542,000	.....	174–175
South Dakota, U.S.A.	77,047	703,000	.....	176–177
Southern Yemen	111,075	1,158,000	E 7	44
South-West Africa (S. Afr.)	317,838	596,000	K16	64–65
Spain	194,896	32,140,036	.....	26–27
Spanish Sahara, Spain	102,702	48,000	D 6	62
Sudan	967,495	14,800,000	M 9	63
Sumatra, Indonesia	164,148	14,982,910	C 6	54
Surinam (Neth.)	55,144	350,000	J 3	69
Svalbard, Norway	23,958	2,828	C 2	18
Swaziland	6,704	374,697	N17	65
Sweden	173,665	7,803,425	J 6	19
Switzerland	15,941	6,025,000	.....	30–31
Syria	71,498	5,450,000	G 5	46
Tadzhik S.S.R., U.S.S.R.	55,251	2,579,000	G 6	38
Tahiti, Fr. Poly.	402	45,430	M 7	56
Taiwan, China	13,048	13,700,000	K 7	51
Tanzania	362,819	12,500,000	N13	65
Tasmania, Aust.	26,215	376,212	J 8	59
Tennessee, U.S.A.	42,244	3,845,000	.....	178–179
Texas, U.S.A.	267,339	10,551,000	.....	180–181
Thailand	198,456	34,800,000	C 3	53
Tibet, China	471,660	1,270,000	C 5	50
Togo	5,765	1,746,000	G10	62
Tokelau Is. (N. Z.)	3.9	1,901	J 6	56
Tonga	270	77,429	J 7	56
Transkei, S. Afr.	16,675	1,439,195	M18	65
Transvaal, S. Afr.	109,621	6,273,477	N17	65
Trinidad & Tobago	1,980	1,000,000	G 5	77
Tristan da Cunha, St. Helena	40	285	O 7	9
Trucial Oman	32,278	150,000	F 5	45
Tuamotu Arch., Fr. Poly.	343	7,097	M 7	56
Tunisia	63,378	4,700,000	H 5	62
Turkey	301,381	31,391,421	.....	46
Turkmen S.S.R., U.S.S.R.	188,456	1,914,000	F 6	38
Turks & Caicos Is. (Br.) ..	166	6,000	D 2	76
Uganda	92,674	7,934,000	N11	65
Ukrainian S.S.R., U.S.S.R.	232,046	45,516,000	D 5	37
Union of Soviet Socialist Republics	8,649,498	253,543,000	.....	36–39
United Arab Republic	386,100	30,907,000	M 6	63
United Kingdom	94,214	55,068,000	.....	16–17
United States of America .... land	3,554,609			
.... land and water	3,615,211	200,996,000	.....	102–103
Upper Volta	105,841	5,054,000	F 9	62
Uruguay	72,172	2,783,000	J10	71
Utah, U.S.A.	84,916	990,000	.....	182
Uzbek S.S.R., U.S.S.R.	173,591	10,581,000	G 5	38
Vatican City	109 acres	1,000	B 6	29
Venezuela	352,143	9,415,000	G 2	68
Vermont, U.S.A.	9,609	397,000	.....	183
Victoria, Aust.	87,884	3,271,993	G 7	59
Vietnam, North	61,293	19,500,000	D 3	53
Vietnam, South	66,263	17,000,000	E 4	53
Virgin Is. (Br.)	59	9,000	H 1	77
Virgin Is. (U.S.A.)	133	56,000	H 1	77
Virginia, U.S.A.	40,815	4,457,000	.....	184–185
Wake I. (U.S.A.)	3	1,097	G 4	56
Wales, U.K.	8,017	2,709,930	E 4	17
Wallis & Futuna (Fr.)	106	8,611	H–J 7	56
Washington, U.S.A.	68,192	2,990,000	.....	186–187
Western Australia, Aust. ..	975,920	863,744	C 4	58
Western Samoa	1,097	135,000	J 7	56
West Irian (Indon. Adm.)..	159,371	800,000	J 6	55
West Virginia, U.S.A.	24,181	1,812,000	.....	188–189
White Russian S.S.R., U.S.S.R.	80,154	8,633,000	C 4	37
Wisconsin, U.S.A.	56,154	4,144,000	.....	190–191
World	57,491,000	3,443,000,000	.....	8–9
Wyoming, U.S.A.	97,914	340,000	.....	192
Yap, Terr. Pac. Is.	46	6,606	D 5	56
Yemen	75,000	5,000,000	D 7	44
Yugoslavia	98,766	20,210,000	C 3	34
Yukon Territory, Canada....	207,076	14,382	C 3	84
Zambia	290,585	3,947,000	M14	65

THE SOLAR SYSTEM

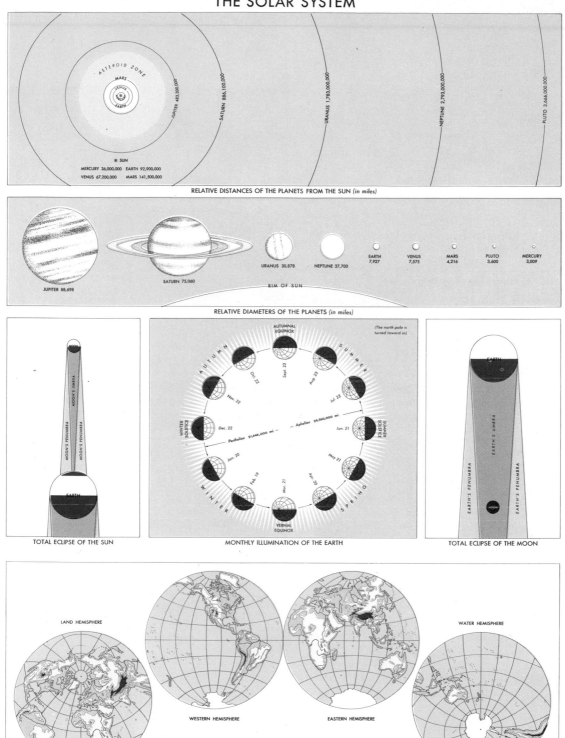

RELATIVE DISTANCES OF THE PLANETS FROM THE SUN (in miles)

MERCURY 36,000,000   EARTH 92,900,000
VENUS 67,200,000   MARS 141,500,000

RELATIVE DIAMETERS OF THE PLANETS (in miles)

JUPITER 88,698   SATURN 75,060   URANUS 30,878   NEPTUNE 27,700   EARTH 7,927   VENUS 7,575   MARS 4,216   PLUTO 3,600   MERCURY 3,009

TOTAL ECLIPSE OF THE SUN

MONTHLY ILLUMINATION OF THE EARTH

TOTAL ECLIPSE OF THE MOON

LAND HEMISPHERE   WESTERN HEMISPHERE   EASTERN HEMISPHERE   WATER HEMISPHERE

EARTH

Longitude East of Greenwich   Longitude West of Greenwich

ARCTIC

OCEAN

Komsomolets I.
SEVERNAYA
ZEMLYA
(NORTH LAND)
October Revolution I.
Bol'shevik I.
C. Chelyuskin

NEW
SIBERIAN IS. DeLong
Is.

Borden I.
SVERDRUP
QUEEN ELIZA
ISLANDS
Melville I.
Bathurst
N. MAG. POLE
Vis. Melville Sd.
Somerset

TAYMYR
PEN.
L. Taymyr
Nordvik

LAPTEV SEA

EAST SIBERIAN SEA

Wrangel I.

Pr. Patrick I.
Lands End

Banks

BEAUFORT
SEA

M'Clure Str.

Victoria I.

Khatanga

Bear Is.

Barrow Pt. Barrow

Amundsen Gulf

UNION OF SOVIET

Verkhoyansk
Srednekolymsk
Arctic Circle

Pt.
Hope

UNITED STATES
Ft. Yukon

Nome
Anadyr
Oymyakon
Gizhiga
Yakutsk

Vilyuysk
Olekminsk

Yukon
Fairbanks
Lawrence
ALASKA
Anchorage

Dawson
Whitehorse

Great
Bear Lake

NORT

Great
Slave Lake

CANA

Churchill

SOCIALIST REPUBLICS

Krasnoyarsk
Irkutsk
Ulan-Ude
L.
Baykal
Chita
Shilka

Okhotsk
Magadan

BERING SEA

SEA OF
OKHOTSK

Komandorskiye

Attu
ALEUTIAN

Pribilof
Is.

Gulf of Alaska
Kodiak I.

Sitka

KURIL IS.
ISLANDS

Petropavlovsk-
Kamchatskiy
Cape
Lopatka

Pr. of Wales I.
QUEEN
CHARLOTTE

Juneau

Prince
Rupert

Edmonton
Saskatoon
Calgary
Regina

AMERI

Peace

Athabasca

Winnip

Winnip

Ulan Bator
MONGOLIA
Paotow
Peking
(Peiping)

Komsomol'sk
Khabarovsk
Sakhalin
Harbin
Changchun
Mukden
Vladivostok
Hokkaido

Vancouver I.
Vancouver

Seattle
Portland

Boise

Salt
Lake City

Minneapolis
Denver

St. P
Chi

GOBI (Desert)

Tientsin
Tsinan
CHINA
Nanking
Chengtu Wuhan
Changsha

SEA OF
JAPAN
Honshu
JAPAN
Nagoya Tokyo
Osaka Yokohama
Kyushu Shikoku

Bonin Is.
(Jap.)

San Francisco

Los Angeles

C. Mendocino

UNITED S

Arkansas

Kansas

Denver

Platte

Colorado

El Paso

Dallas
Houston

Kunming Canton
Chungking
Yangtze Kiang
Foochow
Taipei
Taiwan (Formosa)

EAST
CHINA
SEA

RYUKYU IS.
(U.S. Adm.)

Tropic of Cancer

Guadalupe
(Mex.)

C. San Lucas
Guadalajara

MEXICO

Monterrey Vera

Gul

INDIA
Hanoi MACAO
(Port.)
HONG KONG
(Br.)
Rangoon
BURMA
THAIL. VIETNAM
Bangkok CAMB.
S.VIETNAM
G. of
Siam
SOUTH
CHINA
SEA
MALAYSIA (Br.)
SINGAPORE
Sumatra Borneo

Hainan

Luzon
Manila

Mindanao
Palau

MARIANA
IS.

Guam

CAROLINE IS.

Wake I.
(U.S.)

MARSHALL
IS.

Midway Is.
(U.S.)

UNITED STATES
HAWAII Honolulu
Hawaii

Johnston Atoll
(U.S.)

Revillagigedo Is.
(Mex.)

Clipperton I.
(Fr.)

Mexico City

CENT
AME
Coc

ELS

REPUBLIC OF THE
PHILIPPINES

BRUNEI SABAH
SARAWAK

Celebes

Palmyra I.
(U.S.)
Fanning I.

Washington I. (Br.)

Christmas I. (U.S.& Br.)

Equator

GALÁPAGOS IS.
(Ec.)

Djakarta
INDONESIA
Christmas I.
(Austr.)
Cocos Is.
(Austr.)
SUNDA
ISLANDS
Java
Timor

TERRITORY OF THE PACIFIC ISLANDS
(U.S. Trust Terr.)
New
Guinea
W. IRIAN
(Indon. Adm.)
TERR. OF
NEW GUINEA

NAURU
GILBERT
IS. (Br.)

Howland I. (U.S.)
Baker I. (U.S.)
Canton I. (U.S.)
PHOENIX IS.
(U.S.& Br.)

Jarvis I. (U.S.)

Malden I. (U.S.& Br.)
Starbuck I. (U.S.& Br.)

MARQUESAS IS.
(Fr.)

PAPUA
BISMARCK
ARCH.(Austr.)
SOLOMON IS.
Sta. Cruz
Is. (Br.)

ELLICE I.
(Br.)
Rotuma I. W.SAMOA
(Br.) Tutuila (U.S.)

SOCIETY IS.
(Fr.)
Tahiti Papeete

TUAMOTU
ARCH.
(Fr.)

Darwin
C. York

ARAFURA SEA

CORAL
SEA

NEW
HEBRIDES
(Br.& Fr.)

FIJI IS.
(Br.)
TONGA IS.
(Br.)

COOK
IS.
(N.Z.)

AUSTRALES IS.
(Tubuai) (Fr.)

Tropic of Capricorn

Pitcairn I.
(Br.)

Ducie I.
(Br.)

Easter I.
(Chile)

Sala y Gómez
(Chile)

Port Hedland
INDIAN
OCEAN

Townsville
Rockhampton

AUSTRALIA
Brisbane

Perth Kalgoorlie
Fremantle
C. Leeuwin
Albany

Adelaide
Murray
Melbourne

New
Caledonia
(Fr.)
Loyalty Is.
(Fr.)

Norfolk I.
(Austr.)
Lord Howe I.
(Austr.)

Kermadec Is.
(N.Z.)

SOUTH PACIFIC

OCEAN

Newcastle
Sydney
Canberra

North Cape
Auckland
North I.
NEW
ZEALAND
Wellington
Christchurch
Dunedin

TASMAN
SEA
Tasmania Hobart

Bass Str.

South I.

Chatham Is.
(N.Z.)

Stewart I.

Bounty Is.
(N.Z.)
Antipodes Is.
(N.Z.)

Auckland Is.
(N.Z.)

Campbell I.
(N.Z.)

Macquarie I.
(Austr.)

THE WORLD
MERCATOR PROJECTION
EQUATORIAL SCALES
MILES
0   500   1000   1500   2000   2500
KILOMETRES
0 500 1000 1500 2000 2500
Capitals of Countries .... ⊙
© C.S. HAMMOND & Co., Maplewood, N.J.

ANTARCTICA

Balleny Is.

Scott I.

Antarctic Circle

8

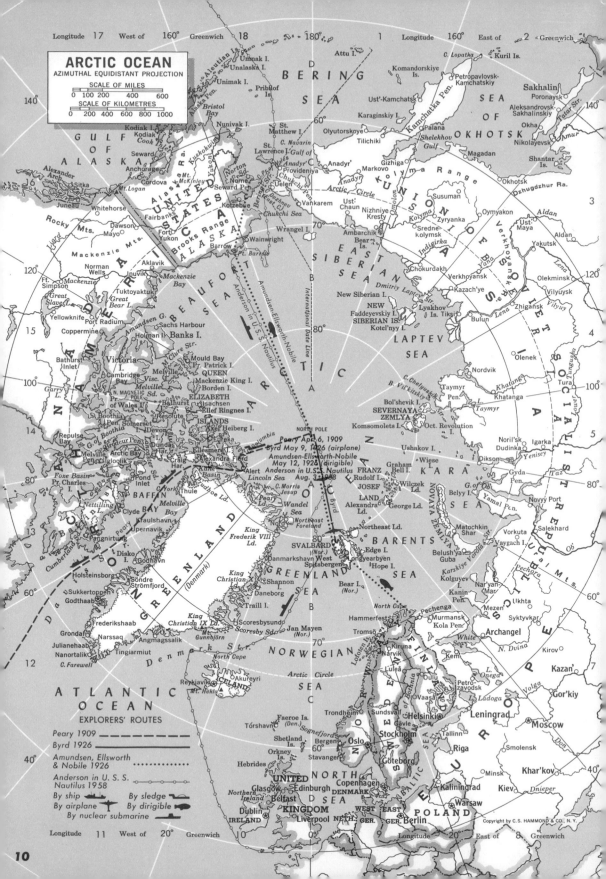

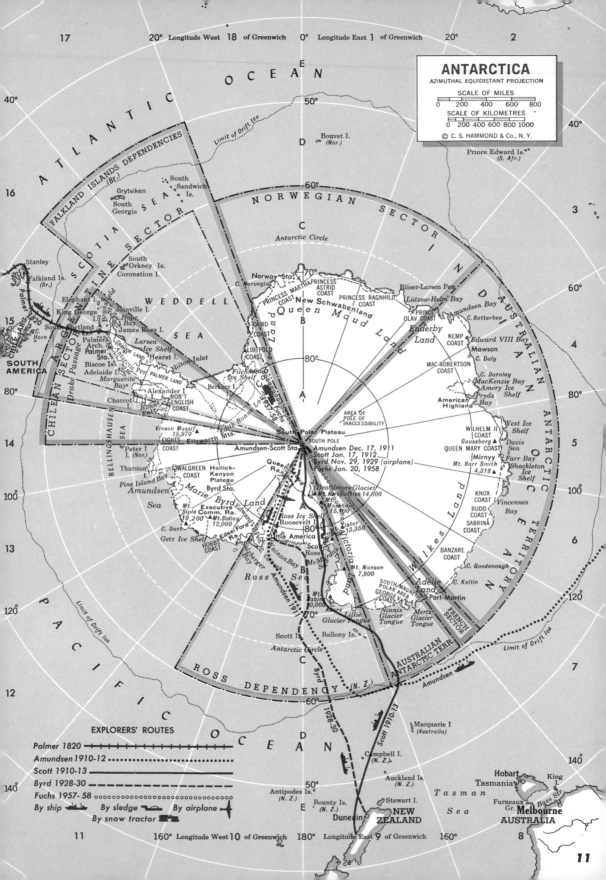

ANTARCTICA

ANTARCTICA
AZIMUTHAL EQUIDISTANT PROJECTION

SCALE OF MILES
0   200   400   600   800

SCALE OF KILOMETRES
0   200   400   600   800   1000

© C. S. HAMMOND & Co., N. Y.

EXPLORERS' ROUTES

Palmer 1820
Amundsen 1910-12
Scott 1910-13
Byrd 1928-30
Fuchs 1957-58
By ship   By sledge   By airplane
By snow tractor

Map of
EUROPE
SCALE OF MILES

0   100   200   300   400

★ Capitals of Countries
● Cities
▬ Boundaries of Countries
▬ Other Boundaries
▲ Mountain Peaks

Mountains   Highlands   Lowlands   Depression   Water

Copyright by C. S. Hammond & Co., N.Y.

ARCTIC

40°   30°   20°   10°   0°   10°

Reykjavik   **ICELAND**

NORWEGIAN
SEA

Faeroe Islands
(Danish)

Shetland Islands
(British)

Trondheim

Bergen

Orkney
Islands

Oslo

Göteborg

Hebrides

Skagerrak

Kattegat

Scotland

Glasgow

GREAT

NORTH

DENMARK

Copenhagen

Northern
Ireland

British Isles

IRELAND
Dublin

IRISH
SEA

Liverpool

Wales

BRITAIN
England

London

Greenwich

SEA

Hamburg

NETHER-
LANDS

The
Hague   Amsterdam

EAST
Berlin

Oder

English Channel

Le Havre

Brussels

BELGIUM
Bonn

WEST

GERMANY

Nantes

Seine R.

Paris

LUXEM-
BOURG

Frankfurt

GERMANY

CZECHO

Pragu

Loire River

Bay of
Biscay

FRANCE

Munich

Danube

Vienna

Rhine R.

AUSTRIA

YU

SWITZER-
LAND

Bern

Lyon R.

Milan   Trieste   Zagreb

Mt.
Blanc

Po

Venice

Oporto

Bilbao

PYRENEES

Bordeaux

Rhone R.

Genoa

Po River

ADRIATIC

Marseille

MONACO

Lisbon

PORTUGAL

Iberian

Madrid

SPAIN

ANDORRA

Barcelona

Corsica
(French)

SAN
MARINO

Rome
VATICAN
CITY

ITALY

Cape
St. Vincent

Peninsula

Valencia   Balearic Islands
(Spanish)

Sardinia
(Italian)

Naples

Seville

GIBRALTAR (British)
Strait of

Gibraltar

MEDITERRAN

Tangier   Ceuta (Spanish)

Algiers

Palermo

Rabat

Melilla
(Spanish)

Tunis

Sicily
(Italian)

MOROCCO

ALGERIA

TUNISIA

MALTA

AFRICA

Longitude West of Greenwich

50°

40°

30°

ATLANTIC   OCEAN

12

Ed Edwen

40° A 30° B 20° C 10° D 0° E 10° F

2

Longitude West of Greenwich   Longitude East of Greenwich

70° Jan Mayen (Nor.)

N O R W E G I A N

60°

North Cape

Breidhifjördhur   Húnaflói
Reykjavík   Akureyri
ICELAND   Seydhisfjördhur
Mt. Hekla
Hornafjördhur

Langanes

Senja
Vesterålen
Lofoten Is.

S E A   Vestfjorden

Arctic Circle   Mo
Trondheimsfjorden
Namsos
3
Faeroe Is. (Den.)   Tórshavn   Kristiansund   Trondheim   Østersund
Rockall   Ålesund   Sundsvall
Shetland Is.   Lerwick   Sognefjord   Lillehammer   Söderhamn
Hebrides   Orkney Is.   Kirkwall   Bergen   Hardangerfjord   Drammen   Fredrikstad   Karlstad   Faluna   Gä
The Minch   Pentland Firth   Haugesund   Oslo   Larvik   Vänern   Uppsala
50°   Inverness   Moray Firth   Stavanger   Halden   Göteborg   Västerås   Eskils
SCOTLAND   Aberdeen   Lindesnes   Skagerrak   Borås   Linköping
BRITISH   Glasgow   Dundee   Kristiansand   Jönköping   Visby
NO. IRELAND   Edinburgh   Ålborg   DENMARK   Halsingborg   Öland
IRELAND   Belfast   UNITED   Newcastle   Aarhus   Kattegat   Lund   Karlskrona
Donegal Bay   Man   upon Tyne   Esbjerg   Copenhagen   Malmö   Bornholm
Galway   Dundalk   Carlisle   Odense   Stralsund
Limerick   Dublin   KINGDOM   Leeds   Flensburg   Kiel   Rostock   Stupsk   Bydg
Waterford   Manchester   Hull   Helgoland   Lübeck   EAST   Szczecin (Stettin)
Cork   Liverpool   Sheffield   The Wash   Frisian Is.   Bremen   Hamburg   BERLIN   Poznań
C. Clear   IRISH SEA   Birmingham   Amsterdam   NETHER-   Hannover   GERMANY   Wrocław
4   WALES   ENGLAND   The Hague   LANDS   Essen   Dortmund   Magdeburg   Leipzig   Dresden (Breslau)
St. George's Chan.   Cardiff   LONDON   Rotterdam   Münster   Kassel   Halle   Erfurt   Częstochowa
Swansea   Bristol   Antwerp   Düsseldorf   Brussels   Cologne   Wiesbaden   Karl-Marx   Prague   Ostrava
Plymouth   Portsmouth   BELGIUM   Liège   Bonn   Frankfurt   Stadt   (Praha)   Olomouc
Land's End   Southampton   Boulogne   Calais   Aachen   Mainz   Mannheim   Pilzen   Brno
English Channel   Lille   LUX.   Saarbrücken   Nuremberg   CHOSLO
Cherbourg   Le Havre   Amiens   Reims   Nancy   Karlsruhe   Regens-   VIENNA   Bratislava
Channel Is. (Br.)   Rouen   Seine   Strasbourg   Stuttgart   burg   (Wien)   Györ
Ushant I.   Brest   PARIS   Marne   Mulhouse   Freiburg   Augsburg   Linz   Sopron   HUN
Rennes   Versailles   Orléans   Dijon   Basel   Zürich   Munich   AUSTRIA   Maribor   Balaton   Pécs
Belle Isle   Angers   Loire   Tours   Bern   SWITZER-   Innsbruck   Ljubljana   Zagreb   Drava   No
St-Nazaire   Nantes   Vichy   FRANCE   Geneva   LAND   L. Geneva   Bolzano   Trieste   GOS
La Rochelle   Limoges   Clermont-Ferrand   Lyon   Mont Blanc   Trento   Venice   Rijeka (Fiume)   Drava
Bay of Biscay   I. d'Oléron   Dordogne   St-Etienne   Grenoble   Turin   Brescia   Verona (Venezia)   Banja Luka   Zadar   Sarajevo
La Coruña   Bordeaux   Garonne   Nîmes   Nice   Milan   Parma   Modena   Ferrara   Split
El Ferrol   C. Finisterre   Bayonne   Toulouse   Marseille   MONACO   Genoa   Bologna   Florence   Ancona   Dubro
40°   Vigo   Oviedo   Santander   San Sebastián   Biarritz   Montpellier   Toulon   Corsica   SAN   (Firenze)   Cetinje   Ragu
Miño   León   Bilbao   Pyrenees   G. of Lions   (Corse)   MARINO   Siena   Perugia   ADR   Shkodë
Oporto   Braga   Burgos   ANDORRA   Ajaccio   Leghorn   IAL
(Porto)   Valladolid   Ebro   (Livorno)   Elba   Tiber   ROME   Durrë
Coimbra   Duero   Saragossa   Barcelona   VATICAN   I   Bari
Lisbon   Sa. de Guadarrama   Tarragona   Sassari   Olbia   CITY   Foggia   Brindisi
(Lisboa)   (Tejo)   MADRID   Elba   Vesuvius
PORTUGAL   Tagus   Toledo   Balearic Is.   Sardinia   Naples   G. of
Setúbal   Guadiana   SPAIN   Valencia   Minorca   (Sardegna)   (Napoli)   Taranto
Évora   Badajoz   Albacete   Majorca   TYRRHENIAN   Catanzaro
C. St. Vincent   Sierra Morena   (Mallorca)   Cagliari   Palermo   Messina   Reggio   IONIA
5   Córdoba   Guadalquivir   Murcia   Palma   Ibiza   SEA   Etna   SEA
G. of Cádiz   Seville   Granada   Lorca   Alicante   Iglesias   Sicily   Catania
Cádiz   Jerez   Sa. Nevada   Cartagena   M E D I T E R R A N   (Sicilia)   Syracuse
Str. of Gibraltar   Málaga   Almería   Pantelleria   MALTA
Tangier   GIBRALTAR (Br.)   Ceuta (Sp.)   Valletta
Kénitra   Oran   Algiers   Skikda   Bizerte   Tunis   C. Bon
Casablanca   Rabat   Melilla (Sp.)   (Alger)   Annaba   TUNISIA   Sousse
Meknès   Fez   Constantine   Tunis
MOROCCO   A L G E R I A   Biskra
Marrakech

14

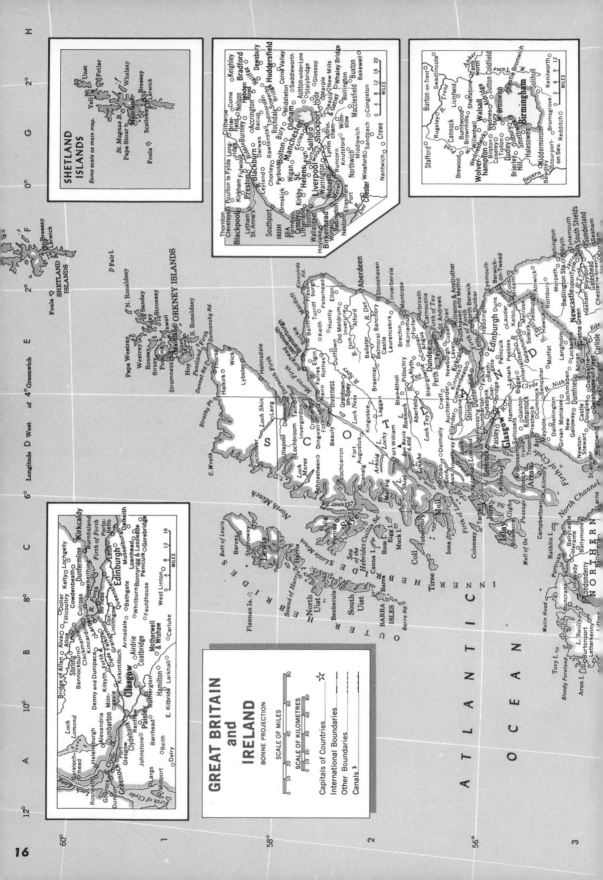

17

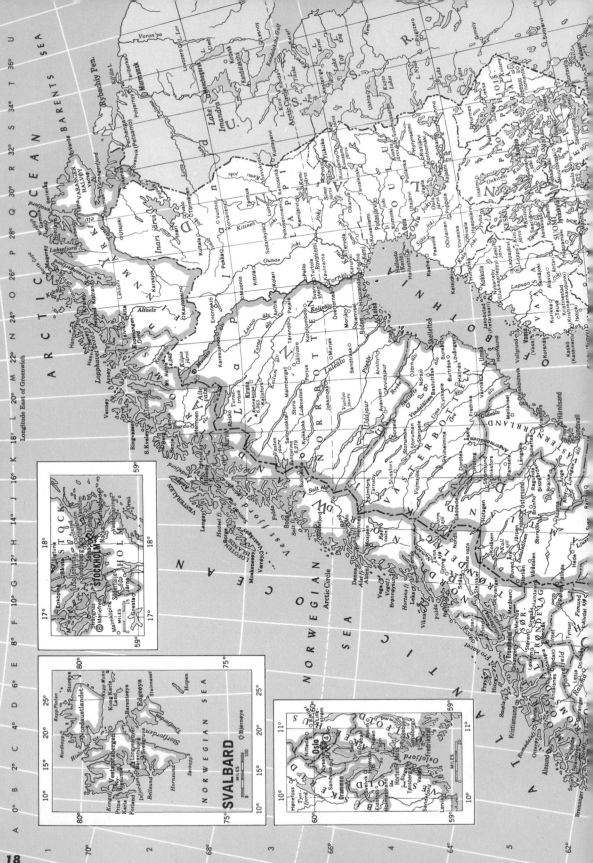

SVALBARD

STOCKHOLM

OSLO

18

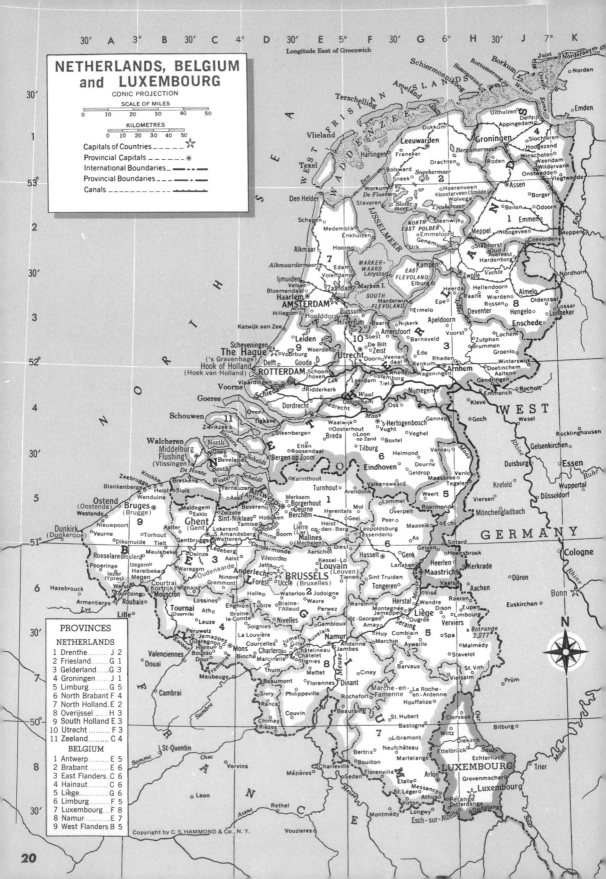

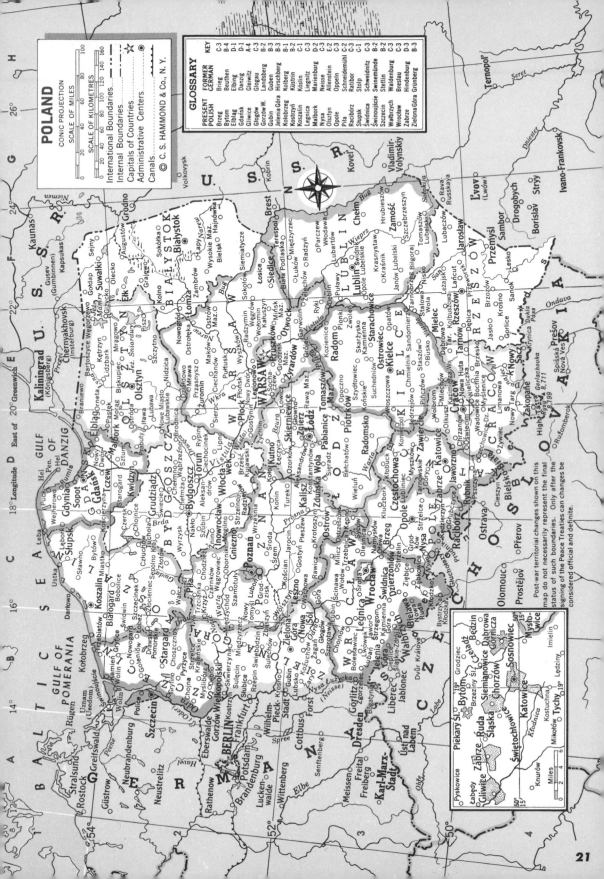

21

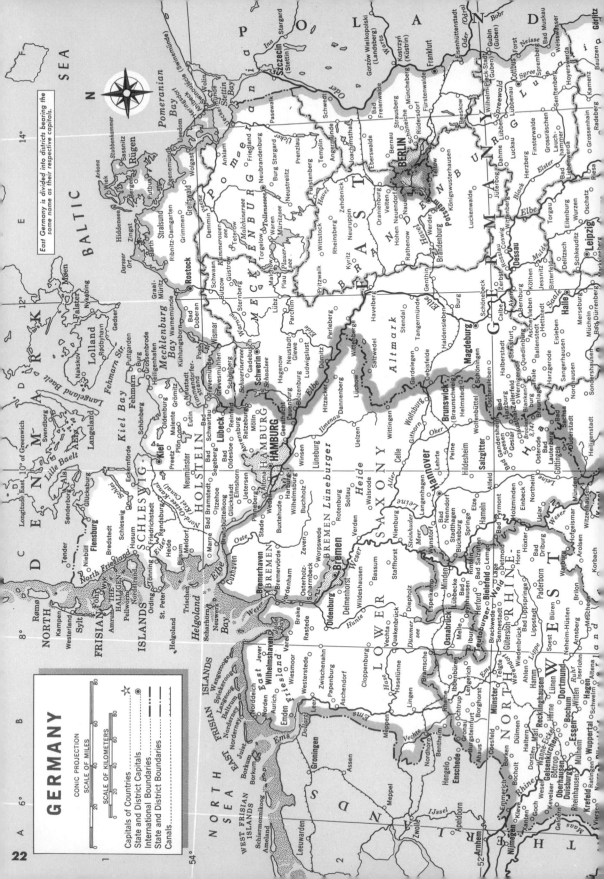

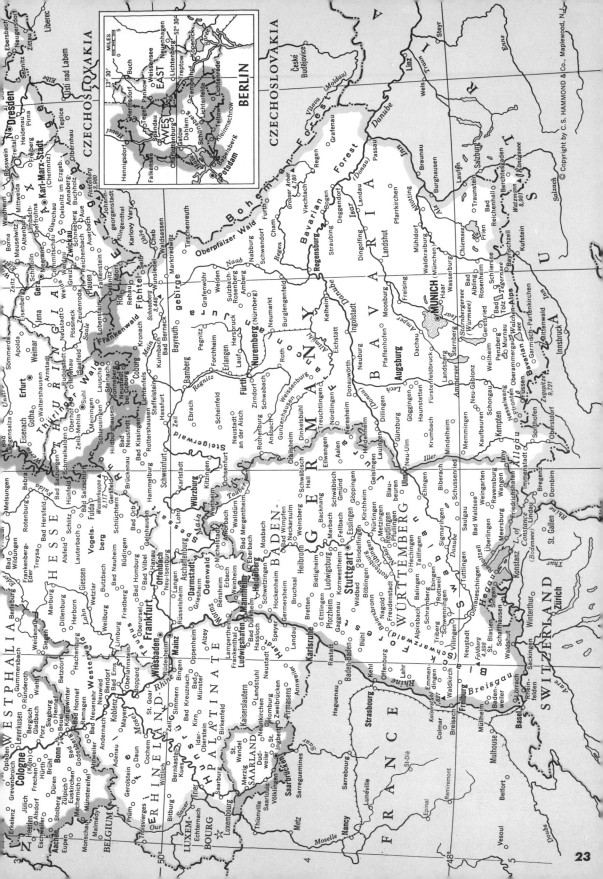

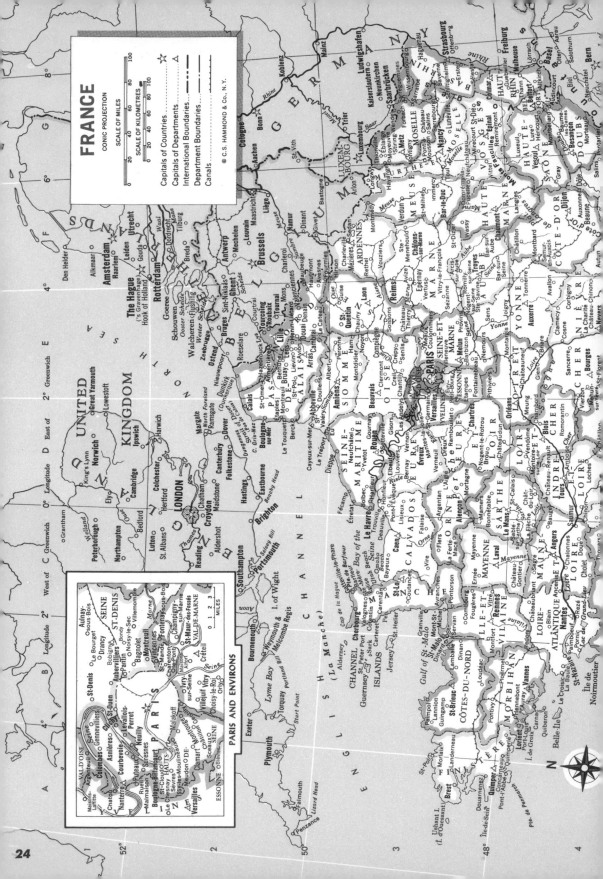

FRANCE

CONIC PROJECTION

SCALE OF MILES

SCALE OF KILOMETRES

Capitals of Countries .... ☆
Capitals of Departments .... △
International Boundaries ......
Department Boundaries ......
Canals ......

© C.S. HAMMOND & CO., N.Y.

PARIS AND ENVIRONS

SPAIN and PORTUGAL

CONIC PROJECTION

SCALE OF MILES
0   20   40   60   80   100

SCALE OF KILOMETRES
0   20   40   60   80   100

Capitals of Countries_____☆
Provincial Capitals_____⌂
International Boundaries_____
Provincial Boundaries_____

© Copyright by C.S. HAMMOND & Co., Maplewood, N.J.

27

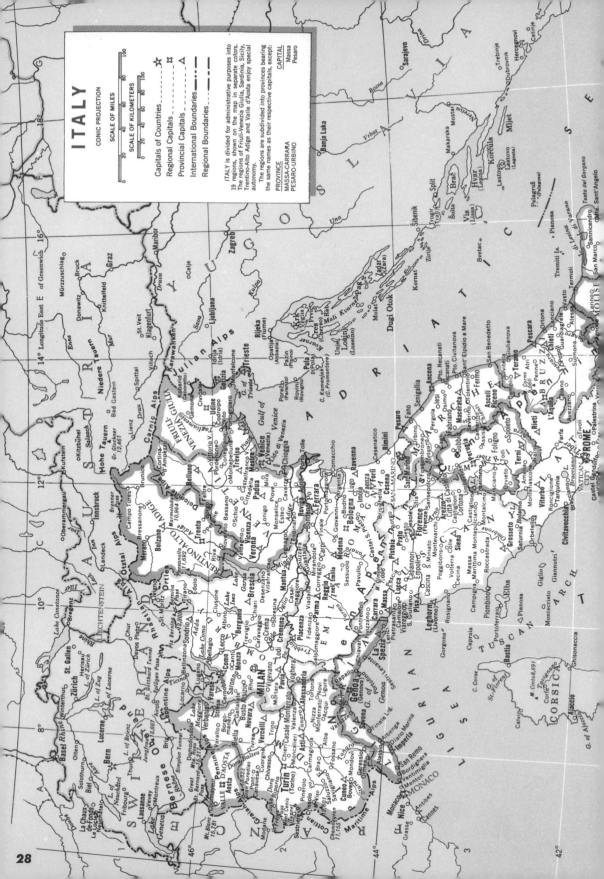

ITALY

CONIC PROJECTION

SCALE OF MILES

SCALE OF KILOMETERS

Capitals of Countries ☆
Regional Capitals ⊞
Provincial Capitals △
International Boundaries ━━━
Regional Boundaries ━━━

CAPITAL
Massa
Pesaro

ITALY is divided for administrative purposes into 19 regions, shown on the map in separate colors. The regions of Friuli-Venezia Giulia, Sardinia, Sicily, Trentino-Alto Adige and Valle d'Aosta enjoy special autonomy.

The regions are subdivided into provinces bearing the same names as their respective capitals, except:

PROVINCE
MASSA-CARRARA
PESARO-URBINO

28

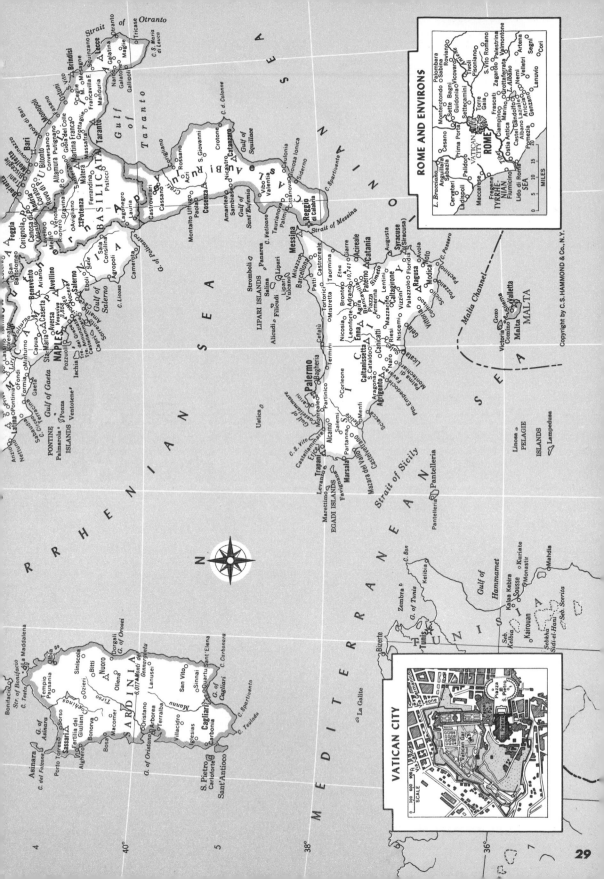

Strait of Otranto
Tricase
C. S. Maria di Leuca

Brindisi
Lecce
Galatina
Maglie
Squinzano
Galatone
Gallipoli
Nardò
Manduria
Francavilla F.
Grottaglie
Mesagne
Ostuni
Fasano
Martina Franca
Monopoli
Massafra
Conversano
Putignano
Mola di Bari
Altamura
Gioia del Colle
Bari
Gravina
U. Bitonto
Modugno
Molfetta
Giovinazzo
Terlizzi
Corato
Ruvo
TARANTO
Gulf of Taranto
C. d. Colonne
Matera
Bitonto
Andria
Barletta
Trani
Canosa di Puglia
Spinazzola
Melfi
Lavello
Cerignola
Foggia
Ferrandina
Pisticci
Policoro
S. Giovanni
Rossano
C. Trionto
Crotone
Gulf of Squillace
C. Rizzuto
BASILICATA
Potenza
Rionero
Lagonegro
Lauria
Castrovillari
Cassano
APENNINES
Catanzaro
Squillace
Caulonia
Siderno
Gioiosa Ionica
C. Spartivento
Montalto Uffugo
Paolo
Cosenza
Amantea
Sambiase
Sant'Eufemia
Gulf of Sant'Eufemia
Vibo Valentia
Palmi
Taurianova
C. Vaticano
Reggio di Calabria
Strait of Messina
Messina
Milazzo
C. Peloro
Patti
Castroreale
Taormina
Giarre
Acireale
Riposto
Catania
Augusta
Syracuse (Siracusa)
Avola
Noto
C. Passero
Pachino
Floridia
Lentini
Palazzolo
Vizzini
Caltagirone
Niscemi
Gela
Mazzarino
Piazza Armerina
Caltanissetta
Enna
Agira
Leonforte
Nicosia
Mistretta
Bronte
Adrano
Etna 10,741
Paternò
Biancavilla
Randazzo
Troina
Centuripe
Cefalù
Termini
Bagheria
Palermo
Monreale
Partinico
Corleone
Misilmeri
Termini Imerese
Roccapalumba
Petralia
Geraci
IONIAN SEA
TYRRHENIAN SEA
Stromboli
Panarea
LIPARI ISLANDS
Salina
Lipari
Vulcano
Alicudi
Filicudi

SICILY
Marsala
Mazara del Vallo
Trapani
Castellammare
Alcamo
Salemi
Partanna
Castelvetrano
Menfi
Sciacca
Ribera
Licata
Agrigento
Porto Empedocle
Canicattì
Naro
Aragona
Favara
S. Cataldo
Montedoro
Pantelleria
Strait of Sicily
EGADI ISLANDS
Levanzo
Favignana
Marettimo
C. S. Vito
Erice
Gulf of Castellammare
Ustica
Cefalù

PELAGIE ISLANDS
Linosa
Lampedusa
Pantelleria
Malta Channel

ROME AND ENVIRONS

Palombara
Palestrina
Monterotondo
Sette Bagni
S. Vito Romano
Guidonia
Vicovaro
Zagarolo
Grottaferrata
Valmontone
Artena
Segni
Cori
Tivoli
Pisoniano
Palidoro
Cesano
Sabazia
Aguzzia
Prima Porta
Torre Gaia
Frascati
Ciampino
Marino
Albano Laziale
Castel Gandolfo
Nemi
Ariccia
Genzano
Velletri
Lanuvio
VATICAN CITY
ROME
Ostia Antica
Lido di Roma
Fiumicino
Pomezia
L. Bracciano
Cerveteri
Ladispoli
Maccarese
Fregene
TYRRHENIAN SEA
Tiber

0 5 10 15
MILES

VATICAN CITY

Via Aurelia
Piazza S. Pietro
Vatican Gardens

0   300   600
SCALE

N

TUNISIA
Tunis
Bizerte
C. Bon
Zembra
G. of Tunis
Kelibia
Nabeul
Hammamet
Gulf of Hammamet
Kalaa Kebira
Sousse
Monastir
Kairouan
Mahdia
Seb. Kebira
Seb. Sidi-el-Hani
Seb. Scerita
La Galite

MEDITERRANEAN SEA

SARDINIA
Bonifacio
Str. of Bonifacio
La Maddalena
C. Testa
Olbia
Tempio Pausania
Siniscola
Dorgali
G. of Orosei
Nuoro
Bitti
Oliena
Gennargentu
Lanusei
Ozieri
Macomer
Monti del Gennargentu
San Vito
Sinnai
Ottana
Tirso
Oristano
G. of Oristano
Terralba
Ghilarza
Arborea
Quartu Sant'Elena
Cagliari
G. of Cagliari
C. Carbonara
C. Spartivento
Villacidro
Iglesias
Carbonia
Sant'Antioco
S. Pietro
Carloforte
C. Teulada
Asinara
C. del Falcone
G. of Asinara
Porto Torres
Sorso
Sassari
Fertilia dei Giuliani
Alghero
Bonorva
Bosa

40°
38°
36°
29

SWITZERLAND
and
LIECHTENSTEIN

CONIC PROJECTION

SCALE OF MILES

0   10   20   30

SCALE OF KILOMETRES

0   5 10   20   30   40   50

Capitals of Countries .... ☆
Capitals of Cantons .... ◉
International Boundaries .... — ∙ — ∙ —
Canals .... — — — —

Copyright by C. S. Hammond & Co., N.Y.

31

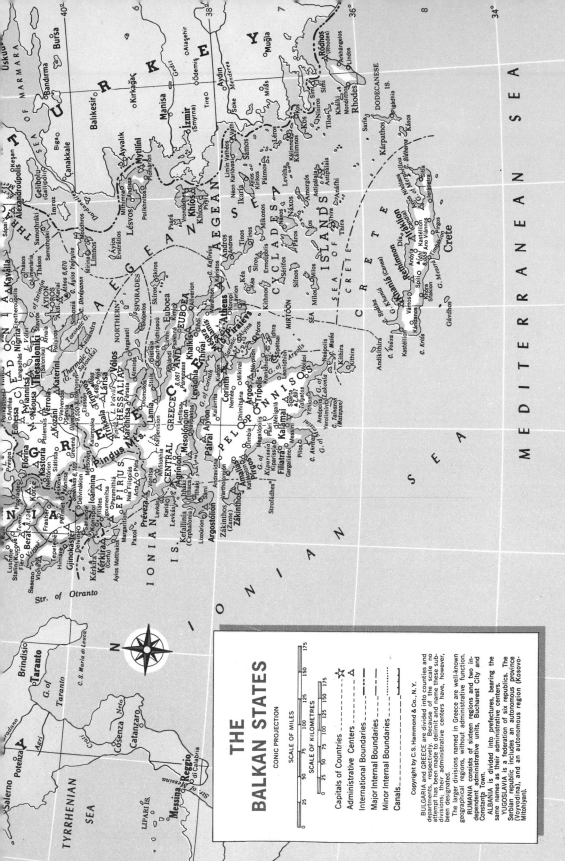

THE BALKAN STATES

CONIC PROJECTION

SCALE OF MILES

0   25   50   75   100   125   150   175

SCALE OF KILOMETRES

0   25   50   75   100   125   150   175

Capitals of Countries	⚝
Administrative Centers	△
International Boundaries	—·—·—
Major Internal Boundaries	—··—··—
Minor Internal Boundaries	·········
Canals	——————

Copyright by C.S. Hammond & Co., N.Y.

BULGARIA and GREECE are divided into counties and departments, respectively. Because of the scale no attempt has been made to delimit and name these subdivisions; their administrative centers have, however, been designated.

The larger divisions named in Greece are well-known geographical regions, without administrative function.

RUMANIA consists of sixteen regions and two independent administrative units, Bucharest City and Constanța Town.

ALBANIA is divided into prefectures, bearing the same names as their administrative centers.

YUGOSLAVIA is a federation of six republics. The Serbian Republic includes an autonomous province (Vojvodina), and an autonomous region (Kosovo-Mitohiyan).

UNION OF SOVIET SOCIALIST REPUBLICS

European Part

CONIC PROJECTION

SCALE OF MILES
0   50   100   200   300

SCALE OF KILOMETRES
0 50 100   200   300

National Capitals .... ☆
Capitals of Union Republics .... ⬡
Administrative Centers .... △
International boundaries .... ▬▬▬
Union Republic boundaries .... ▬ ▪ ▬
A.S.S.R. Oblast, Kray boundaries .... ▬ ▪ ▬
Autonomous Oblast boundaries .... ▪▪▪▪▪▪
National Okrug boundaries .... ▪▪▪▪▪▪
Canals ....

The government of the United States has not recognized the incorporation of Estonia, Latvia and Lithuania into the Soviet Union, nor does it recognize as final the de facto western limit of Polish administration in Germany (the Oder-Neisse line).

ARCTIC OCEAN

GULF OF OB'

KARA SEA

WHITE SEA

BARENTS SEA

NORWAY

SWEDEN

FINLAND

GULF OF BOTHNIA

GULF OF FINLAND

Novaya Zemlya

Yamal Pen.

Kanin Pen.

Kola Pen.

Timan Ridge

Ural Mts.

Northern Ural

Central Ural

Arctic Circle

LENINGRAD

Archangel

Murmansk

Petrozavodsk

Vologda

Yaroslavl'

Ivanovo

Kostroma

Rybinsk

Kalinin

Sverdlovsk

Perm' (Molotov)

Izhevsk

Kirov

Syktyvkar

Chelyabinsk

Nizhniy Tagil

ESTONIAN S.S.R.
Tallinn

LATVIAN S.S.R.
Riga

LITHUANIAN S.S.R.

Helsinki

Stockholm

L. Onega

L. Ladoga

Longitude East of Greenwich

Narodnaya 6,184

Telposiz 5,535

Administrative Divisions bear same names as their respective Capitals or Centers, except:

Administrative Division	Capital/Center	Grid
Abkhaz A.S.S.R.	Sukhumi	F6
Adygey Aut. Oblast	Maykop	F6
Adzhar A.S.S.R.	Batumi	F6
Bashkir A.S.S.R.	Ufa	J4
Chechen-Ingush A.S.S.R.	Grozny	G6
Chuvash A.S.S.R.	Cheboksary	G3
Crimean Oblast	Simferopol'	D6
Dagestan A.S.S.R.	Makhachkala	G6
Kabardin-Balkar A.S.S.R.	Nal'chik	F6
Kalmuck A.S.S.R.	Elista	F5
Karachay-Cherkess Aut. Obl.	Cherkessk	F6
Karelian A.S.S.R.	Petrozavodsk	D2
Komi A.S.S.R.	Syktyvkar	H2
Komi-Permyak Nat'l Okrug	Kudymkar	H3
Mari A.S.S.R.	Yoshkar-Ola	G3
Mordvinian A.S.S.R.	Saransk	G4
Nagorno-Karabakh Aut. Obl.	Stepanakert	G7
Nenets Nat'l Okrug	Nar'yan-Mar	H1
North Ossetian A.S.S.R.	Ordzhonikidze	F6
South Ossetian Aut. Obl.	Tskhinvali	F6
Tatar A.S.S.R.	Kazan'	G3
Trans-Carpathian Oblast	Uzhgorod	B5
Udmurt A.S.S.R.	Izhevsk	H3
Volyn Oblast	Lutsk	C4

Copyright by C. S. HAMMOND & CO., N.Y.

37

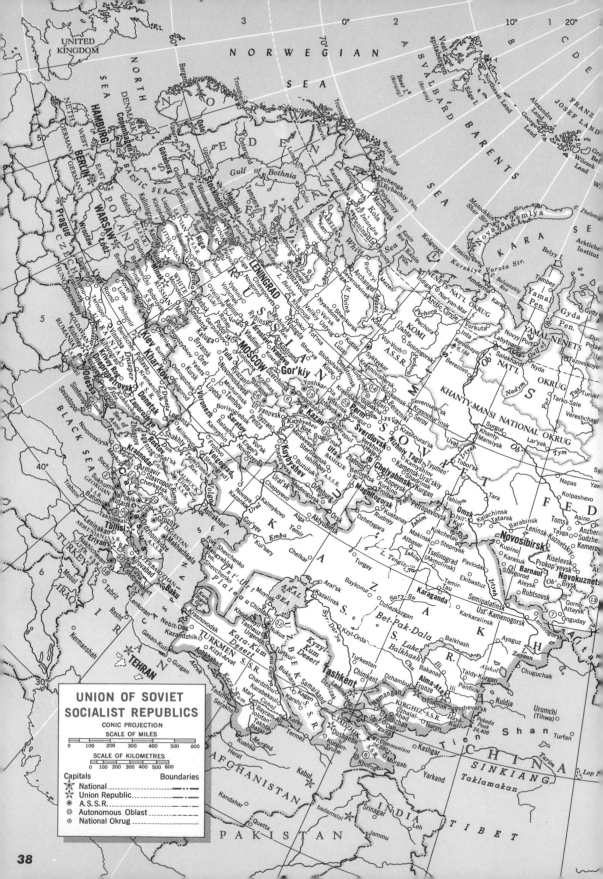

ARCTIC OCEAN

Longitude East of Greenwich
40° 60° 80° 100° 120° 140° 160° 170° 180° 1 170° Longitude West of Greenwich 2 160° 3

UNITED STATES
ALASKA
Nome

H J K L M N O P Q R S T U
Bering Str.
St. Lawrence I. (U.S.)

Komsomolets I.
SEVERNAYA
Pioner Is. October Revolution I.
ZEMLYA
Bol'shevik I.
Vil'kitskiy Str.
Boris C. Chelyuskin

LAPTEV

NEW SIBERIAN
ISLANDS
Faddeyevskiy I.
Novaya
Sibir' I.
Kotel'nyy I.
Bol'shoy Lyakhov I.
Dmitriy Laptev Str.

EAST SIBERIAN
SEA
De Long Str.
Wrangel I.
CHUKCHI
SEA

Bering Str.
C. Dezhnev
Gulf Pen.
Beringovskiy
C. Navarin

Taymyr
Peninsula
Lake
Taymyr
Kozhevnikovo
Nordvik
Olenek
Bay
Tiksi
Kazach'ye
Allaykha
Indigirka
Druzhina
Nizhniye Kresty
Kolyma
Srednekolymsk
Omolon
Markovo

Ust'-
Chaun
Ayon
Ambarchik

CHUKCHI NAT'L OKRUG (Gyda)
Anadyr' Range
CHUKCHI REPUBLIC
Anadyr
KORYAK
Oyutorskiy

Pyasina
chikha
TAYMYR
NAT'L
Noril'sk Medvezhiy Yar
Volochanka
Khatanga
Dzhelinda
OKRUG
Kheta
Yessey

Olenek
Bulun
Kyusyur
Verkhoyansk
Yana
Verkhoyansk
Ege-Khaya
Arctic Circle
Zyryanka
Y. A. S. S. R.
Cherskiy Range
Taskan
Omsukchan
Penzhino
Kamenskoye
Gizhiga
Palana
NAT'L OKRUG
Ust'-Kamchatsk

Sukhana
Zhigansk
Siktyakh
Vilyuy Range
EVENKI
NAT'L OKRUG
Tura
Poligus
Baykit
Strelka
Stony Tunguska
Chunya
Vanavara
Nakanna
Nyurba
Markha
Vilyuysk
Verkhne-Vilyuysk
Yakutsk
Pokrovsk
Lena
Aldan
Zhatay
El'dikan
Ust'-Maya
Amga
Khandyga
Allakh-
Yun'
Oymyakon
Ust'-
Nera
Srednekan
Magadan
Ola
Atka
Yamsk
Shelekhov
Gulf

Klyuchevskaya Sopka
15,912
Petropavlovsk-
Kamchatsky
Industrial'nyy

KOMANDORSKIYE
IS.

YAKUT
SOVIET
SOCIALIST
FEDERATED
REPUBLIC

SEA OF
OKHOTSK

BERING SEA

KURIL ISLANDS

PACIFIC OCEAN

Yeniseysk
Makl'akovo
Kezhma
Upper Tunguska
Chuna
Ilimsk
Kirensk
Mama
Bodaybo
Nepa
Peleduy
Olekma
Tommot
Aldan
Chul'man
Aldan
Plateau
Nagornyy
Nel'kan
Chagda
Ayan
Shantar
Is.
Udskoye
Nikolayevsk
Okha
Aleksandrovsk-Sakhalinskiy
Sakhalin
Poronaysk
Kansk
Tayshet
Nizhneudinsk
Minusinsk
Tulun
Zima
Ilanskiy
Bratsk
Nizhne-
Angarsk
Baunt
Bagdarin
Muya
Kalakan
Chara
Tyndinskiy
Skovorodino
Zeya
Magdagachi
Svobodnyy
Belogorsk
Zavitinsk
Birobidzhan
Khabarovsk
Komsomol'sk
Sovetskaya Gavan'
Vanino
Dolinsk
Yuzhno-Sakhalinsk
Kholmsk
Korsakov
La Pérouse Str.

Krasnoyarsk
B'sk Mts
Cheremkhovo
Tayshet
Kachug
Kyzyl
Örlik
Shagonar
Samagaltay
Tannu-Ola Ra.
Baykal
Irkutsk
Angarsk
Ust'-Ordynskiy
Ulan-Ude
BURYAT A.S.S.R.
Petrovsk-
Zabaykal'skiy
Khilok
Aginskoye
Borzya
Zabaykal'sk
Manchouli
Nerchinsk
Shilka
Sretensk
Chita
Chernyshevsk
Moho
Dzalinda
Shimanovsk
Mogocha
Raychikhinsk
Obluch'ye
Leninskoye
Blagoveshchensk
Amur
Bureya
Tsitsihar
MANCHURIA
Sikhote-Alin' Ra.
Iman
Lesozavodsk
Spassk-
Dal'niy
Ussuriysk
Artem
Nakhodka
Vladivostok
Ch'ŏngjin
Sapporo
HOKKAIDO
Hakodate
Morioka
Sendai

Kyzyl
Shagonar
Gusinoozersk
Kyakhta
Gorodok
Selenga
Orkhon
Altan Bulak
Menza
Choibalsan
Uliassutai
Ulan Bator

MONGOLIA

INNER
MONGOLIA

CHINA
Harbin
Changchun
Kirin
Fushun
Mukden
Anshan
Liaoyang
Huozhou
Hamhŭng
Wŏnsan
NORTH
KOREA
P'yŏngyang
SEOUL
Inch'ŏn
SOUTH
KOREA
Taegu
Pusan
Korea Strait
SEA OF
JAPAN
TOKYO
Yokohama
Kobe
Kyoto
Nagoya
OSAKA
Fukuoka
Kumamoto
Kyushu
Shikoku
Hiroshima

Peking
Tientsin
Tsinan
Tsingtao
Huang Ho
Sinsiang
Cheju
YELLOW
SEA

© C. S. HAMMOND & CO., Maplewood, N.J.

39

ATLANTIC OCEAN

ARCTIC OCEAN

PACIFIC OCEAN

BERING SEA

Aleutian Islands

UNITED STATES
Alaska

Bering Strait

Anadyr

Kamchatka Peninsula

SEA OF OKHOTSK

Sakhalin I. (to U.S.S.R.)

Kuril Islands (to U.S.S.R.)

Hokkaido

Honshu

Tokyo

Osaka

Shikoku

Kyushu

Ryukyu Islands (to U.S.)

JAPAN

SEA OF JAPAN

Vladivostok

Khabarovsk

NORTH KOREA

SOUTH KOREA

Pyongyang

Seoul

Lutta

PONYGYANG SEA OF

YELLOW SEA

Tientsin

Tsingtao

EAST CHINA SEA

Shanghai

Nanking

Wuhan

Foochow

Yangtze Kiang

Manchuria

Amur River

Harbin

Mukden

Peking

Lanchow

Sian

Hwang Ho

Chungking Kiang

CHINA

Chita

Irkutsk

Lake Baikal

Ulan Bator

MONGOLIA

Gobi Desert

ALTAY MOUNTAINS

TIEN SHAN

Sinkiang

Urumchi

Kashgar

KUNLUN MOUNTAINS

Tibet

Verkhoyansk

Yakutsk

Lena River

Igarka

Yenisey River

Novosibirsk

Karaganda

Lake Balkhash

Alma-Ata

KASHMIR

Islamabad

Kabul

Siberia

Soviet Socialist Republics

RUSSIA

Ob River

Irtysh

River

Omsk

Sverdlovsk

Tashkent

Syr-Dar'ya R.

Amu-Dar'ya

Ashkhabad

AFGHANISTAN

North Pole

180°

160°

140°

120°

100°

80°

60°

40°

20°

0°

Severnaya Zemlya (to U.S.S.R.)

New Siberian Is. (to U.S.S.R.)

Franz Josef Land (to U.S.S.R.)

Novaya Zemlya (to U.S.S.R.)

KARA SEA

Svalbard (Norwegian)

GREENLAND (Danish)

ICELAND

Arctic Circle

NORWAY

SWEDEN

FINLAND

Moscow

Volga River

Ural R.

Ural River

URAL MOUNTAINS

UNION OF SOVIET

EUROPE

Aral Sea

CASPIAN SEA

IRAN

Tehran

Tabriz

Baghdad

Basra

KUWAIT

Persi

Riyadh BAH.

SAUDI

Tigris R.

Euphrates R.

GREAT BRITAIN

IRELAND

NORTH SEA

DEN.

BALTIC SEA

NETH.

BELG.

WEST GER.

EAST GER.

POLAND

CZECHO.

SWITZ.

AUSTRIA

HUNG.

YUGOSLAVIA

RUMANIA

BULG.

ALB.

GREECE

ITALY

FRANCE

BLACK SEA

TURKEY

Ankara

Asia Minor

CYPRUS

Crete (Greek)

LEB.

SYRIA

ISRAEL

Jerusalem

JORDAN

U.A.R.

MEDITERRANEAN SEA

Suez Canal

Egypt

Nile River

RED SEA

50°

60°

70°

80°

80°

70°

60°

50°

40°

30°

40°

40°

40°

40°

Map of
ASIA

SCALE OF MILES

0 200 400 600 800 1000

Capitals of Countries
Cities
Boundaries of Countries
Other Boundaries
Mountain Peaks
Canals

Water
Lowlands
Depression
Highlands
Mountains

Copyright by C.S. Hammond & Co., N.Y.

Longitude   East of   Greenwich
50°   60°   70°   80°   90°   100°   110°   120°

AUSTRALIA

Molucca I.
BANDA SEA
CELEBES SEA
Celebes
Flores
Timor
Sumba
Sumbawa
Bali
Java
JAVA SEA
I N D O N E S I A
Sumatra
Djakarta
Medan
SINGAPORE
Borneo
Sabah
BRUNEI (British)
Sarawak
M A L A Y S I A
Kuala Lumpur
Malaya
Gulf of Siam
SOUTH CHINA SEA
Saigon
Phnom Penh
CAMBODIA
SOUTH VIET-NAM
Bangkok
THAILAND
BURMA
Hainan
Canton
HONG KONG (British)
Kunming
NORTH VIET-NAM
Hanoi
Mekong R.
Salween R.
Irrawaddy R.
Rangoon
ANDAMAN SEA
Andaman Is. (Indian)
Nicobar Is. (Indian)
BAY OF BENGAL
Calcutta
Madras
CEYLON
Colombo
Dondra Head
Cape Comorin
DECCAN PLATEAU
Hyderabad
Bombay
Ahmadabad
New Delhi
INDIA
NEPAL
Katmandu
BHUTAN
Mt. Everest
Ganges R.
Laccadive Is. (Indian)
MALDIVE ISLANDS
Tropic of Cancer
Karachi
PAK.
Indus R.
ARABIAN SEA
OMAN
MUSCAT
TRUCIAL OMAN
Rub' al Khali Desert
A R A B I A
Mecca
Gulf of Aden
Socotra (So. Yemen)
SOUTHERN YEMEN
Madinat ash Sha'b
YEMEN
San'a
Ta'izz
T. A. S. (Fr.)
ETHIOPIA
SOMALI REP.
SEYCHELLES (British)
BRITISH INDIAN OCEAN TERR.
MAURITIUS
Réunion (French)
Madagascar
MALAGASY REP.

Equator

Tropic of Capricorn

I N D I A N   O C E A N

PHILIPPINES
REPUBLIC OF THE PHILIPPINES
Luzon
Quezon City
Manila
Mindanao
Taiwan (Formosa)

Yangtze

10°   0°   10°   20°   30°   40°

41

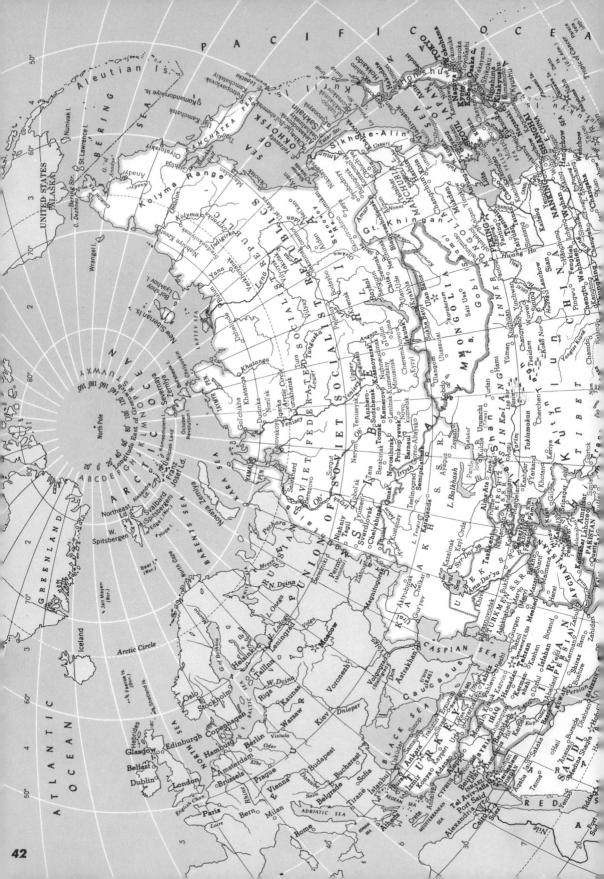

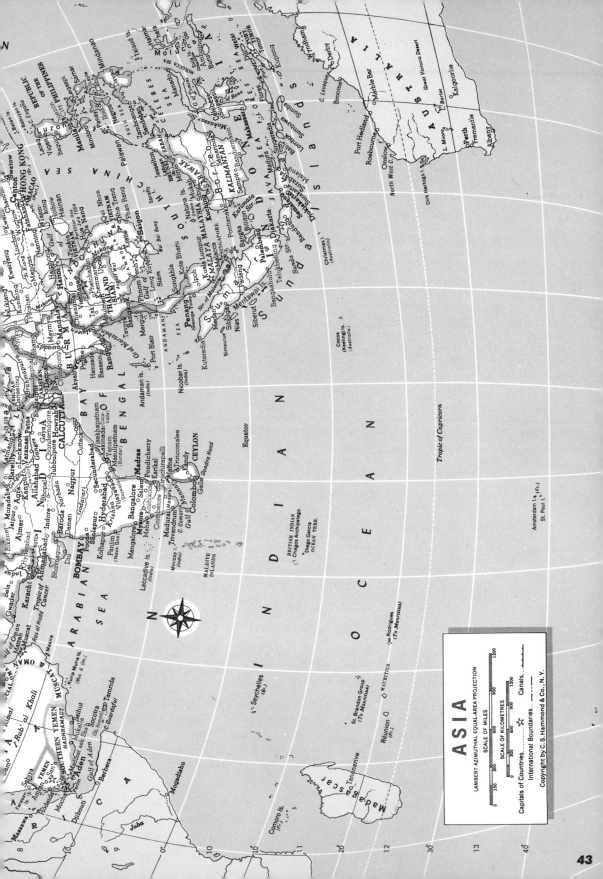

ASIA

LAMBERT AZIMUTHAL EQUAL-AREA PROJECTION

SCALE OF MILES

SCALE OF KILOMETRES

Capitals of Countries..........✪   Canals............

International Boundaries............

Copyright by C. S. Hammond & Co., N. Y.

43

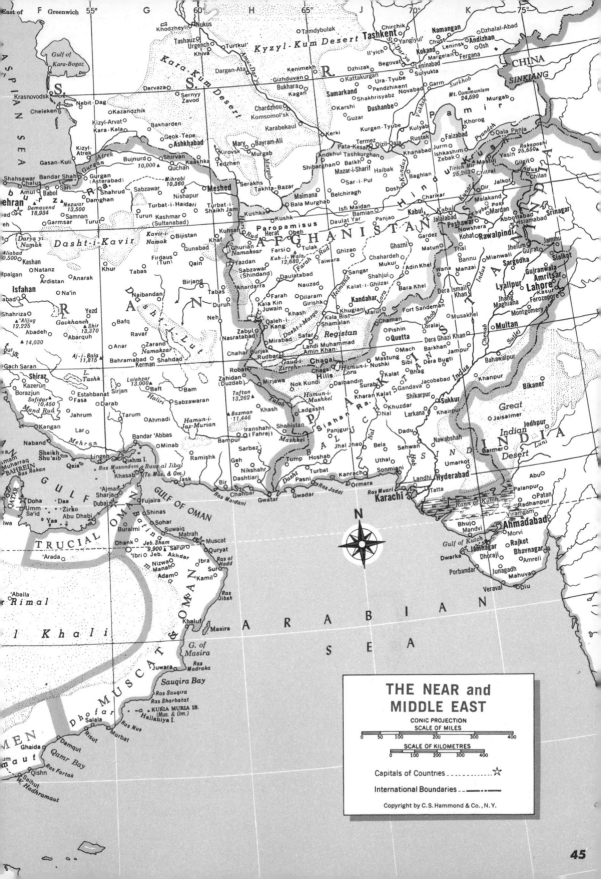

THE NEAR and
MIDDLE EAST

CONIC PROJECTION
SCALE OF MILES

0   50   100   200   300   400

SCALE OF KILOMETRES
0   100   200   300   400

Capitals of Countries .... ☆

International Boundaries _ . _ . _

Copyright by C. S. Hammond & Co., N. Y.

45

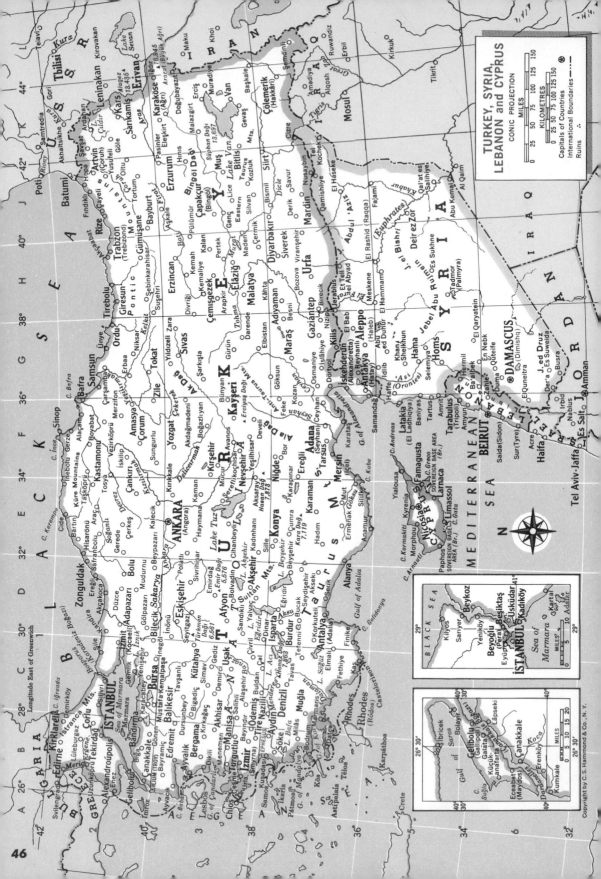

TURKEY, SYRIA,
LEBANON and CYPRUS

CONIC PROJECTION

MILES
0 25   50   75   100   125   150

KILOMETRES
0   25 50 75 100 125 150

⊕ Capitals of Countries
International Boundaries ....
Ruins .....

Copyright by C.S. Hammond & Co., N.Y.

ISRAEL and JORDAN
CYLINDRICAL PROJECTION
Copyright by C.S. Hammond & Co., N.Y.
SCALE OF MILES
0 5 10 15 20 25 30
SCALE OF KILOMETRES
0 5 10 15 20 25 30

Capitals of Countries .... ☆
District and Provincial Capitals .... ◉
International Boundaries ....
District and Provincial Boundaries ...._.._
Demilitarized Zone Boundaries ....
Neutral Zone Boundaries ....

47

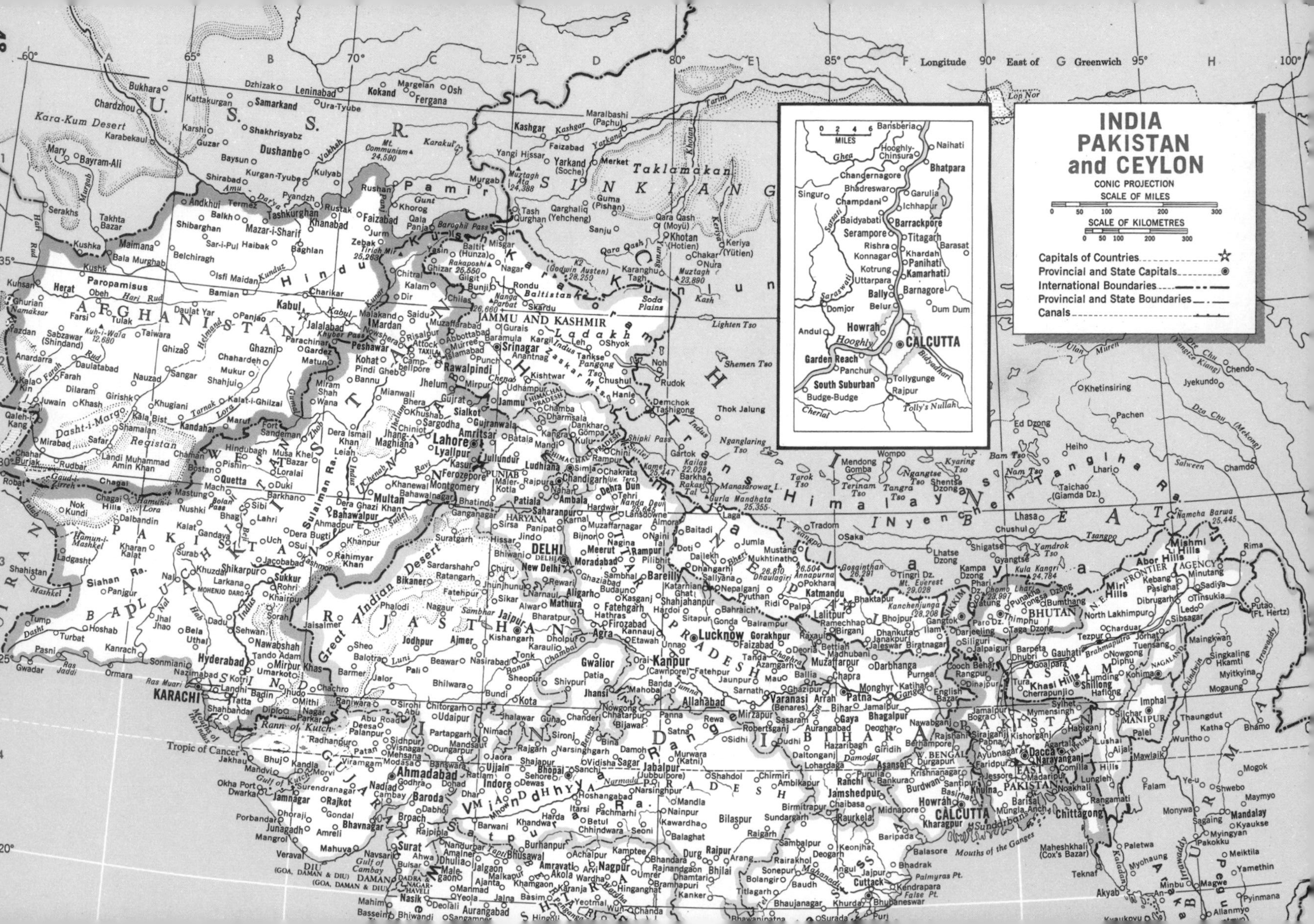

INDIA PAKISTAN and CEYLON

CONIC PROJECTION

SCALE OF MILES
0   50   100   200   300

SCALE OF KILOMETRES
0   50 100   200   300

Capitals of Countries .... ✪
Provincial and State Capitals .... ◉
International Boundaries .... ———
Provincial and State Boundaries .... ———
Canals .... ----

MILES
0 2 4 6

CALCUTTA

Nahati
Barisberiac
Bhatpara
Ganjul
Ichhapur
Hooghly-Chinsura
Barasat
Baidyabati
Titagarh
Barrackpore
Serampore
Rishra
Panihati
Changernagore
Konnagar
Khardah
Chamdoni
Dum Dum
Uttarpara
Kotrung
Baidyabati
Barnagore
Bally
Belur
Howrah
HOWRAH
Hooghly R.
Rajpur
Tollygunge
Garden Reach
Panchur
South Suburban
Domjur
Andul
Chetal
Budge-Budge

PAKISTAN
AFGHANISTAN
KASHMIR
JAMMU AND KASHMIR
RAJASTHAN
U.P.
BIHAR
WEST BENGAL
ASSAM
BHUTAN
NEPAL
SIKKIM
PUNJAB
HARYANA
DELHI
GUJARAT
MADHYA PRADESH
ORISSA
SINKIANG
TIBET
U.S.S.R.

KARACHI
DELHI
New Delhi
Lahore
Kabul
Herat
Kandahar
Quetta
CALCUTTA
Howrah
Kanpur
Lucknow
Agra
Gwalior
Allahabad
Benares
Patna
Ahmadabad
Surat
Nagpur
Jaipur
Jodhpur
Amritsar
Rawalpindi
Peshawar
Hyderabad
Multan
Indore
Baroda

Tropic of Cancer

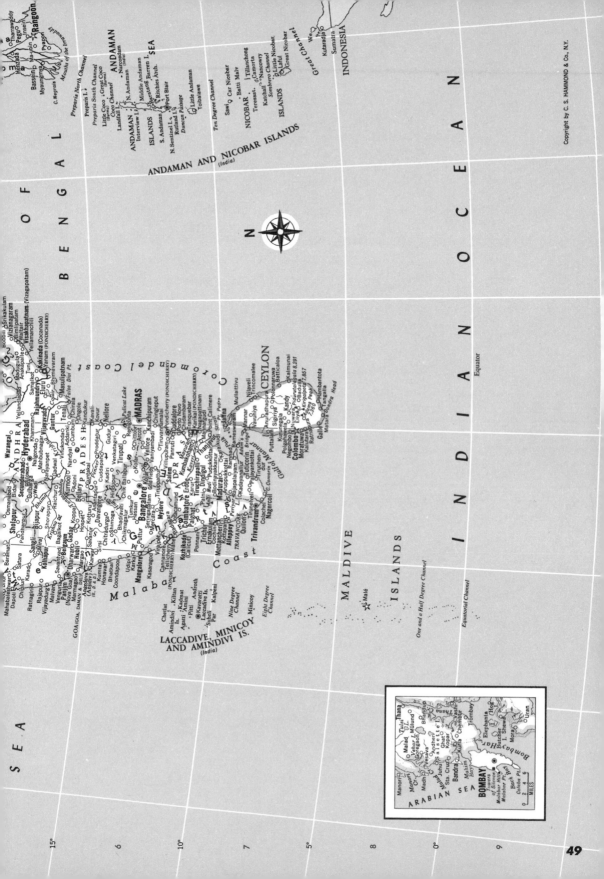

CHINA and MONGOLIA

CONIC PROJECTION

SCALE OF MILES

0   100   200   300   400   500

SCALE OF KILOMETRES

0   100   200   300   400   500

Capitals of Countries....★...   International Boundaries ....
Provincial Capitals........◉   Provincial Boundaries....----
Canals ....┅┅┅   Walls ....ᴧᴧᴧᴧᴧ

Copyright by C.S. Hammond & Co., N.Y.

*Wuhan municipality consists of
Hankow, Hanyang and Wuchang
†Lüta municipality includes
Port Arthur and Dairen

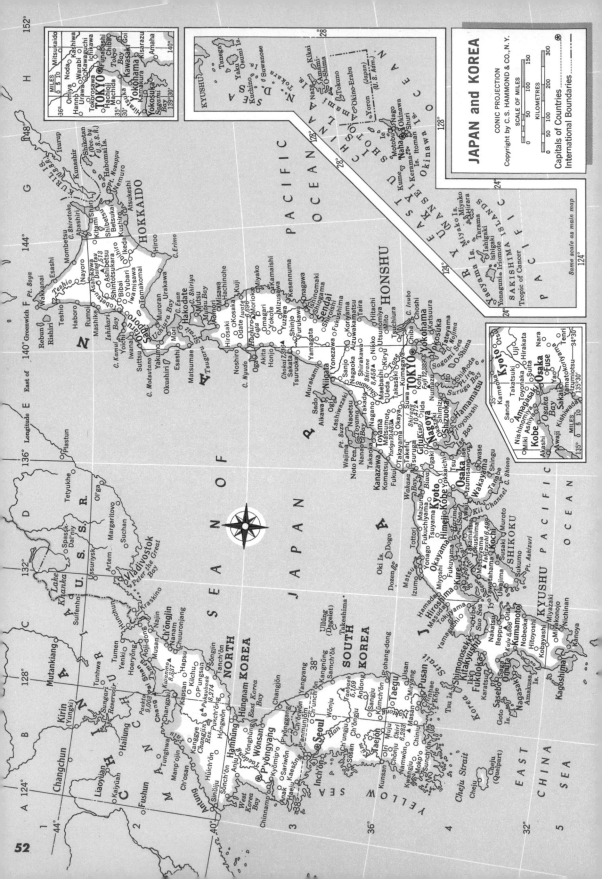

JAPAN and KOREA

CONIC PROJECTION

Copyright by C. S. HAMMOND & CO., N.Y.

SCALE OF MILES

MILES
0   50   100   150

KILOMETRES
0   50   100   200   300

Capitals of Countries ⊛
International Boundaries ....

TOKYO (inset)

MILES
0 5 10

KYOTO – OSAKA (inset)

MILES
0   5   10

Same scale as main map

PACIFIC OCEAN

SEA OF JAPAN

YELLOW SEA

EAST CHINA SEA

NORTH KOREA

SOUTH KOREA

U. S. S. R.

M A N C H U R I A

HOKKAIDO

HONSHU

SHIKOKU

KYUSHU

KURILE IS.

RYUKYU ISLANDS

SAKISHIMA ISL.

Tropic of Cancer

Seoul

Pyŏngyang

Tokyo

Kyoto

Osaka

Nagoya

Yokohama

BURMA, THAILAND, INDOCHINA and MALAYA

CONIC PROJECTION

SCALE OF MILES
0 50 100   200   300

SCALE OF KILOMETRES
0 50 100   200   300

Capitals of Countries .... ⊛
Capitals of States .... ◉
International Boundaries .... ____ ____

53

54

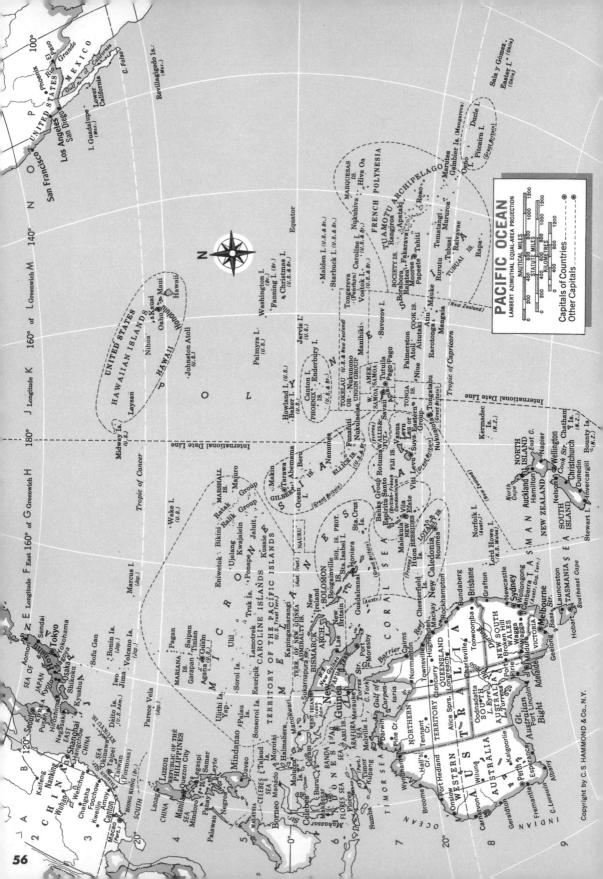

PACIFIC OCEAN

LAMBERT AZIMUTHAL EQUAL-AREA PROJECTION

NAUTICAL MILES

STATUTE MILES

KILOMETERS

Capitals of Countries
Other Capitals

Copyright by C.S. HAMMOND & Co., N.Y.

56

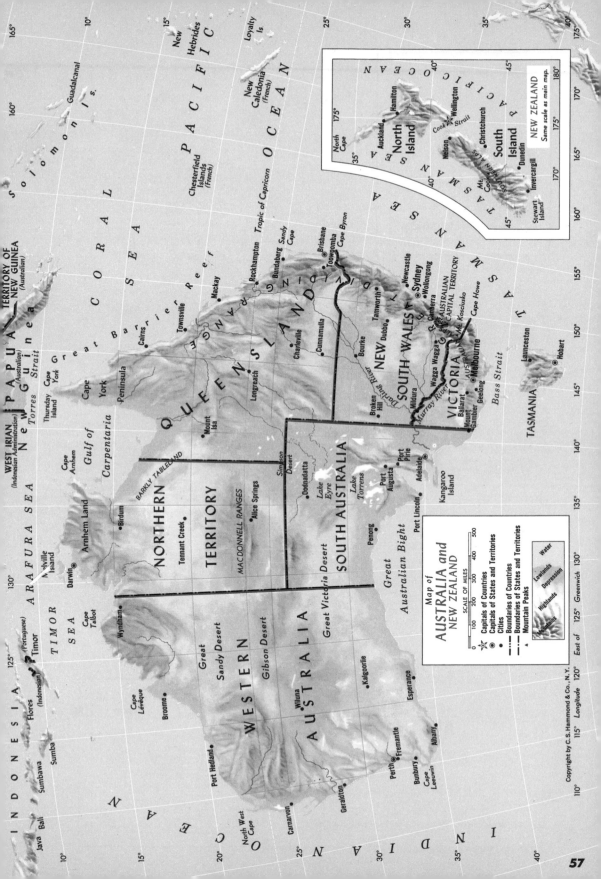

165° 10° 15° New Loyalty 25° 30° 35° 40°
Hebrides Is.

PACIFIC OCEAN

New New **NEW ZEALAND**
Guadalcanal Caledonia *Same scale as main map.*
(French) (French)

PACIFIC OCEAN 45°

Solomon Is. Hamilton 40°
North Wellington 180°
Cape Auckland Cook Str. Nelson Christchurch
North South Dunedin
TERRITORY OF Chesterfield **Island** **Island**
NEW GUINEA Islands Invercargill
(Australian) (French) Mt. 170°
35° Tropic of Capricorn Stewart 45°
Island 175° SOUTHERN ALPS Kosciusko

PAPUA CORAL SEA TASMAN SEA
(Australian)

New Guinea Torres Strait Great Barrier Reef Brisbane Cape Byron
Thursday Cape Toowoomba Newcastle
WEST IRIAN Island York Rockhampton Sandy Sydney
(Indonesian Administration) Cape Bundaberg Cape Wollongong
Cape York Mackay **NEW** AUSTRALIAN
Arnhem Peninsula Townsville **QUEENSLAND** Tamworth CAPITAL TERRITORY
ARAFURA SEA Cairns Charleville Dubbo **SOUTH WALES** Canberra
Cape Cunnamulla Bourke Mt. Kosciusko Cape Howe
Melville Arnhem Longreach Broken Wagga Launceston
Island Land Hill Wagga VICTORIA Hobart
Darwin Gulf of Mount Isa Mildura Melbourne
TIMOR SEA Carpentaria Bass Strait
Cape Barkly Tableland Murray River Ballarat Geelong
Talbot Simpson Mount **TASMANIA**
TIMOR Birdum **NORTHERN** Desert Gambier
(Portuguese) MACDONNELL RANGES Oodnadatta
Flores Tennant Creek **TERRITORY** Alice Springs Lake Lake
(Indonesian) Eyre Torrens
Wyndham Port
INDONESIA Cape **SOUTH AUSTRALIA** Pirie
Léveque Port Adelaide
Sumba Broome Augusta Kangaroo
Sumbawa Great Port Lincoln Island
Bali Sandy Desert Great Victoria Desert Penong
Java **WESTERN** Gibson Desert Great Australian Bight

Port Hedland **Map of**
North West Wiluna **AUSTRALIA and**
Cape **AUSTRALIA** Kalgoorlie **NEW ZEALAND**
Carnarvon SCALE OF MILES
Geraldton Esperance 0 100 200 300 400 500
Perth ⊛ Capitals of Countries
Fremantle Bunbury ◉ Capitals of States and Territories
Cape Albany ● Cities
Leeuwin ---- Boundaries of Countries
--- Boundaries of States and Territories
▲ Mountain Peaks

Water
Lowlands
Depression
Highlands
Mountains

INDIAN OCEAN

Copyright by C. S. Hammond & Co., N.Y.

East of Greenwich
110° 115° 120° 125° 130° 135° 140°

57

Inset map (upper left):

MILES
0 10 20 30 40

116°

Moore R.
Darling Ra.
Gingin
Muchea
Toodyay
Northam
York
Subiaco
Nedlands
Perth
Midland
Fremantle
Rottnest
Garden I.
Rockingham
C. Bouvard
Mandurah
Pinjarra
Peel Inlet
L. Preston
Mt. Keats
Warpona
Swan R.
Avon R.
Mt. Dale ▲1,780
Armadale
Kwinana
Jarrahdale
Brookton
Beverley
Pingelly
Hotham R.
Williams R.
Williams
Goomalling

32°

INDIAN OCEAN

Main map labels:

INDONESIA
ARAFURA SEA
Frederik Hendrik I.
Wetar   Babar Is.   Selaru
Flores   Alor   Dili   PORTUGUESE
Solor   OE-CUSSE   TIMOR
SAWU SEA
Kūpang
Sawu Is.   Roti
TIMOR   SEA
TERR. OF ASHMORE
Ashmore Is. & Cartier Is.
Cartier I.
Melville I.
C. Van Diemen   Dundas Str.
Bathurst I.   Croker I. Miss.   C. Wessel I.
Van Diemen   Goulburn   Wessel Is.
Clarence Str.   Gulf   Is.   C. Arnhem
DARWIN
Rum Jungle   Arnhem
Adelaide River   Land
Pine Creek
RESERVE   C. Grey
Katherine   Groote
Mataranka   Cape Be.
Rope R.   Limmen Bight   CARP
Urapunga   Sir Edward
Larrimah   Group
Borroloola   Vande
NORTHERN
Coolibah
Daly Waters
Victoria River Downs
Wave Hill   L. Woods   Anthony
Newcastle Waters   Powell Creek   Lagoon
RES.   Alexandria   Tableland
TERRITORY
Tanami Desert   Barkly
The Granites   Tennant Creek   Hatches Creek   Cam
Tanami   RESERVE   Barrow Creek
L. Mackay   Mount Doreen   Harts Range
Alice Springs   Hay
RESERVE   Macdonnell   Ranges
Hermannsburg   Ewaninga
L. Macdonald   Mission
Hopkins L.   Finke   Rodinga
Petermann   L. Amadeus   Bundooma   Simpson
Ranges   Ayers Rock   Rumbalara   Desert
▲2,845   Kulgera   Charlotte Waters
Musgrave Ranges   Isabella
ABORIGINAL   RESERVE   The   Peer
Mt. Woodroffe   Alberga   Macumba   Pool
Birksgate   4,970   Oodnadatta
Range   Algebuckina
SOUTH
Warrina
Coober Pedy   Lake
Great Victoria Desert   Eyre
Forrest   Anna Creek
Lakes   Stuart   Farina
AUSTRAL
Maralinga   Range
Hughes   Wynbring   Mt.
Reid   Fisher   Ooldea   Kingoonya   Leigh
Rawlinna   Forrest   Woomera
Lake   Eba   Lake
RES.   Madura   Harris   Torrens
Eucla   L. Everard
RESERVE   C. Nuyts   Iron Knob
Nullarbor Plain   Penong   Eyre   Whyalla   Wa.
Ceduna   Port   Quor
Streaky B.   Gawler Ra.   Augusta
Streaky Bay   Buckleboo   Iron Baron
Investigator   Elliston   Port Pirie
Group   Eyre   Port   Spencer
Pen.   Port Lincoln   Edithburg   Adel
GREAT   Yorke Pen.
C. Spencer   Investigator Str.
AUSTRALIAN   Kangaroo I.   Victor   Kingsc
BIGHT   Encounter   Lac

WESTERN
Port Hedland   Thou P.
De Grey   Bamboo
Roebourne   Mundabullangana   Marble Bar
Dampier Arch.   Yule R.   RES.
Monte Bello Is.   Fortescue   Nullagine
Barrow I.   Onslow   Wittenoom Gorge
Muiron Is.   Hamersley Ra.   L. Disappointment
North West C.   Mt. Bruce 4,024
Learmonth   Ashburton R.
Exmouth Gulf   Gibson   Desert
Pt. Cloates   L. Macdonald
C. Farquhar   Hopkins L.
C. Cuvier   Lyons R.   Petermann
Geographe Chan.   Gascoyne R.   Ranges
L. McLeod   Robinson Ranges
Bernier I.   Wooramel R.   Mt. Hale   L. Carnegie
Dorre I.   2,400
Carnarvon   Mt. Margaret   L. Wells
Naturaliste Chan.   Meekatharra   Miss.
Dirk Hartog I.   Nannine   L. Yeo
Steep Pt.   Wiluna   Laverton
Big Bell   RESERVE   ABORIGINAL
Cue   Leonora
Shark B.   Mt. Magnet   L. Barlee
Ajana   Sandstone   Menzies   L. Raeside
Yuna   Yalgoo   Youanmi
AUSTRALIA
Northampton   Mingenew   Morawa
Geraldton   Dongara   L. Moore   Broad Arrow
Houtman Abrolhos   Dalwallinu   Kalgoorlie
Greenough   Ballidu   Boulder   Zanthus
Darling   Mukinbudin   Coolgardie
Muchea   Moora   Southern Cross   L. Cowan
Perth   Northam   Meredin   L. Lefroy   Balladonia
Fremantle   Bruce Rock   Norseman   Madura
Kwinana   York   Hyden   L. Dundas
Corrigin   Widgiemooltha
Range   Narrogin   Lake Grace
Bunbury   Wagin   Newdegate   Ravensthorpe
Collie   Katanning   Hopetoun   Pt. Culver
Geographe B.   Borden   Esperance
C. Naturaliste   Bridgetown   Cap Le Grand   C. Arid
Busselton   Nannup   Archipelago
Augusta   Northcliffe   Albany   of the Recherche
C. Leeuwin   Flinders B.   Bald Head
Pt. D'Entrecasteaux

Kimberley Plateau
Turkey Creek
King Leopold Ra.
RESERVES   Ord
Fitzroy Crossing   Nicholson
Halls Creek   Ord River
C. Talbot   C. Londonderry
Pt. Blaze   Peron I.   Anson B.   C. Ford
C. Rulhieres   Joseph
C. Bougainville   Bonaparte
Long Reef   Admiralty Gulf   Gulf
Montague Sound
Browse I.
York Sound
Adele I.   Collier B.   Drysdale R.
Brunswick B.   Koolan I.
Buccaneer Arch.   RESERVES
C. Leveque   Yampi Sound
Lacepede Is.   Derby   St. George
Dampier Land   Ranges
Broome   Fitzroy R.
Roebuck B.   RESERVE
C. Latouche Treville   La Grange
Eighty Mile Beach
Great Sandy Desert
Pardoo

INDIAN   OCEAN

115°   B   120°   Longitude   C   East of   125°   Greenwich   D   130°   E   135°   F
10°   15°   20°   25°   30°   35°   40°

Legend box (lower left):

AUSTRALIA
and
NEW ZEALAND
BONNE PROJECTION

SCALE OF MILES
0   50   100   200   300   400   500

SCALE OF KILOMETRES
0   50   100   200   300   400   500

Capital of Country _ _ ☆   State and Territorial Capitals_ _ △

Inset map (lower right) — Adelaide area:

138° 30'

MILES
0   5   10   15

Gawler   Williamstown
Gawler R.   Q
Elizabeth
Outer   S. Para R.
Harbor   Salisbury   Mt. Pleasant
Port Adelaide   Woodville   Gumeracha
Hindmarsh   Kensington   Lobethal
West Torrens   Adelaide   and Norwood   Woodside
Marion   Unley   Torrens R.
Mitcham   Mt. Lofty
   ▲2,384
Reynella   Onkaparinga   Nairne
Noarlunga   Echunga   Hahndorf
McLaren Vale   Mt. Barker
   Strathalbyn   Bremer R.

Gulf   St. Vincent
35°

138° 30'
Me.
Mo.
C. No.

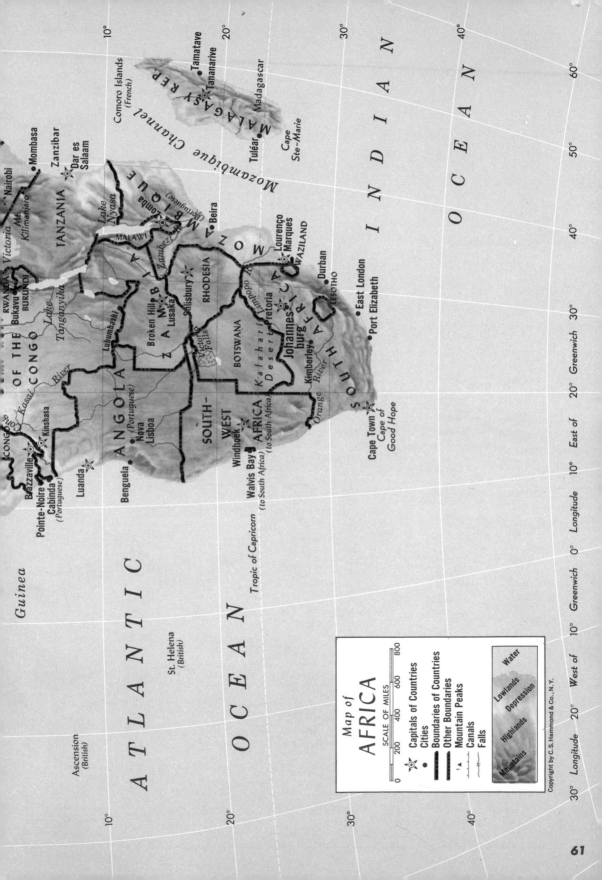

10°
20°
30°
40°

Tamatave
Tananarive

Comoro Islands
(French)

MALAGASY REP.

Madagascar

Tuléar

Cape
Ste-Marie

Mombasa
Zanzibar
Dar es
Salaam

Mozambique Channel

INDIAN

OCEAN

Nairobi

Mt.
Kilimanjaro

TANZANIA

Lake
Nyasa

MALAWI

Lake
Tanganyika

RWANDA
Bukavu
BURUNDI

OF THE CONGO

Lubumbashi

Beira

Zambezi
(Portuguese)

MOZAMBIQUE

RHODESIA

Salisbury

Broken Hill
Lusaka

Z A M B I A

Victoria
Falls

Limpopo R.

Lourenço
Marques

SWAZILAND

Pretoria

Johannes-
burg

SOUTH AFRICA

Durban

LESOTHO

East London

Port Elizabeth

Kasai

River

Congo

Brazzaville

Pointe-Noire
Cabinda
(Portuguese)

Kinshasa

CONGO

Luanda

Benguela

ANGOLA
(Portuguese)

Nova
Lisboa

BOTSWANA

Kalahari

Desert

Kimberley

Orange
River

SOUTH-
WEST
AFRICA
(to South Africa)

Windhoek

Walvis Bay
(to South Africa)

Cape Town
Cape of
Good Hope

Guinea

St. Helena
(British)

Ascension
(British)

ATLANTIC

OCEAN

Tropic of Capricorn

10°
20°
30°
40°

30° Longitude 20° West of 10° Greenwich 0° Greenwich 10° East of 20° Longitude 30° 40° 50° 60°

Map of
AFRICA
SCALE OF MILES
0   200   400   600   800

⬥ Capitals of Countries
• Cities
▬ Boundaries of Countries
▬ Other Boundaries
▲ Mountain Peaks
═ Canals
⌐ Falls

Water
Lowlands
Depression
Highlands
Mountains

Copyright by C. S. Hammond & Co., N.Y.

61

MAP CONTINUED ON

AFRICA
NORTHERN PART
LAMBERT AZIMUTHAL EQUAL-AREA PROJECTION

SCALE OF MILES
0   100   200   400   600

SCALE OF KILOMETRES
0 100 200   400   600

Capitals of Countries _____ ☆
Other Capitals _____ ◉
International Boundaries _____.__.__
Internal Boundaries _____
Canals _____ ⌄_____ Wells ⌄

Copyright by C. S. HAMMOND & Co., N.Y.

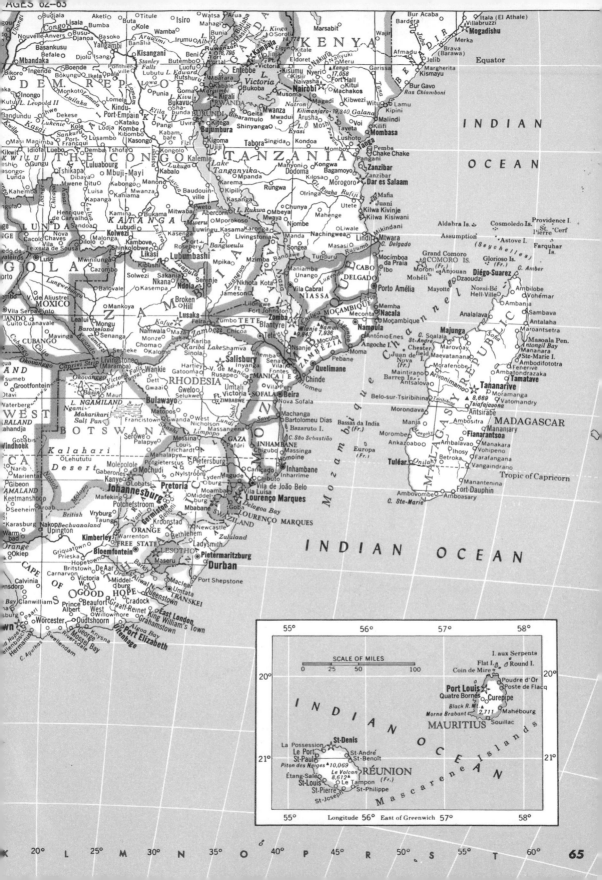

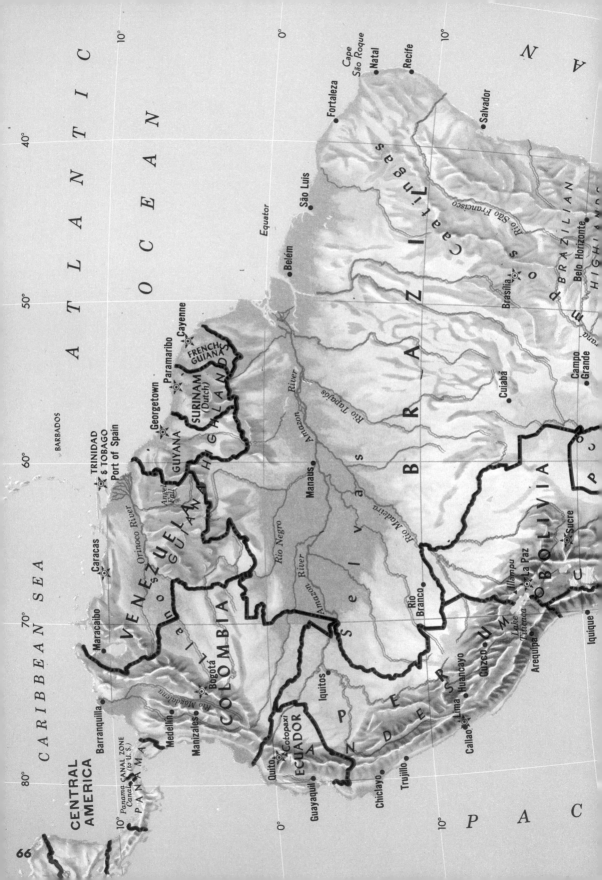

CENTRAL
AMERICA

CARIBBEAN SEA

ATLANTIC OCEAN

ATLANTIC

BARBADOS

TRINIDAD & TOBAGO
Port of Spain

Barranquilla

Maracaibo

Caracas

VENEZUELA

Llanos

Orinoco River

Angel Fall

GUIANA HIGHLANDS

GUYANA

Georgetown

Paramaribo

SURINAM
(Dutch)

Cayenne

FRENCH GUIANA

Medellín

Manizales

Bogotá

Rio Magdalena

COLOMBIA

Rio Negro

Amazon River

Manaus

Amazon River

Belém

Equator

São Luís

Fortaleza

Cape São Roque

Natal

Recife

Caatingas

Rio São Francisco

Salvador

Belo Horizonte

BRAZILIAN HIGHLANDS

Brasília

BRAZIL

Rio Tapajós

Selvas

Rio Madeira

Cuiabá

Campo Grande

Quito

Cotopaxi

ECUADOR

Guayaquil

Chiclayo

Trujillo

Iquitos

Rio Branco

PERU

ANDES

Callao

Lima

Huancayo

Cuzco

Lake Titicaca

Arequipa

Illampu

La Paz

Sucre

BOLIVIA

PANAMA

CANAL ZONE
(to U. S.)
Panama Canal

PACIFIC

N

80°

70°

60°

50°

40°

10°

0°

10°

Equator

10°

0°

10°

A T L A N T I C   O C E A N

Rio de Janeiro

São Paulo
Santos
Curitiba

Pôrto Alegre

Iguassú Falls

A G U A Y

Asunción

Rio Paraná

Rio Uruguay

URUGUAY
Montevideo
Rio de la Plata

Rosario
La Plata
Buenos Aires

Santa Fe

Tucumán

Córdoba

Mendoza
Aconcagua

Bahía Blanca

Río Colorado

P a t a g o n i a

Falkland Islands (British)

Strait of Magellan
Tierra del Fuego

Cape Horn

Antofagasta

Atacama Des.

Coquimbo

Valparaíso
Santiago

Concepción

Puerto Montt

Punta Arenas

Juan Fernández Islands (Chilean)

P A C I F I C   O C E A N

Map of
SOUTH AMERICA

SCALE OF MILES
0 100 200 300 400 500 600

☆ Capitals of Countries
● Cities
▬ Boundaries of Countries
▲ Mountain Peaks
Canals
Falls

Water
Lowlands
Depression
Highlands
Mountains

Copyright by C. S. Hammond & Co., N.Y.

CARIBBEAN SEA

NETH. ANTILLES
WEST INDIES

Martinique (Fr.)

15°   85°   D   80°   E   75°   F   70°   G   65°   H

Grena

St. George's   Grenada

C. Gracias a Dios

C. Grande

Isla de Providencia (Col.)

Isla de San Andrés (Col.)

1   NICARAGUA

L. de Perlas

Bluefields   Pta. Mico

Bahía de San Juan del Norte

Pen. de Paraguaná   Pta. de Gallinas

Guajira Pen.

Aruba   Curaçao   Willemstad   Bonaire

Los Roques

La Orchila

I. de Margarita   La Asunción

La Tortuga

I. de Coche

Carúpano   Tucupita   Caribe

St.

Port

Trinidad

Serpents

Uribia

Santa Marta

Riohacha

Pto. Cumarebo

Amuay   Pto. Cabello

San

Coro   Nirgua

La Guaira   Caracas   Pto. La Cruz   Cumaná

COSTA RICA   San José

PANAMA   Panamá

Gulf of Panamá

Punta Mala

C. Matapalo   Golfo Dulce   Punta Burica

G. de Chiriquí   I. Coiba

G. de Montijo   Punta Mariato

Pta. San Blas

Colón   Cristóbal

CANAL ZONE (U.S.)

Magdalena   Ciénaga

Barranquilla   Pto. Colombia   Calamar

Cartagena

Sincelejo   Mompós

Turbo   Montería

Ayapel   San Marcos

Quibdó   Antioquia

C. Corrientes   Itsmina

Buenaventura

Medellín   Manizales

Pereira   Ibagué

Cali   Palmira   Buga   Tuluá

Popayán   Neiva

Huila 18,865

Pasto   Florencia

Tumaco   Barbacoas   Bolívar   Guapí

Esmeraldas   Pta. Galera   Ibarra   Tulcán   Mocoa

Bahía de Caráquez   Portoviejo   Quito

Manta   Jipijapa   Latacunga   Tena

ECUADOR   Ambato   Riobamba

Guaranda   Guayaquil   Alausí   Macas

Gulf of Guayaquil   Azogues   Cuenca

Santa Elena   Salinas   Machala   Pasaje

Tumbes   Pto. Bolívar   Ta. Rosa

Loja   Zamora

Talara   Sullana   Barranca   Marañón

Punta Pariñas   Paita   Piura   Jaén

Catacaos   Requena

B. de Sechura   Chachapoyas   Moyobamba

Pta. Aguja

I. Lobos de Tierra   Pimentel   Chiclayo   Cajamarca

Is. Lobos de Afuera   Puerto Eten   Ascope

Pacasmayo

Trujillo   Salaverry   Pucallpa

Chimbote   Huascarán 22,205   Masisea

Huarás

Supe   Huanuco   Pto. Bermúdez

Cerro de Pasco   Atalaya

Huacho   Tarma   San Ramón

La Oroya   Jauja

Callao   Lima   Huancayo

Lurín   Huancavelica   Ayacucho

Cañete   Chincha Alta   Cuzco

Pisco   Ica

Pen. Paracas   Nasca   Abancay

Coracora   Sicuani

Lomas   Atico   El Misti 19,199

Camaná   Arequipa   Juliaca

Matarani   Mollendo

Moquegua   Titicaca

Tacna   Corocoro

Arica   Puquios

Tarapacá   Desaguadero

Pisagua   Iquique

CHILE

NETH. ANTILLES

VENEZUELA

Coro   Nirgua   Villa de Cura   Barcelona   Maturín

Valencia   Aragua de Barcelona

San Felipe   Valera   Guanare   Calabozo   El Tigre   Ciudad Guayana

Trujillo   Barinas   El Tocuyo

Mérida   Barquisimeto   Bruzual   El Pao   Ciudad Bolívar

San Cristóbal   San Carlos   San Fernando   Caicara   Ciudad Piar   El Callao

Cúcuta   Arauca   Aro

Pamplona   Tame 18,022

Bucaramanga   Alto Ritacuva   Casanare

Barrancabermeja   Puerto Carreño   Angel Fall

COLOMBIA

Tunja   Sogamoso   Orocué   Pto. Nariño

Bogotá   Villavicencio   Vichada

Facatativá   Guaviare

Ibagué   Tolima 18,438

San Fernando de Atabapo   Orinoco

Serra Pacaraima

Boa Vista

Mitú   Taracuá   Sa. Imeri

Iauareté   Uaupés   Tapuruquara   Boiaçu

Mocoa   Ipiales

Otavalo   Cayambe   Cotopaxi 19,347   Napo

Chimborazo 20,561   Pantoja   Curaray   Pto. Arturo   Putumayo

AMAZON   Moura

São Gabriel   Marié   Lago de Maracaí

São Antônio do Içá   Barcelos

L. Amanã   Manacapuru   Anamã

Iquitos   Loreto   Tefé   Coari   Codajás

Nauta   São Paulo de Olivença

Pevas   Tabatinga   Benjamin Constant   Carauari

Leticia   Coari

Yavarí   Requena   Jutaí   Juruá

Itacoaí   Eirunepé   Purus   Lábrea   Humaitá

Juruá   Tapauá   Calama

Contamana   Cruzeiro do Sul   Taracuá   Sena Madureira   Bôca do Acre

Tarauacá   Embira   Pôrto Velho

Pucallpa   Purus   Alto Madeira   Ariquemes   Rondônia

Pto. Pardo   Iaco   Rio Branco   Abunã

Cocama   Brasiléia   Villa Bella   Guajará-Mirim

Cobija   Riberalta   Guayaramerín   BRAZIL

Dios   Pto. Heath   Cavinas   San Joaquín

Puerto Maldonado   Lago Rogaguado   Sta. Ana

Machupicchu   Reyes   Yacuma   Trinidad

Vilcanota 20,664   Illampu 21,276

Sorata   Ascención   Concepción

Puno   Achacachi   La Paz   Santa Cruz   L. Concepción

Juli   Guaqui   Oruro   Cochabamba   Punata   Portachuelo

Corocoro   Quillacollo   Vallegrande

BOLIVIA   Uncía   Colquechaca

Lago Poopó   Challapata   Sucre   Camiri

Salar de Uyuni   Potosí   Villa Montes

Salar de Uyuni   Huanchaca   Pulacayo   PARAG

Uyuni   Tupiza   Villazón   Tarija   Mariscal Estigarribia

Tocopilla   Oruro   La Quiaca   Yacuiba   Fn. Bo.

Gatico   Chuquicamata   Rinconada   Orán   Tartagal

GALÁPAGOS ISLANDS
(Archipiélago de Colón)
(To Ecuador)

I. Wolf

I. Pinta

I. Marchena   I. Genovesa   Equator

Pta. Albemarle   Equator

Isla Fernandina   Isla San Salvador

Isla Isabela   Isla Santa Cruz   San Cristóbal

Villamil   Pto. Baquerizo

I. Santa María   I. Española

Same scale as main map

90°

SOUTH AMERICA
NORTHERN PART
LAMBERT AZIMUTHAL EQUAL-AREA PROJECTION

SCALE OF MILES
0   100   200   300   400   500

SCALE OF KILOMETRES
0   100   200   300   400   500

Capitals of Countries............☆
Other Capitals ....△
International Boundaries.......-·-·-·
Other Boundaries..............-·-·-·

Copyright by C. S. Hammond & Co., N.Y.

Tropic of Capricorn

I. de San Félix • I.San Ambrosio
(Chile)   (Chile)

JUAN FERNÁNDEZ IS.
(Chile)
I. Robinson
Crusoe
I. Alejandro,   I. Santa Clara
Selkirk

SOUTH AMERICA
SOUTHERN PART
LAMBERT AZIMUTHAL EQUAL-AREA PROJECTION

SCALE OF MILES
0   100   200   300   400   500

SCALE OF KILOMETRES
0   100   200   300   400   500

Capitals of Countries .... ☆
Other Capitals .... △
International Boundaries ... — · —
Other Boundaries .... — · —

Copyright by C.S. Hammond & Co., N.Y.

ARCTIC OCEAN

ANTIC OCEAN

ICELAND

GREENLAND
(Danish)

Davis Strait

Thule

Baffin
Bay

Baffin Island

Ellesmere Island

North
Pole

120° 100° 80° 60° 40°20°
0°
20°
40°
60°
80°
100°
120°
140°
140°
160°
180°
160°

80°

70°

60°

ARCTIC
OCEAN

North
Magnetic
Pole

Victoria
Island

Arctic Circle

Great
Bear Lake

Great
Slave Lake

Mackenzie River

Labrador

Goose
Airport

Hudson
Bay

Churchill

C
A
N
A
D
A

Lake
Winnipeg

Winnipeg

Edmonton

Calgary

R
O
C
K

M
O
U
N

Vancouver

Seattle

Portland

CASCADE RANGE

Columbia R.

Great
Salt Lake

Great
Salt Lake City

SIER

San
Franci

Vancouver
Island

Queen
Charlotte
Islands

Jumeau

Whitehorse

Mt.
McKinley

Anchorage

Yukon

UNITED STATES
Alaska

Al. River

Point
Barrow

Bering Strait

ASIA

Newfoundland

St. Pierre &
Miquelon
(French)

Halifax

Nova
Scotia

Boston

New York

Philadelphia
ington

MOUNTAINS

Toronto
Cleveland

Montreal
Ottawa

Detroit
Chicago

Minneapolis

St. Lawrence River

Great Lakes

Missouri R.

Grea

PACI

North Pole

40°

70°

80°

50°

40°

60°

70°

80°

90°

60°

72

Map of
NORTH AMERICA
SCALE OF MILES
0 200 400 600 800
Capitals of Countries
Cities
Boundaries of Countries
Mountain Peaks
Canals
Mountains
Highlands
Lowlands
Depression
Water
Los Angeles
San Diego
Phoenix
Mt. Whitney
Colorado
El Paso
Rio Grande
Plains
Dallas
Houston
Memphis
Mississippi River
New Orleans
Atlanta
Mt. Mitchell
Jacksonville
Cape Kennedy
Miami
Hatteras
Bermuda (British)
Bahama Islands (British)
Tropic of Cancer
Lower California
Monterrey
Gulf of Mexico
Guadalajara
Mexico City
Veracruz
Havana
CUBA
HAITI
DOMINICAN REPUBLIC
PUERTO RICO (to U. S.)
West Indies
JAMAICA
Yucatán Peninsula
BRITISH HONDURAS
CARIBBEAN SEA
HONDURAS
GUATEMALA
EL SALVADOR
NICARAGUA
COSTA RICA
CENTRAL AMERICA
CANAL ZONE (to U.S.)
PANAMA
Panama Canal
VENEZUELA
COLOMBIA
ECUADOR
SOUTH AMERICA
PERU
BRAZIL
BOLIVIA
Galápagos Islands (Ecuadoran)
Equator
OCEAN
MEXICO
UNITED STATES
Longitude West of Greenwich
130° 120° 110° 100° 90° 80° 70°
30° 20° 10° 0° 10°

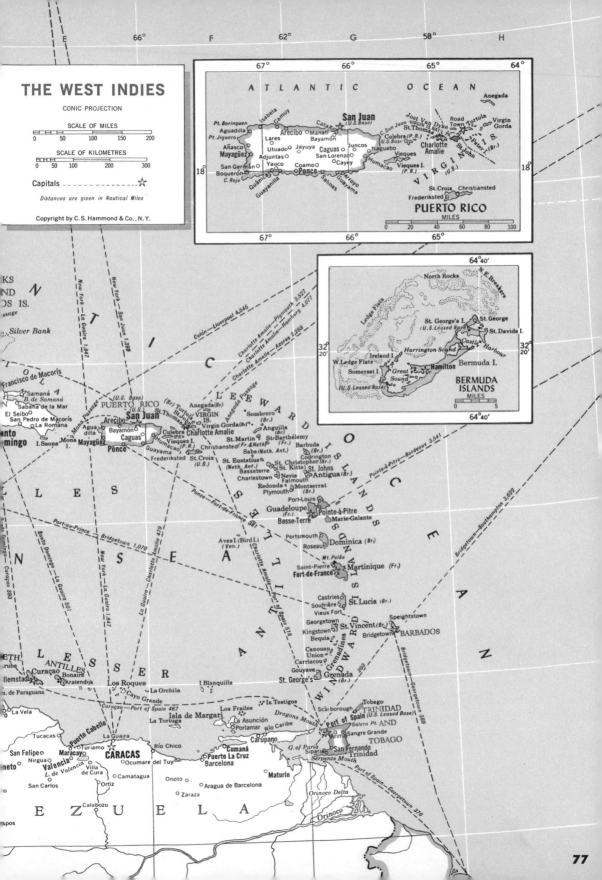

CENTRAL AMERICA

CONIC PROJECTION

SCALE OF MILES

0   25   50   100   150

SCALE OF KILOMETRES

0   25 50   100   150

Capitals of Countries .... ☆
International Boundaries .... ━ ━ ━
Canals .... ━•━•━•━

Copyright by C.S. Hammond & Co., N.Y.

78

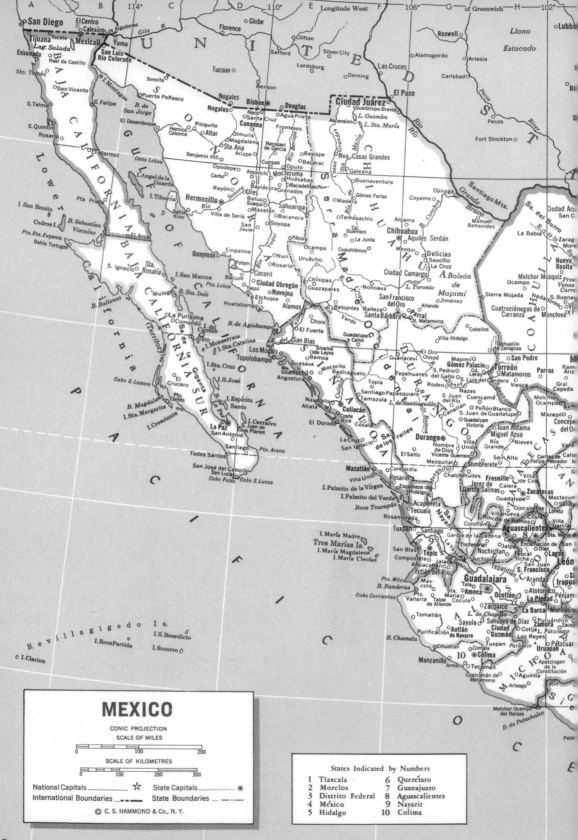

MEXICO

CONIC PROJECTION

SCALE OF MILES

0 — 200

SCALE OF KILOMETRES

0 — 100 — 200 — 300

National Capitals .... ☆ State Capitals .... ◉
International Boundaries ---- State Boundaries ----

© C. S. HAMMOND & Co., N. Y.

States Indicated by Numbers

1	Tlaxcala	6	Querétaro
2	Morelos	7	Guanajuato
3	Distrito Federal	8	Aguascalientes
4	México	9	Nayarit
5	Hidalgo	10	Colima

Inset map (top):

SCALE OF MILES
0 10 20 30 40

HIDALGO

99° 98° 97° 96°

MÉXICO
MEXICO CITY
Coyoacán
Xochimilco
Tlalpan
Ixtapalapa
DISTRITO FEDERAL
Azcapotzalco
Coyotepec
Zumpango
Cuautitlán
Tlainepantla de Comonfort
Naucalpan
Almoloya del Río
Tepetlaoxtoc
Texcoco de Mora
Chicoloapan de Juárez
Chalco
Amecameca de Juárez
Tlalmanalco de Velásquez
Tlayacapan
MORELOS
Cuernavaca
Yautepec
Cuautla Morels
Miacatlán
Coatetelco
Puente de Ixtla
Jojutla de Juárez
Tlatizapan
Tlaquiltenango
Jantetelco
Jonacatepec Huehuetlán
Tepoztlán
Tepalcingo
Tizayuca
Temascalapa
Tultepec de Arista
Tepeapulco
Apan
Tepetitlán
Otumba de Gómez Farías
Nanacamilpa
Calpulálpan
TLAXCALA
Apizaco
Chiautempan
Tlaxco de Morelos
S. Nicolás Terrenate
S. Martín Xaltocan
Huejotzingo
Cholula
Vicente Guerrero
S. Martín Texmelucan
Sta. Inés Zacatelco
S. Juan Ixtenco
Zacatlán
Chignahuapan
Zacapoaxtla
Chignautla Teziutlán
Tlapacoyan
Misantla
Tezuitlán
San Juan Xiutetelco
Jalacingo
Altotonga
Las Vigas
Perote 13,411
Naucampatépetl
Jico
PUEBLA
Huamantla
El Carmen
Oriental
Zacatepec
Nopalucan
Amozoc de Mota
Tepatlaxco de Hidalgo
Aljojuca
Acatzingo
Tepeaca
Quecholac
Palmar de Bravo
Morelos Cañada
Xochitlán
Tepexi de Rodríguez
Chietla
Izúcar
Huaquechula
Atlixco
Metepec
Tulcingo del Valle
Presa Valsequillo
Acatlán
Chapulco
Tehuipango
Zongolica
Nogales
Ciudad Mendoza
Orizaba
Ciudad Serdán
Citaltépetl (Orizaba) 18,700
Tenango de R. Blanco
Tlacotepec de Mejía
Huatusco de Chicuellar
Coscomatepec de Bravo
Chocamán
Amatlán de los Reyes
Fortín de las Flores
Córdoba
Cuitlahuac
R. Blanco
Tlalixcoyan
Medellín de Bravo
Soledad de Doblado
Boca del Río
Veracruz Llave
Úrsulo Galván
Actopan
Jalapa Enríquez
Coatepec
Teocelo
Tlacotepec de Mejía
Tepetlán
Naolinco de Victoria
Juchique de Ferrer
Yecuatla
VERACRUZ
Antigua
GULF OF MEXICO
Ignacio de la Llave

19°

HIDALGO
Zacatlán
Chignahuapan
Zacapoaxtla
Chignautla Teziutlán
Tlapacoyan
Misantla

Main map (bottom):

K 98° L M 94° N 90° P Q 86°

Abilene
Brownwood
Eagle Pass
Uvalde
Corpus Christi
Corpus Christi Bay
Kingsville
Cd. Guerrero
evo Laredo
Laredo
Falcon Res.
Cd. Miguel Alemán
Cd. Camargo
Mier
McAllen
Reynosa
San Benito
Brownsville
Cerralvo
El Azúcar Res.
Guadalupe
China
Cadereyta Jiménez
Gral Bravo
Río Bravo
Valle Hermoso
Matamoros
Montemorelos
Linares
San Carlos
S. Nicolás
Villagrán
Hidalgo
Burgos
Cruillas
S. Fernando
Barra San Rafael
Barra San Antonio
Barra Jesús María
Santander Jiménez
Soto la Marina
Padilla
Güémez
Ciudad Victoria
Jaumave
Llera de Canales
Xicoténcatl
Aldama
Ocampo
González
Morelos
Altamira
Antiguo Morelos
Cd. Mante
Ciudad Madero
Tampico
Pánuco
Ozuluama
Naranjos
Tamiahua
Tuxpan de Rodríguez Caño
Tihuatlán
Poza Rica de Hidalgo
Papantla de Olarte
Gutiérrez Zamora
Nautla
Martínez de la Torre
Yecuatla
Pta. Delgada
Jalapa Enríquez
Huauchinango
Zacapoaxtla
Coatepec
Huatusco
Orizaba
Córdoba
Veracruz Llave
Alvarado
Tlacotalpan
Cosamaloapan de Carpio
Santiago Tuxtla
San Andrés Tuxtla
Catemaco
Loma Bonita
Tierra Blanca
Tehuacán
Ajalpan
Tuxtepec
Teotitlán
Huajuapan de León
Cuicatlán
Cosoleacaque
Minatitlán
Coatzacoalcos
Puerto México
Barra de Sta. Ana
Frontera
Paraíso
Pelizada
Carmen
Lag. de Términos
Cd. del Carmen
Mamantel
Champotón
Sabancuy
Escárcega
CAMPECHE
Candelaria
Balancán
Tenosique de Pino Suárez
Palenque
Simojovel
Chiapa de Corzo
S. Cristóbal de las Casas
Comitán
Gulf of Honduras
Pto. Barrios
Pto. Cortés
Livingston
S. Pedro Sula
Belize City
Stann Creek
BR. HONDURAS
Turneffe I.
Ambergris Cay
Xcalak
Chetumal
Chetumal Bay
Bacalar
L. Bacalar
Felipe Carrillo Puerto
Pto. Herrero
Pta. Herrero
QUINTANA ROO (Territory)
Cozumel
Cozumel I.
Isla Mujeres
Puerto Juárez
Cabo Catoche
I. Holbox
Río Lagartos
Tizimín
Espita
Valladolid
CHICHEN-ITZÁ (Ruin)
Temax
Izamal
Motul
Progreso
DZIBILCHALTUN
Mérida
Hunucmá
Celestún
Umán
Maxcanú
Halachó
Muna
Ticul
Tekax
Sotuta
Peto
Oxkutzcab
Tekit
Tenabo
Hecelchakán
Calkiní
Bolonchén de Rejón
Hopelchén
Iturbide
Pustunich
Tixmucuy
Champotón
YUCATÁN
Mérida
GULF OF CAMPECHE
Campeche Bank
Arrecife Alacrán
I. Pérez
Cayo Arenas
Cayo Nuevo
Triángulo Oeste
Triángulo Este
Cayo Arcas
GULF OF CAMPECHE
Tropic of Cancer
MEXICO
GULF OF MEXICO

MEXICO CITY
Toluca
Tenancingo
Cuernavaca
Valle de Bravo
Ixtapan de la Sal
Tlaxiaco
Teloloapan
Zumpango del Río
Chilapa
Tixtla
Chilpancingo
Ayutla de los Libres
Acapulco de Juárez
Azoyú
Ometepec
San Marcos
Santiago Pinotepa Nacional
Pta. Maldonado
Pta. Galera
Toluca
Cuautla
Izúcar
Ciudad de Alarcón
San Gabriel Chilac
Acatlán
Coyotepec
Tlapa de Comonfort
Tamazulapan
Asunción Nochixtlán
Sta. María Juxtlahuaca
Putla
Tlaxiaco
Tamazulapan
GUERRERO
OAXACA
Zaachila
Zimatlán de Álvarez
Ocotlán de Morelos
Ejutla de Crespo
Miahuatlán
Pochutla
Puerto Ángel
San Agustín Loxicha
Tlacolula
MITLA (Ruin)
Sta. María del Tule
Oaxaca
Etla
Ixtepec
Unión Hidalgo
Juchitán de Zaragoza
Salina Cruz
Tehuantepec
Laguna Superior
Mar Muerto
Gulf of Tehuantepec
Matías Romero
Isthmus of Tehuantepec
Jaltipán
Acayucan
Jáltipan
Hueyapan de Ocampo
Cunduacán
Cárdenas
Villahermosa
Teapa
Tacotalpa
Macuspana
Jalapa
Jonuta
TABASCO
Huimanguillo
S. Fernando
Pichucalco
Yajalón
Ocosingo
L. Petén-Itzá
Flores
La Libertad
Dolores
San Luis
Chinaja
Cobán
Panzós
L. de Izabal
Salamá
Zacapa
Sta. Rosa
HONDURAS
La Esperanza
Quezaltenango
Jalapa
Amatitlán
GUATEMALA
Totonicapán
Quiché
Huehuetenango
Nentón
Mapastepec
Salinas
Omotepa de Mendoza
Huixtla
Tapachula
Escuintla
CHIAPAS
Tuxtla Gutiérrez
Venustiano Carranza
La Concordia
La Trinitaria
Arriaga
Tonalá
Cintalapa
Jiquipilas
Frontera Comalapa

N

81

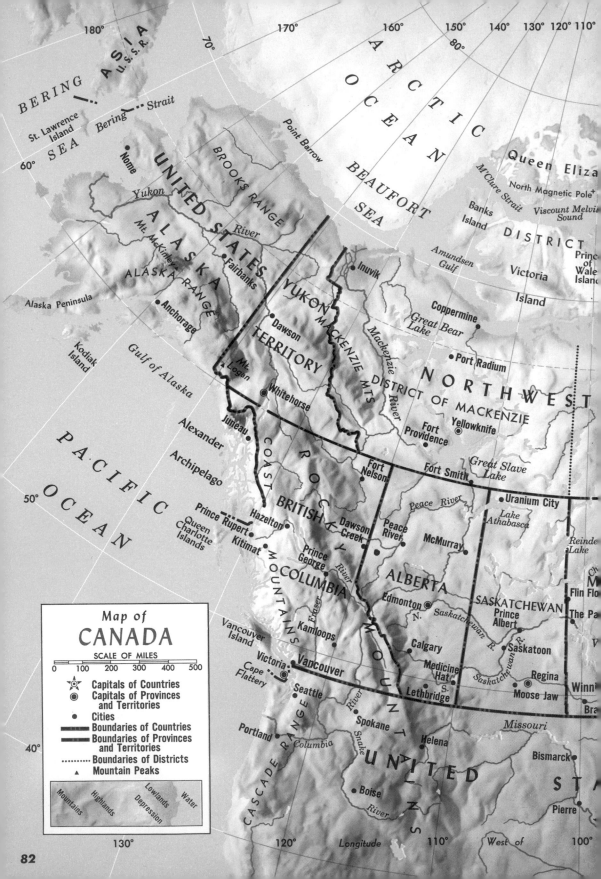

Map of
CANADA
SCALE OF MILES

0   100   200   300   400   500

✪ Capitals of Countries
◎ Capitals of Provinces
   and Territories
• Cities
━━ Boundaries of Countries
▰▰▰ Boundaries of Provinces
   and Territories
······ Boundaries of Districts
▲ Mountain Peaks

Mountains Highlands Lowlands Depression Water

BERING
ASIA
U.S.S.R.
St. Lawrence
Island
SEA
Nome
Bering Strait
60°
180°
70°
Point Barrow
170°
ARCTIC
160°
OCEAN
80°
150°
140°
130° 120° 110°
Queen Eliza
M'Clure Strait
North Magnetic Pole
Viscount Melvi
Sound
Banks
Island
DISTRICT
Prince
of
Wale
Island

BEAUFORT
SEA
Amundsen
Gulf
Victoria
Island

UNITED STATES
ALASKA
BROOKS RANGE
Yukon
River
Fairbanks
ALASKA RANGE
Mt. McKinley▲
Anchorage
Kodiak
Island
Alaska Peninsula
Gulf of Alaska
PACIFIC
OCEAN
50°
130°
40°

Inuvik
Coppermine
Great Bear
Lake
Port Radium

YUKON
MACKENZIE
TERRITORY
Dawson
Mt.
Logan▲
Whitehorse
MTS
Mackenzie
River
DISTRICT OF MACKENZIE
NORTHWEST
Fort
Providence
Yellowknife

Juneau
Alexander
Archipelago
COAST
ROCKY
Fort
Nelson
Fort Smith
Great Slave
Lake

Prince Rupert
Hazelton
Queen
Charlotte
Islands
Kitimat
BRITISH
COLUMBIA
Prince
George
MOUNTAINS
Dawson
Creek
Peace
River
Peace River
McMurray
Uranium City
Lake
Athabasca
Reinde
Lake

Vancouver
Island
Kamloops
Fraser
River
ALBERTA
Edmonton ◎
N.
Saskatchewan R.
SASKATCHEWAN
Prince
Albert
Flin Flo
The Pa
M

Victoria ◎
Cape
Flattery
Vancouver
Seattle
Calgary
Saskatoon
R.
Medicine
Hat
S.
Saskatchewan
Lethbridge
Regina ◎
Moose Jaw
Winn
Bra

CASCADE RANGE
Portland
Columbia
River
Spokane
Snake
River
UNITED
Helena
STA
Bismarck
Missouri
120°
Boise
River
110°
Longitude
West of
100°
Pierre

82

90° 80° 70° 60° 50° 40° 30° 20°

ICELAND

Reykjavik

G R E E N L A N D
(Danish)

70°

60°

Thule

BAFFIN

Devon Island

th Islands

BAY

Arctic Circle

Lancaster Sound

FRANKLIN

Davis Strait

Baffin

Gulf of Boothia

Foxe

Island

Godthaab

Basin

Cape
Farewell

STRICT

OF T E R R I T O R I E S

Frobisher Bay

ATLANTIC

EWATIN

Southampton
Island

Hudson Strait

Chesterfield
Inlet

Ungava
Peninsula

OCEAN

50°

HUDSON

Port Harrison

Fort
Chimo

Nain

Battle
Harbour

BAY

LABRADOR

Churchill

Scheffervile

Goose Airport

Newfoundland

Port
Nelson

Belcher
Islands

Grand
Falls

Gander

St.
John's

River

Fort George

Seven
Islands

Corner
Brook

TOBA

Severn

James

Anticosti
Island

St. Pierre &
Miquelon
(French)

eg

River

Bay

Q U É B E C

Lake
Mistassini

Gaspé
Peninsula

Gulf of
St. Lawrence

PRINCE
EDWARD
ISLAND

Charlottetown

Sydney

Moosonee

Chicoutimi

NEW
BRUNSWICK

Cape Breton
Island

Sable Island

O N T A R I O

Lake Nipigon

Rouyn

Trois
Rivières

Québec

Moncton

Kenora

Kapuskasing

Timmins

Fredericton

NOVA SCOTIA

Halifax

Lake of
the Woods

Port
Arthur

Montréal

Saint
John

Fort William

Sault-
Ste-Marie

Sudbury

Sherbrooke

Cape Sable

Duluth

Lake Superior

North
Bay

St. Lawrence

MTS.

Yarmouth

ES

St. Paul

Ottawa

Cornwall

APPALACHIAN

Minneapolis

Mississippi R.

Milwaukee

Toronto

Lake
Ontario

Boston

Detroit
Windsor

Lake Erie

Buffalo

New York

Greenwich

90°

80°

70°

40°

Copyright by C. S. HAMMOND & Co. N.Y.

83

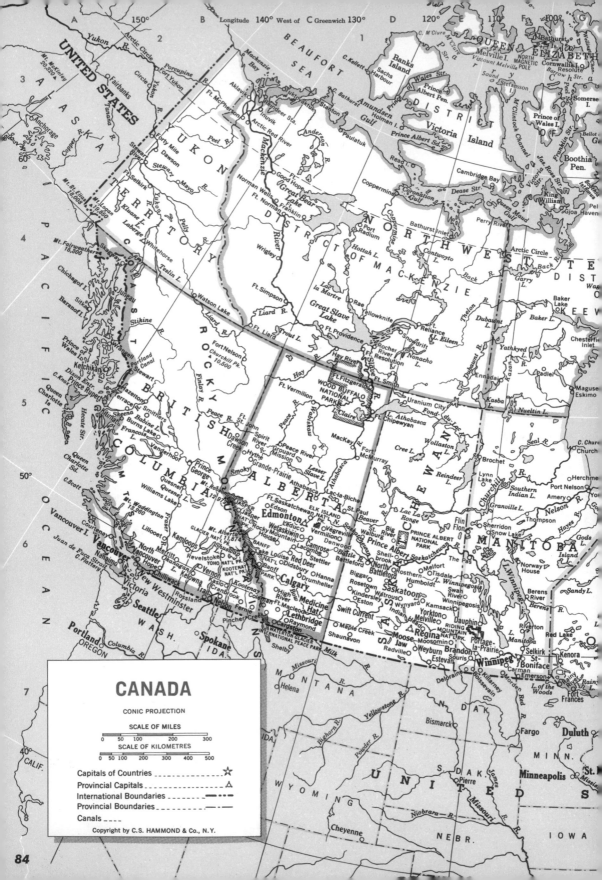

CANADA

CONIC PROJECTION

SCALE OF MILES

0 50 100   200   300

SCALE OF KILOMETRES

0 50 100   200   300   400   500

Capitals of Countries _____ ☆
Provincial Capitals _____ △
International Boundaries _____
Provincial Boundaries _____
Canals _ _ _ _

Copyright by C.S. Hammond & Co., N.Y.

84

MARITIME PROVINCES

SCALE OF MILES

0   10   20   30   40   50

Provincial Capitals	⊛	Provincial Boundaries
County Seats	⊚	County Boundaries
International Boundaries		

Copyright by C.S. Hammond & Co., N.Y.

QUEBEC
SOUTHERN PART

SCALE OF MILES

0   5 10   20   30   40

National Capital _____ ⊛ Provincial & State
Provincial Capital _____ ⊛ Boundaries _____
County Seats _____ ⊙ International
County Boundaries _____ Boundaries _____

Copyright by C. S. Hammond & Co., N. Y.

GASPÉ PENINSULA

MILES

0 5 10   20   30   40

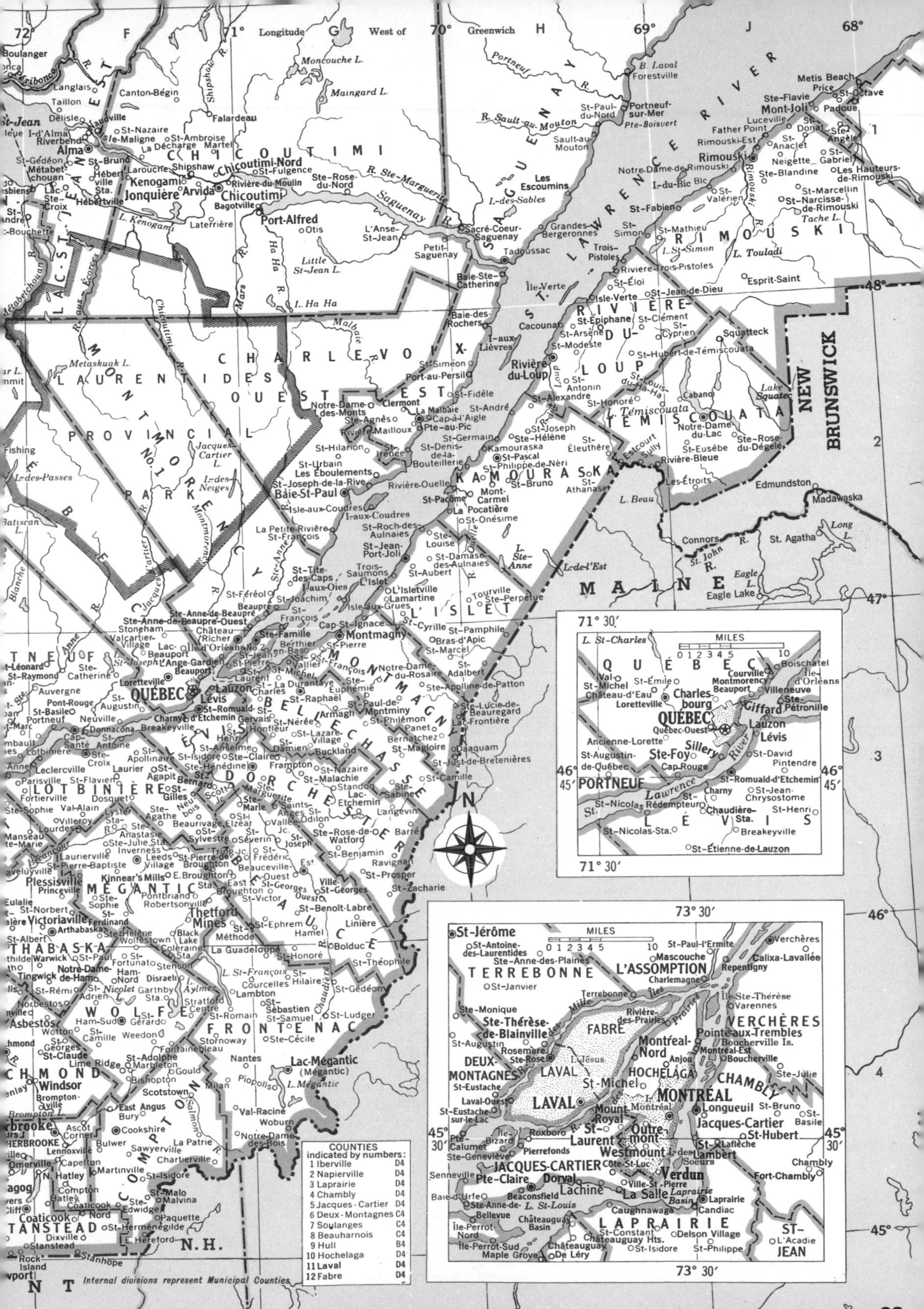
72°
71° Longitude West of 70° Greenwich
69°
68°
48°
47°
46°
45°
CHICOUTIMI
LAC-ST-JEAN-EST
CHARLEVOIX-EST
CHARLEVOIX-OUEST
LAURENTIDES PROVINCIAL PARK
MONTMORENCY No. 1
MONTMORENCY
SAGUENAY
ST. LAWRENCE RIVER
RIMOUSKI
RIVIÈRE-DU-LOUP
TÉMISCOUATA
KAMOURASKA
L'ISLET
MONTMAGNY
BELLECHASSE
DORCHESTER
BEAUCE
LÉVIS
LOTBINIÈRE
MÉGANTIC
FRONTENAC
WOLFE
COMPTON
ARTHABASKA
RICHMOND
STANSTEAD
SHERBROOKE
NEW BRUNSWICK
MAINE
N.H.
Chicoutimi
Jonquière
Arvida
Kenogami
Alma
Port-Alfred
Bagotville
Tadoussac
Forestville
Rimouski
Mont-Joli
Rivière-du-Loup
Baie-St-Paul
La Malbaie
Montmagny
Lévis
Lauzon
QUÉBEC
Loretteville
Beauport
Thetford Mines
Victoriaville
Plessisville
Asbestos
Lac-Mégantic (Mégantic)
Windsor
East Angus
Cookshire
Coaticook
Edmundston
71° 30′
L. St-Charles
MILES
0 1 2 3 4 5 10
QUÉBEC
PORTNEUF
LÉVIS
Charlesbourg
Sillery
Ste-Foy
Québec-Ouest
St. Lawrence River
73° 30′
MILES
0 1 2 3 4 5 10
TERREBONNE
L'ASSOMPTION
VERCHÈRES
DEUX-MONTAGNES
LAVAL
FABRE
HOCHELAGA
CHAMBLY
JACQUES-CARTIER
LAPRAIRIE
ST-JEAN
MONTRÉAL
Montréal-Nord
St-Michel
Mount Royal
Outremont
Westmount
St-Laurent
Verdun
Lachine
Dorval
Pte-Claire
Longueuil
Jacques-Cartier
St-Jérôme
COUNTIES indicated by numbers:
1 Iberville D4
2 Napierville D4
3 Laprairie D4
4 Chambly D4
5 Jacques-Cartier D4
6 Deux-Montagnes C4
7 Soulanges C4
8 Beauharnois C4
9 Hull B4
10 Hochelaga D4
11 Laval D4
12 Fabre D4
Internal divisions represent Municipal Counties

MANITOBA
NORTHERN PART
SCALE OF MILES
0   40   80   120

MANITOBA
SOUTHERN PART
SCALE OF MILES
0 5 10   20   40   60

Provincial Capital .... ⊛
International Boundaries ─ ── ─ ──
Provincial Boundaries ─ ─ ─ ── ─

Copyright by C.S. HAMMOND & Co., N.Y.

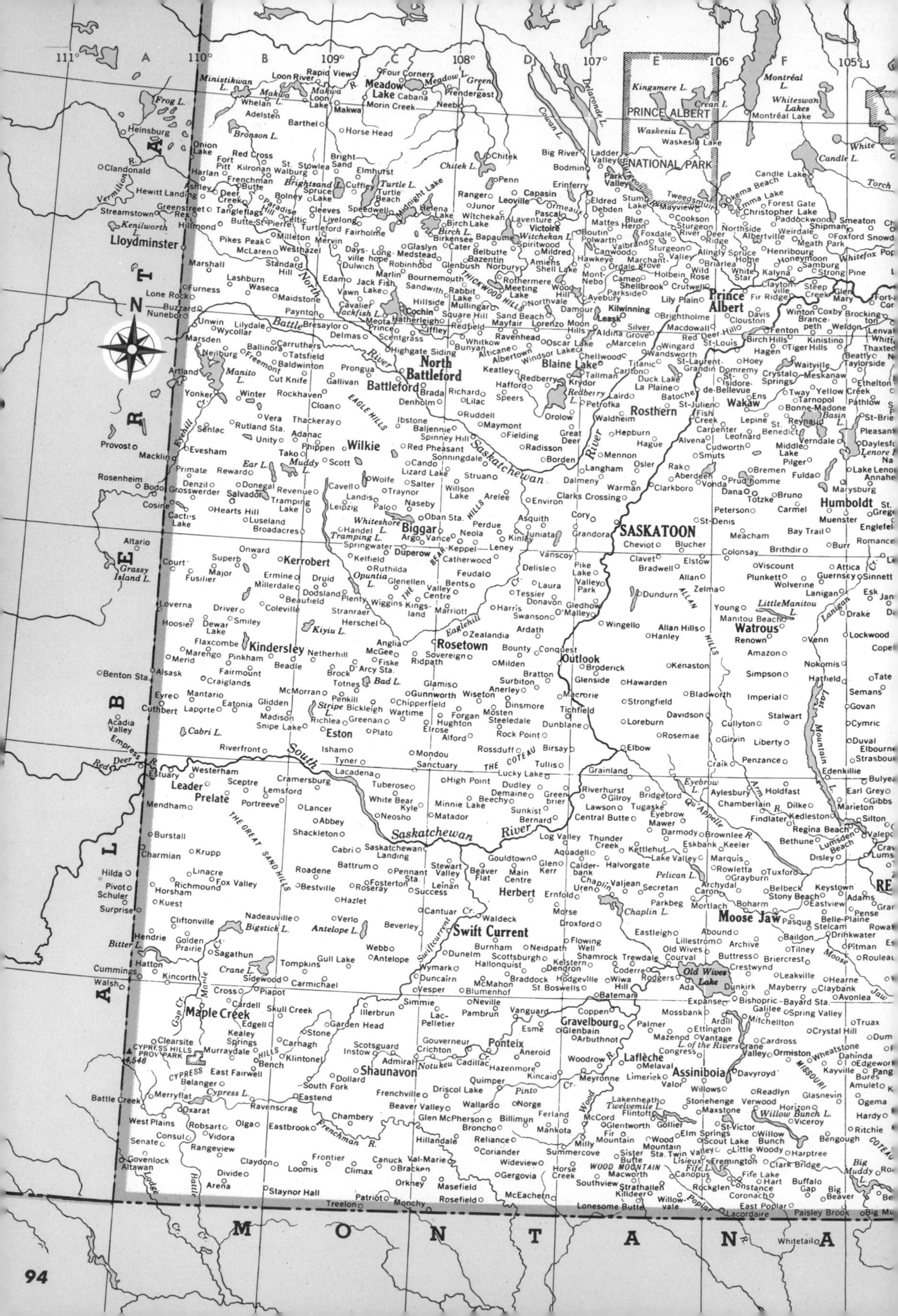

MONTANA

PRINCE ALBERT

PRINCE ALBERT NATIONAL PARK

North Battleford

Battleford

SASKATCHEWAN

Saskatoon

Rosthern

Wakaw

Humboldt

Watrous

Biggar

Rosetown

Outlook

Kindersley

Kerrobert

Wilkie

Lloydminster

Leader

Prelate

Maple Creek

Swift Current

Herbert

Gravelbourg

Ponteix

Shaunavon

Assiniboia

Laflèche

Moose Jaw

Meadow Lake

North Saskatchewan River

South Saskatchewan River

EAGLE HILLS

CYPRESS HILLS PROV PARK 4,548

THE GREAT SAND HILLS

THE COTEAU

WOOD MOUNTAIN

MISSOURI COTEAU

SASKATCHEWAN
NORTHERN PART

SASKATCHEWAN
SOUTHERN PART
SCALE OF MILES

Provincial Capital .... ⊛
International Boundaries ___.___
Provincial Boundaries ___ ___

Copyright by C.S. HAMMOND & CO., N.Y.

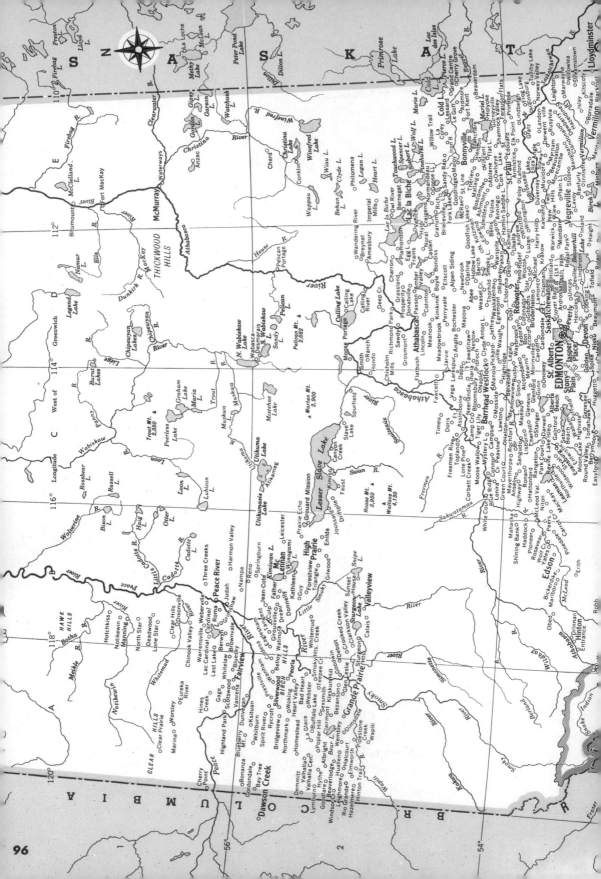

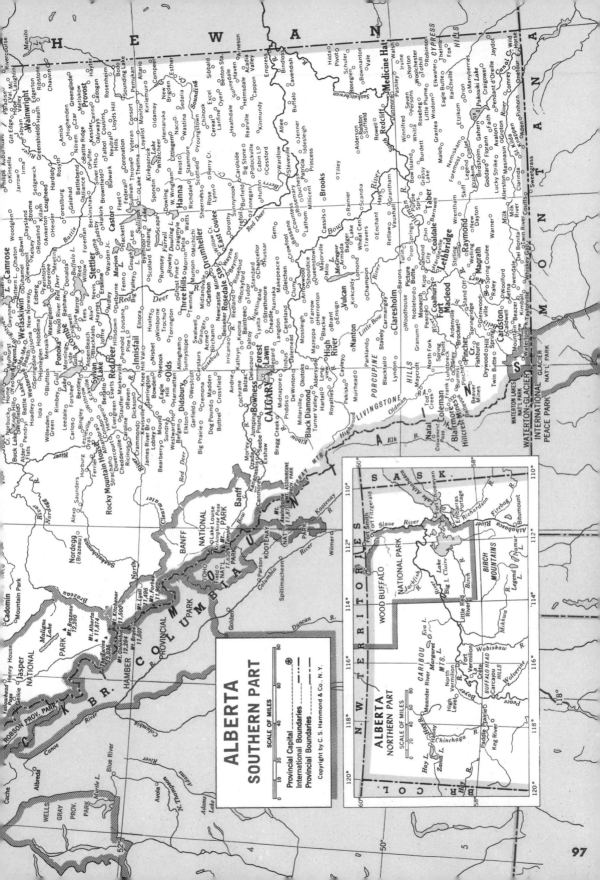

ALBERTA
SOUTHERN PART

SCALE OF MILES

Provincial Capital ⊕
International Boundaries — · — · —
Provincial Boundaries — — — —

Copyright by C. S. Hammond & Co., N.Y.

ALBERTA
NORTHERN PART

SCALE OF MILES

97

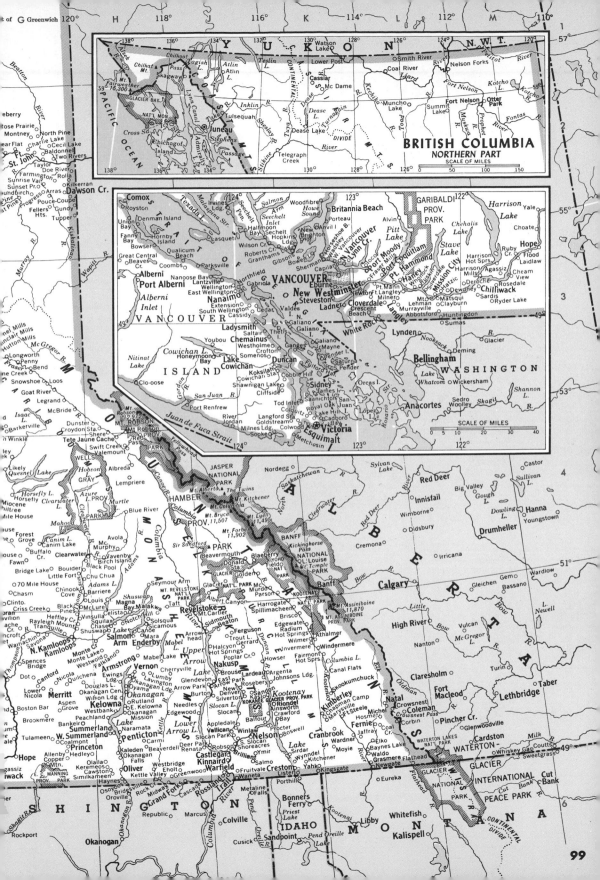

This is a map of British Columbia and surrounding regions, including Vancouver Island, the Lower Mainland, Alberta, Washington, Idaho, and Montana.

BRITISH COLUMBIA
NORTHERN PART
SCALE OF MILES
0   50   100   150

GARIBALDI PROV. PARK

VANCOUVER

New Westminster

ISLAND

VANCOUVER ISLAND

WASHINGTON

Juan de Fuca Strait

SCALE OF MILES
0 5 10 15 20 25 30 35 40

JASPER NATIONAL PARK

BANFF

A L B E R T A

Calgary

Revelstoke

Banff

Kamloops

Kelowna

Penticton

Nelson

Cranbrook

Lethbridge

WASHINGTON   IDAHO   MONTANA

WATERTON LAKES NAT'L PARK

GLACIER NATIONAL PARK

PEACE PARK

Map of
UNITED STATES
LAMBERT CONFORMAL CONIC PROJECTION
Copyright by C. S. Hammond & Co., N.Y.
SCALE OF MILES
0   50   100   200   300

Capitals of Countries .... ✵
State and Provincial Capitals .... ☆
International Boundaries ....
State Boundaries ....
Provincial Boundaries ....

Copyright by C. S. Hammond & Co., N.Y.

APPROXIMATE ELEVATIONS

10,000 ft. ....
5,000 ft. ....
2,000 ft. ....
1,000 ft. ....
500 ft. ....
Sea level ......
Depression ......

Longitude 90° West of Greenwich

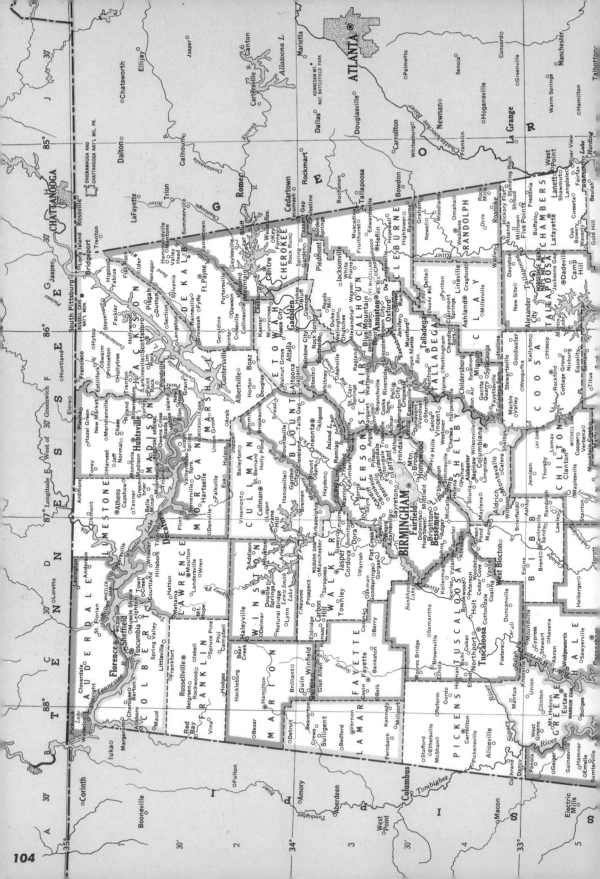

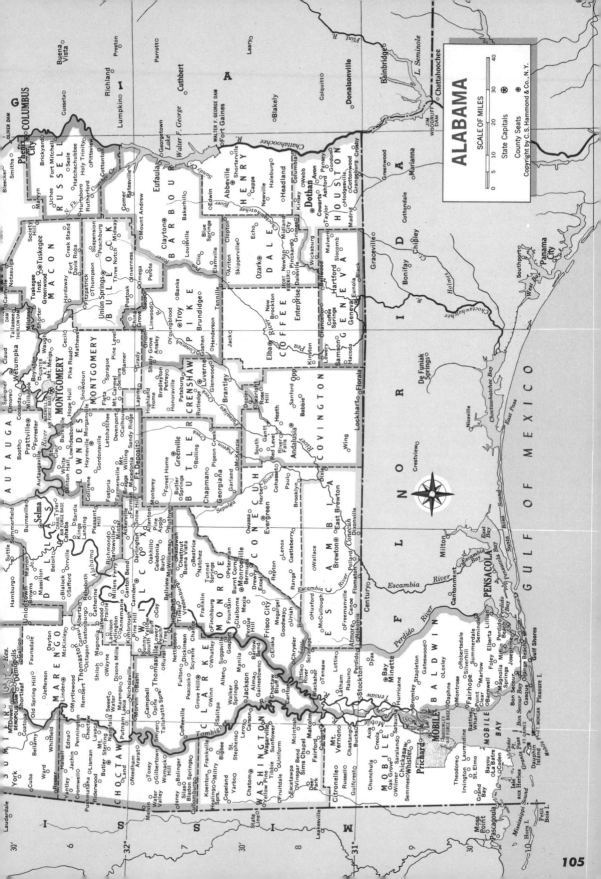

ALABAMA

SCALE OF MILES

State Capitals ⊛
County Seats ⊙

Copyright by C. S. Hammond & Co., N. Y.

GULF OF MEXICO

105

ALASKA

POLYCONIC PROJECTION

SCALE OF MILES

| 0 | 50 | 100 | 150 | 200 |

State and Territorial Capitals ⊛
Court Houses ⊙
International Boundaries
Senatorial District Boundaries

© C. S. HAMMOND & Co., Maplewood, N. J.

106

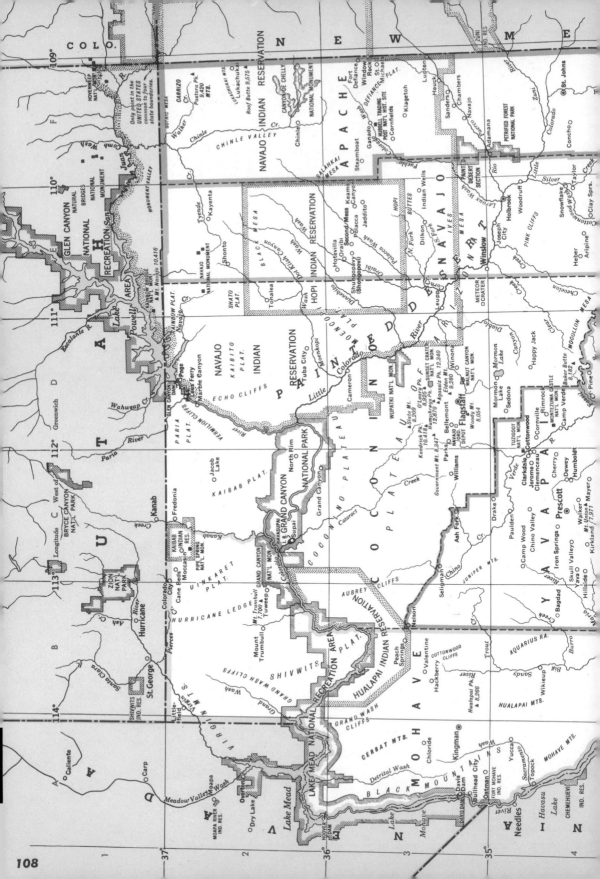

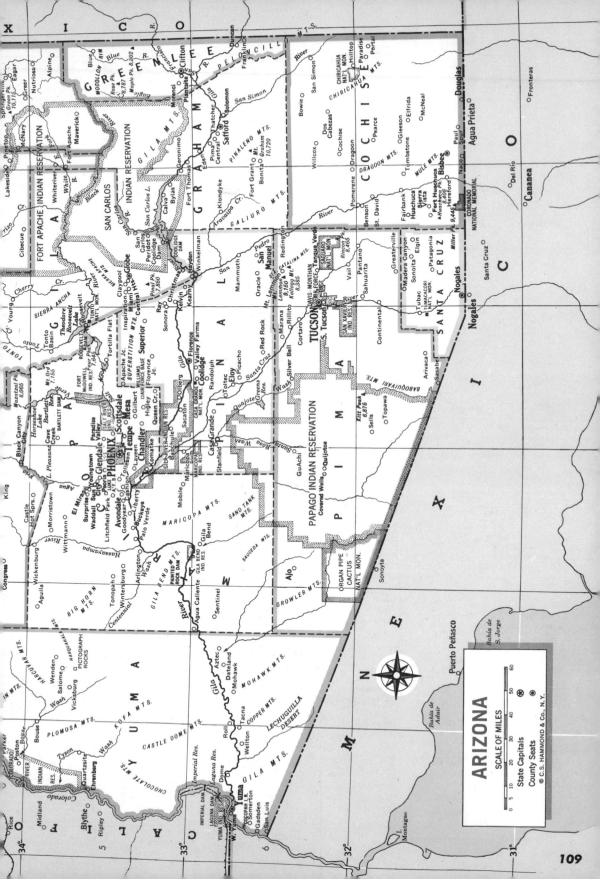

ARIZONA

DEATH VALLEY NATIONAL MONUMENT

PANAMINT VALLEY

SAN BERNARDINO

JOSHUA TREE NAT'L MON.

IMPERIAL

MEXICO

PACIFIC OCEAN

Los Angeles
San Diego
Long Beach
Santa Barbara

RIVERSIDE

SACRAMENTO AND VICINITY

LOS ANGELES AND VICINITY

COLORADO

SCALE OF MILES

0 5 10   20   30   40

State Capitals ⊛   County Seats ◉

Canals

114

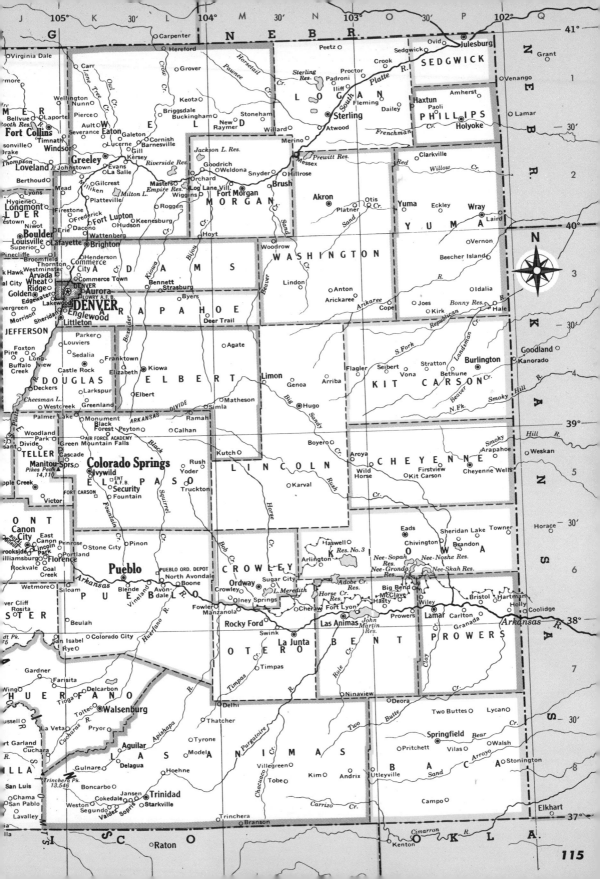

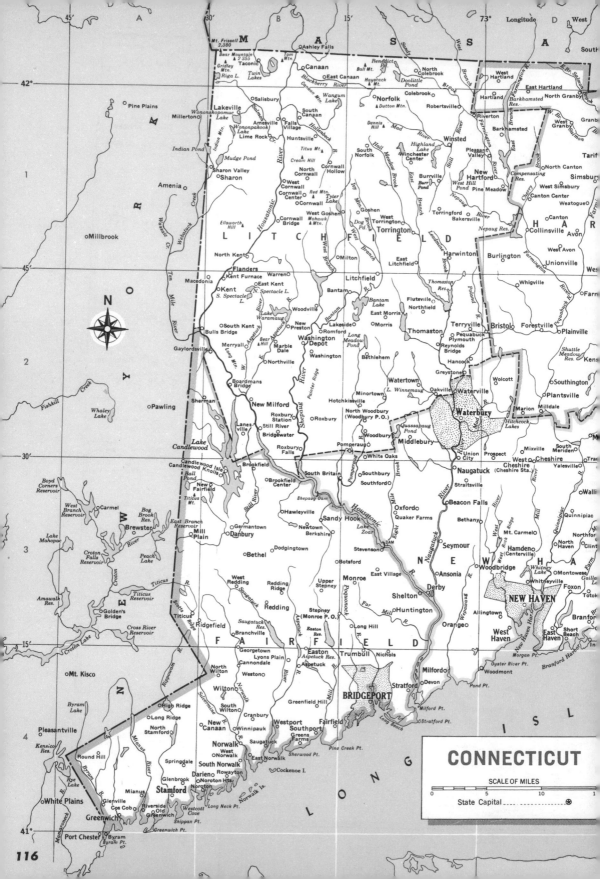

CONNECTICUT

SCALE OF MILES

0 — 5 — 10 —

State Capital ⊛

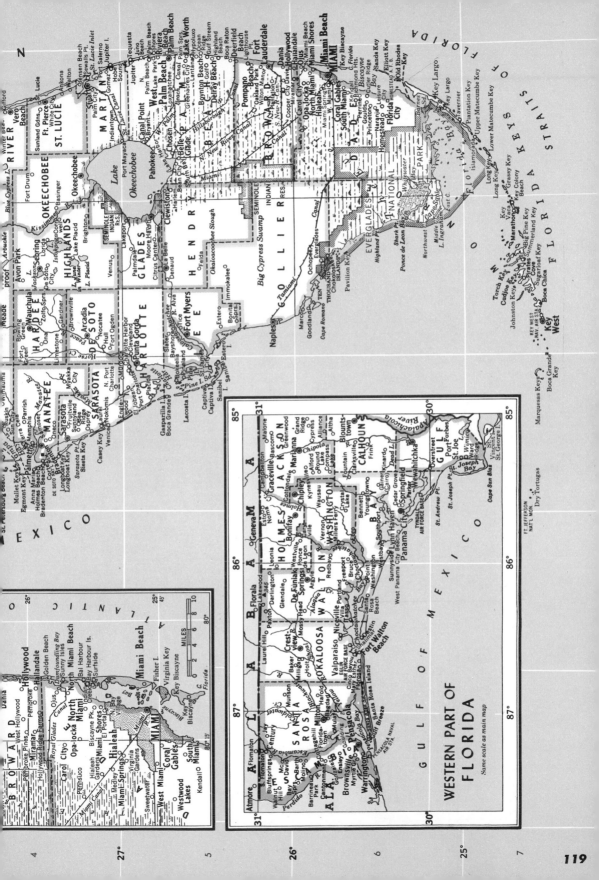

WESTERN PART OF FLORIDA

Same scale as main map

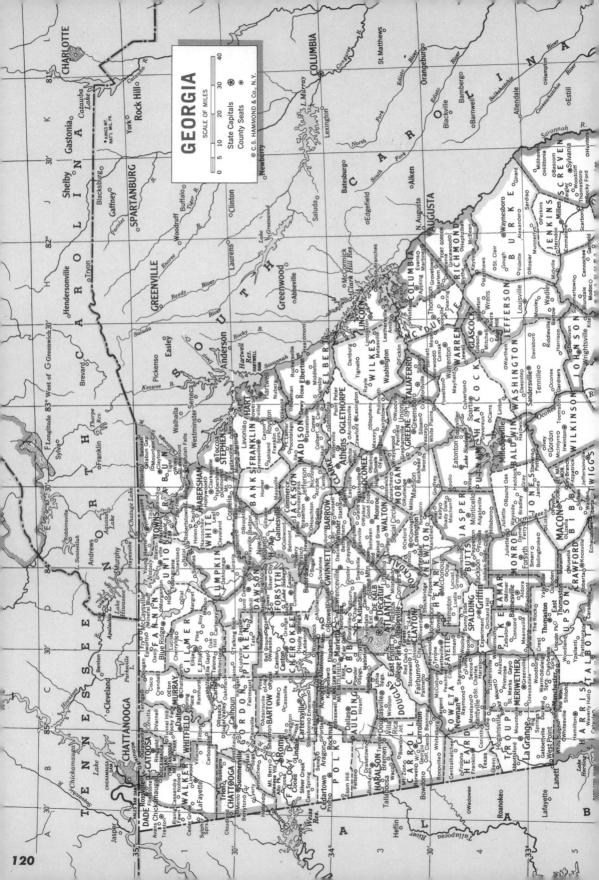

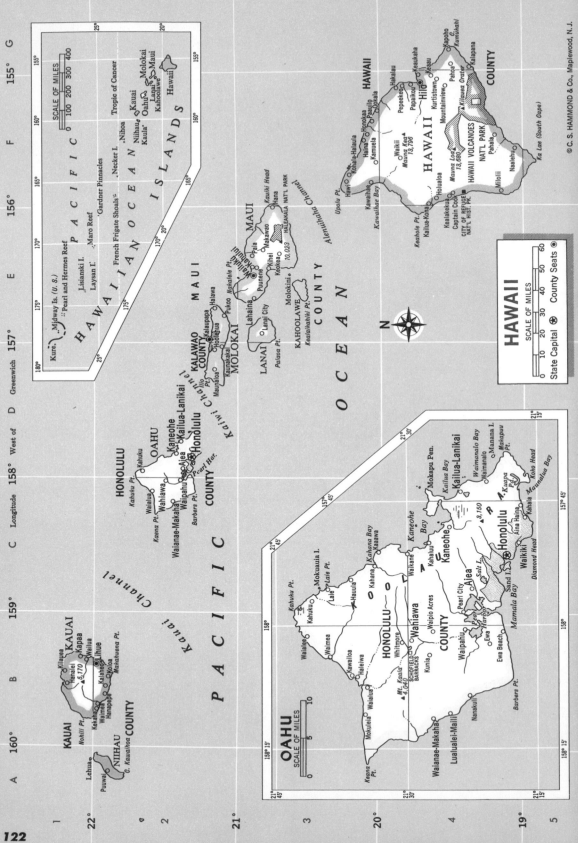

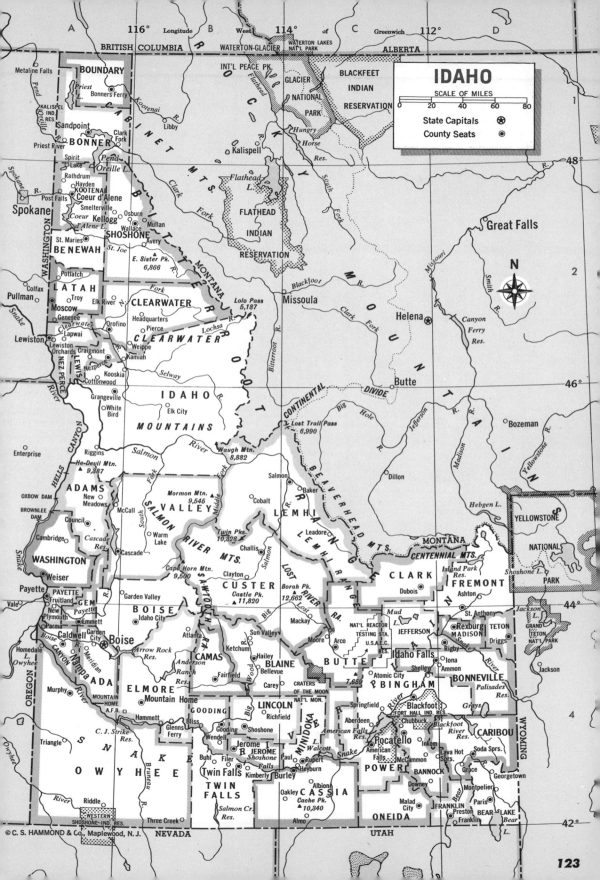

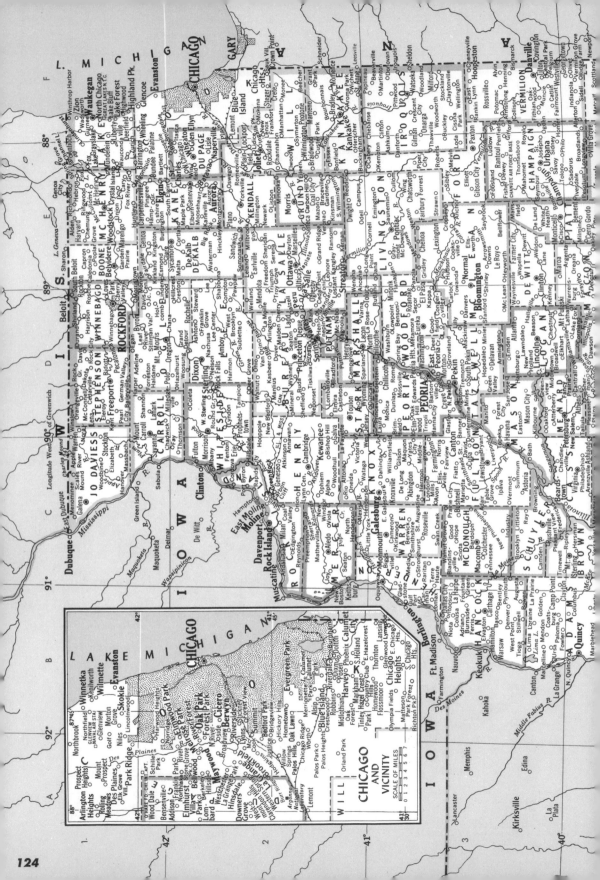

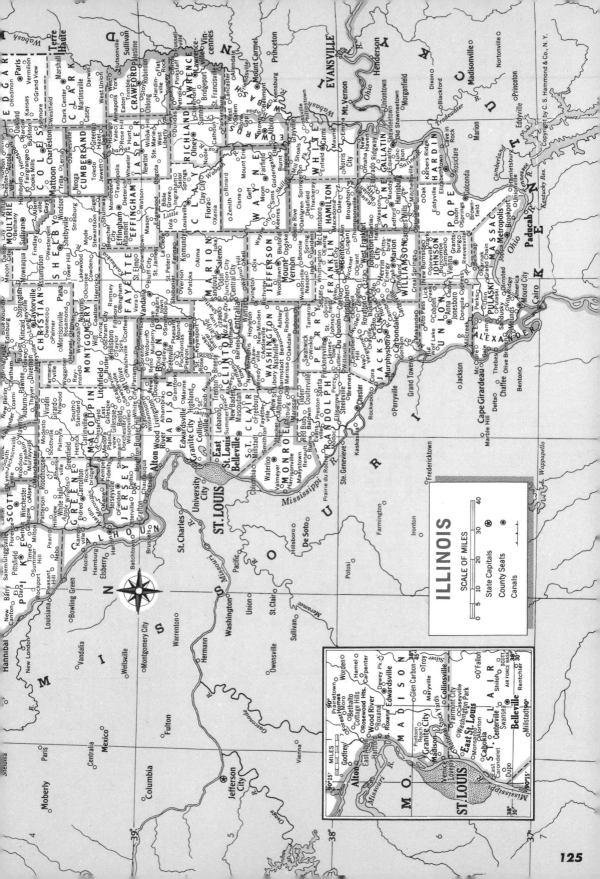

ILLINOIS

SCALE OF MILES

| 5 | 10 | 20 | 30 | 40 |

⊗ State Capitals
◉ County Seats
Canals

125

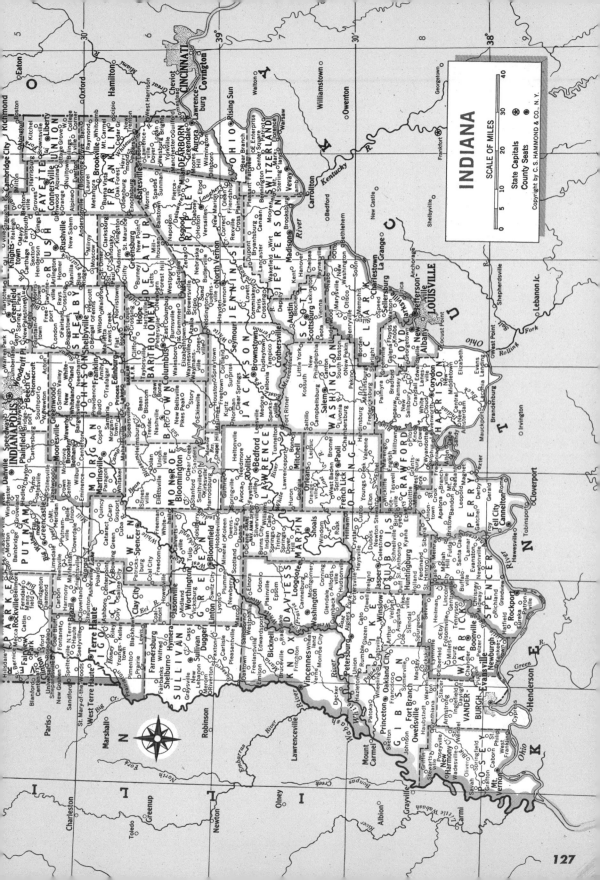

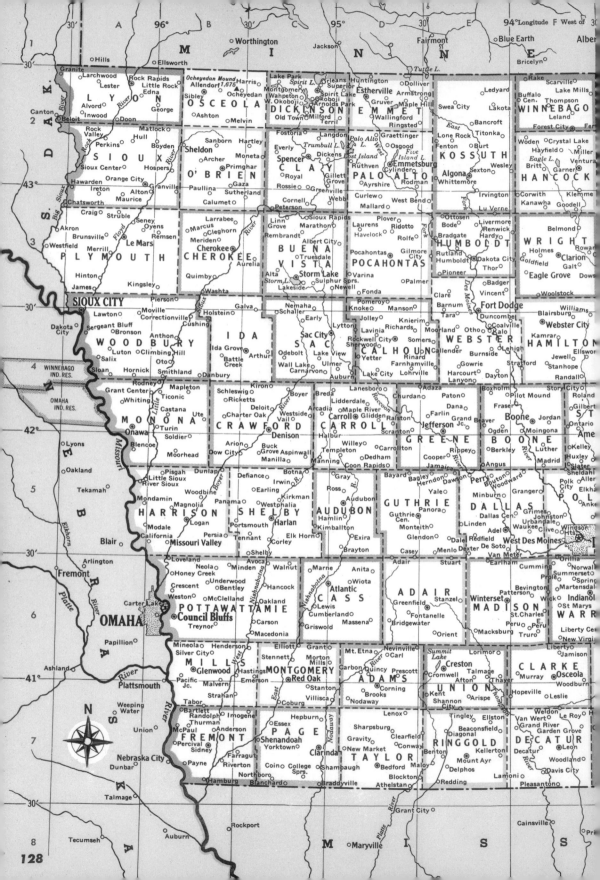

IOWA

SCALE OF MILES

0 5 10   20   30   40

State Capitals ⊛
County Seats ⊙

129

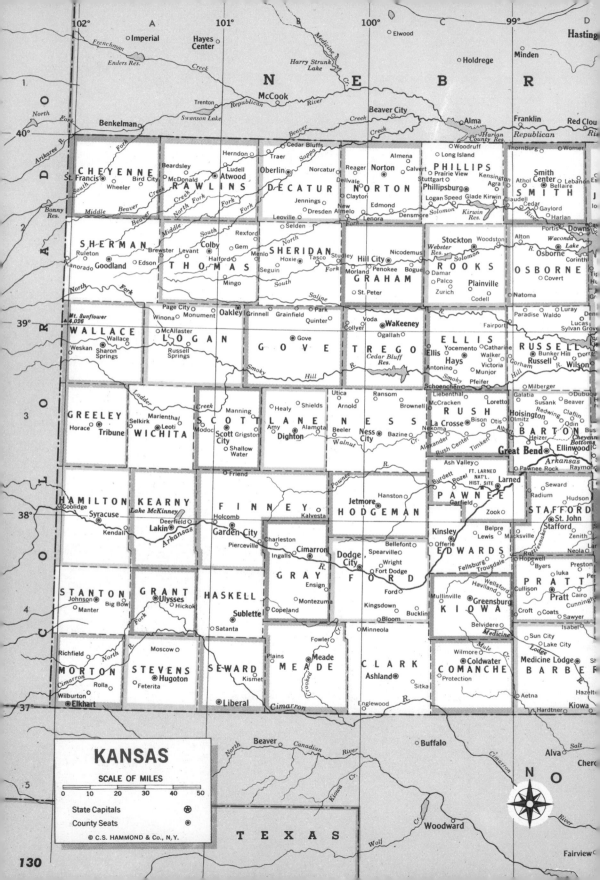

131

WESTERN PART OF KENTUCKY
Same scale as main map

ILLINOIS

MISSOURI

INDIANA

TENNESSEE

Zeigler · West Frankfort · Greenfield
Herrin · Eldorado · Connersville
Marion · Harrisburg · Rushville
Shawneetown · Hope · Bates
Cobden · Uniontown · Morganfield · Waverly
Anna · Grove Center · U N I O N
Jonesboro · Vienna · Henshaw · Dekoven · Pride · Tilden · North Vernon
Jackson · Rosiclare · Sturgis · Wheatcroft
Cape Girardeau · Elizabethtown · Sullivan · Clay · Dixon · WEBSTER · Osgood · Versailles
Golconda · Tolu · Blackford · HOPKINS
Carrsville · Joy · Providence
Shady · CRITTENDEN · Dawson Sprs · Hopkins
Bayou · Lola · Hampton · Marion · Crayne · Crider · CALDWELL · North Vernon
Birdsville · Salem · Burna · Fredonia · Princeton · Madison · Carrollton
Metropolis · Brookport · Mexico · Eddyville · Scottsburg · Austin · Scottsburg · TRIMBLE
Paducah · West Paducah · Kevil · Smithland · Iuka · Kuttawa · Cobb · Cerulean · Bedford
Cairo · BALLARD · McCRACKEN · Calvert City · L Y O N · Wallonia · CARR
Charleston · Wickliffe · Blandville · Lovelaceville · Melber · Grand Rivers · Golden Pond · Cadiz · Milton · Prestonsville
Sikeston · Bardwell · Cunningham · MARSHALL · Canton · TRIGG · English
Columbus · CARLISLE · Burkley · Milburn · Lowes · Viola · Benton · Brewers · Hardin · Canton · Lake · Turners Sta.
East Prairie · GRAVES · Boaz · Fancy · Farm · Dexter · Kentucky · Almo · Barkley · OLDHAM
HICKMAN · Dublin · Mayfield · Kirksey · Lake · Sellersburg · Goshen · Crestwood
New Madrid · Clinton · Pryorsburg · Farmington · CALLOWAY · Pleasureville
Gakton · Moscow · Wingo · Sedalia · Murray · Hamlin · Crestwood · Cropper
Hickman · Crutchfield · Water Valley · Lynn · Grove · New · Concord · Lake · Anchorage
Cayce · Fulton · Hazel · Barkley

Copyright by C. S. HAMMOND & CO., N. Y.

132

KENTUCKY

SCALE OF MILES

0   5   10   20   30   40

State Capitals ⊛
County Seats ⊙

LOUISIANA

SCALE OF MILES

0 5 10   20   30   40

State Capitals   ⊗   Canals

Parish Seats   ⊙

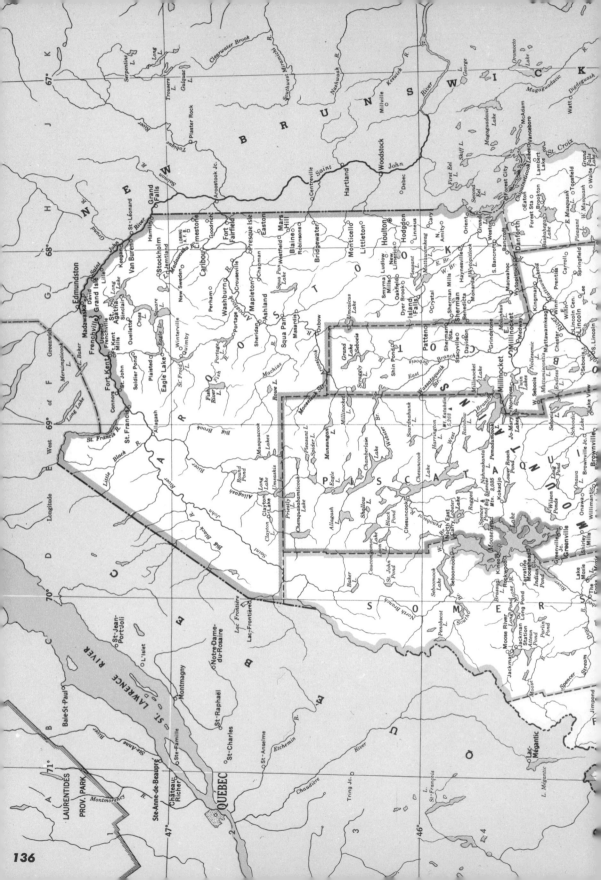

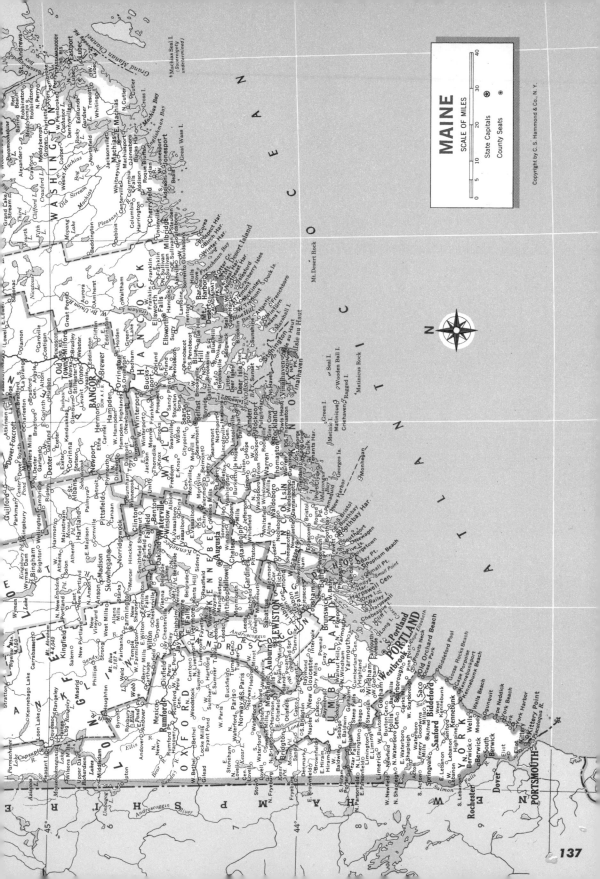

MAINE

SCALE OF MILES

⊛ State Capitals
⊙ County Seats

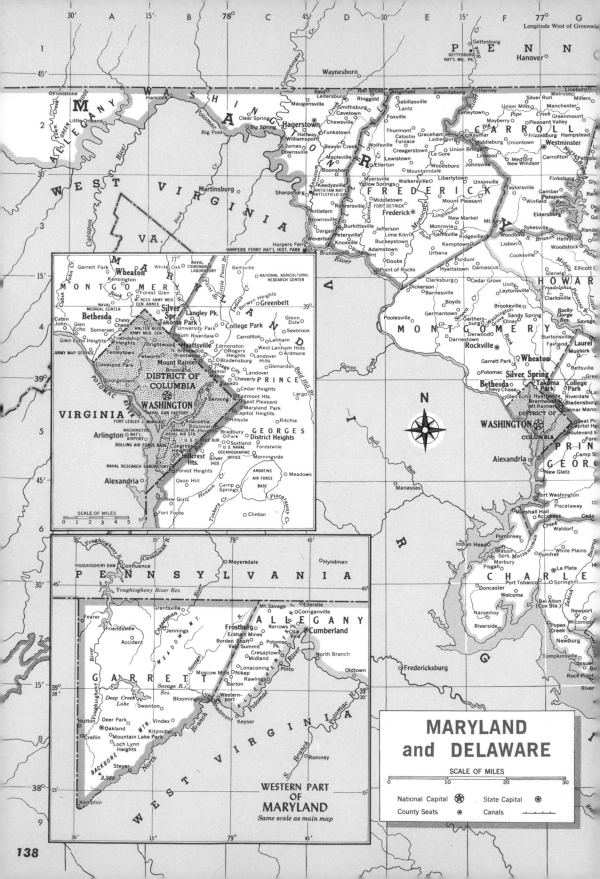

MARYLAND and DELAWARE

SCALE OF MILES

National Capital
County Seats

State Capital
Canals

WESTERN PART
OF
MARYLAND
Same scale as main map

138

MASSACHUSETTS and RHODE ISLAND

SCALE OF MILES

0   10   20

State Capitals ⊕   Canals

County Seats & Courthouses ◉

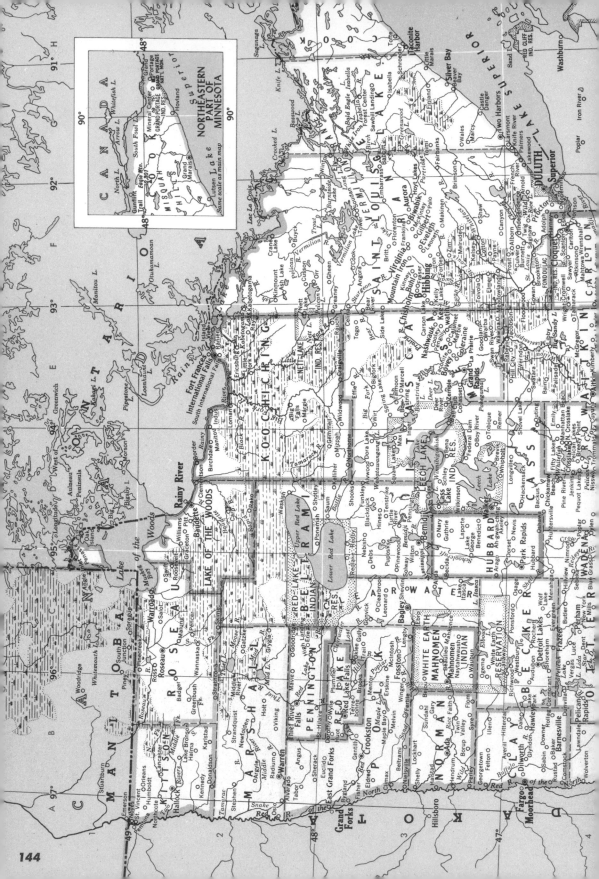

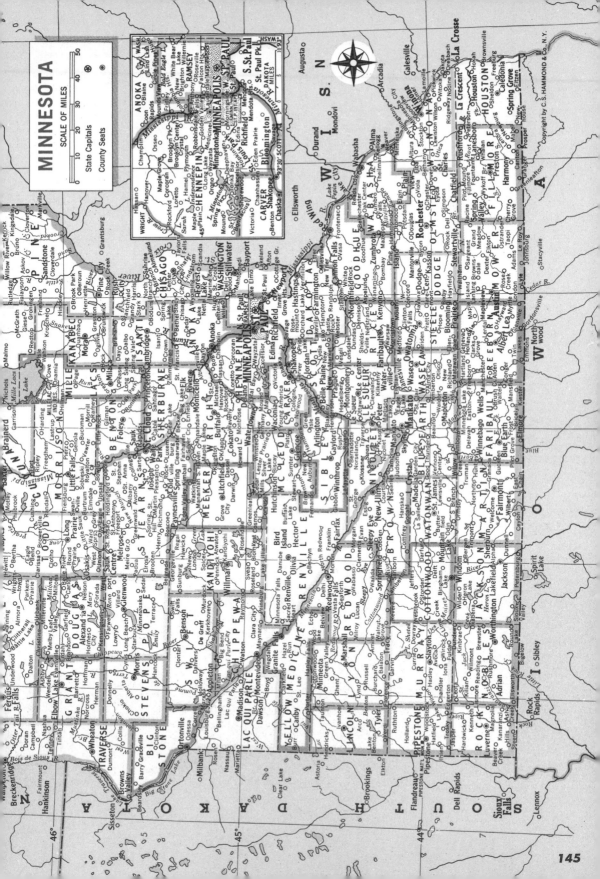

MINNESOTA

SCALE OF MILES

0 10 20 30 40 50

⊕ State Capitals
⊙ County Seats

145

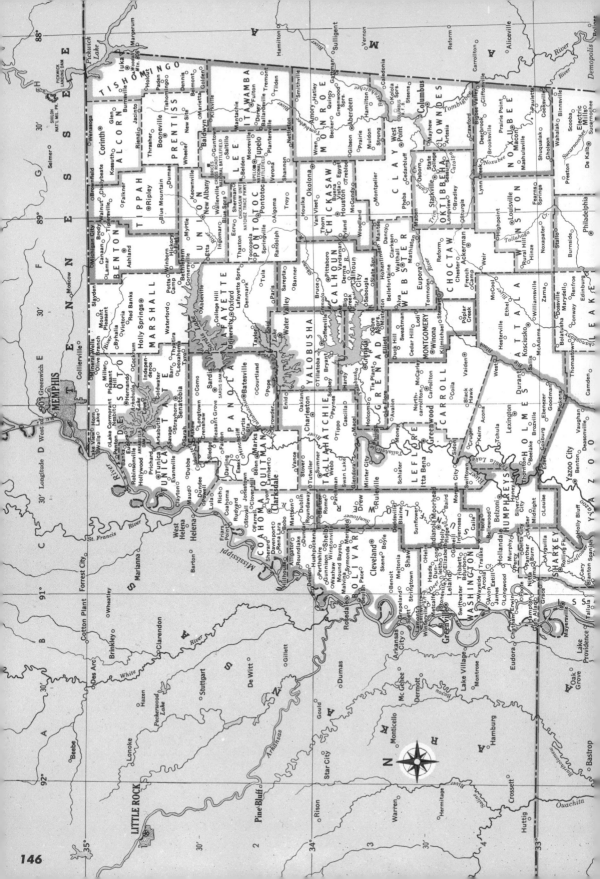

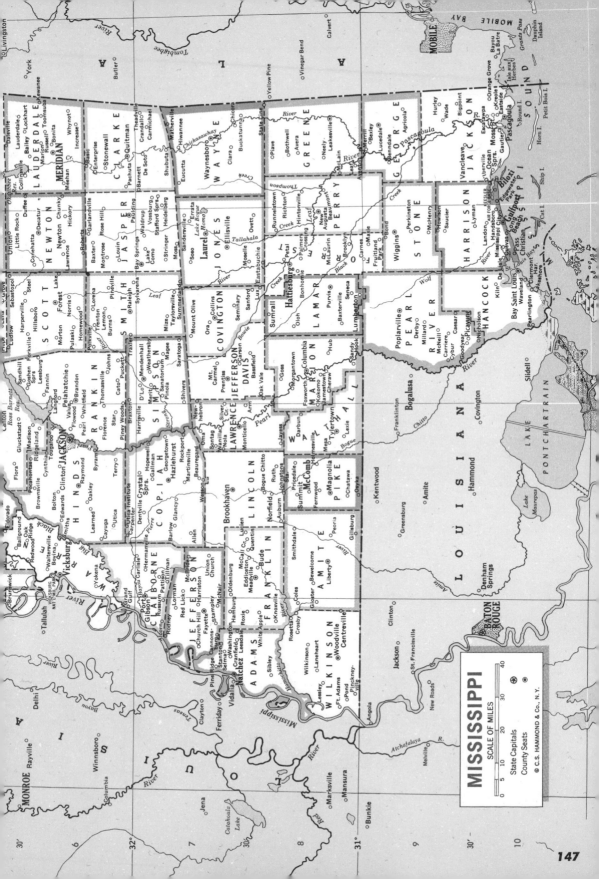

MISSISSIPPI

SCALE OF MILES

State Capitals ⊛
County Seats ◉

© C. S. HAMMOND & CO., N.Y.

MISSOURI

SCALE OF MILES

State Capitals ⊛
County Seats ⊙

© C.S. HAMMOND & Co., N.Y.

149

MONTANA

SCALE OF MILES

10 20   40   60   80

⊗ State Capitals
⊙ County Seats

Copyright by C.S. HAMMOND & CO., N.Y.

150

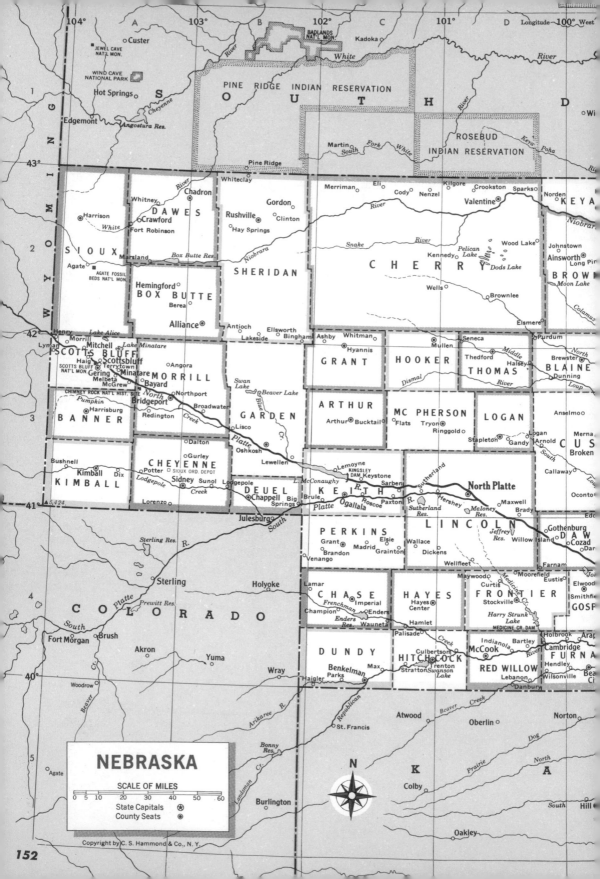

NEBRASKA

SCALE OF MILES

0 5 10   20   30   40   50   60

State Capitals ⊛

County Seats ⊙

Copyright by C. S. Hammond & Co., N. Y.

152

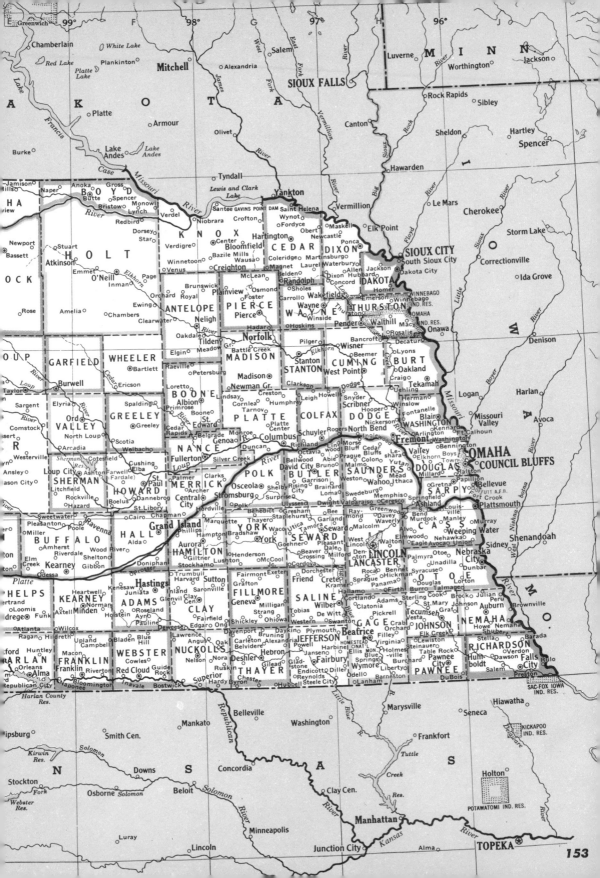

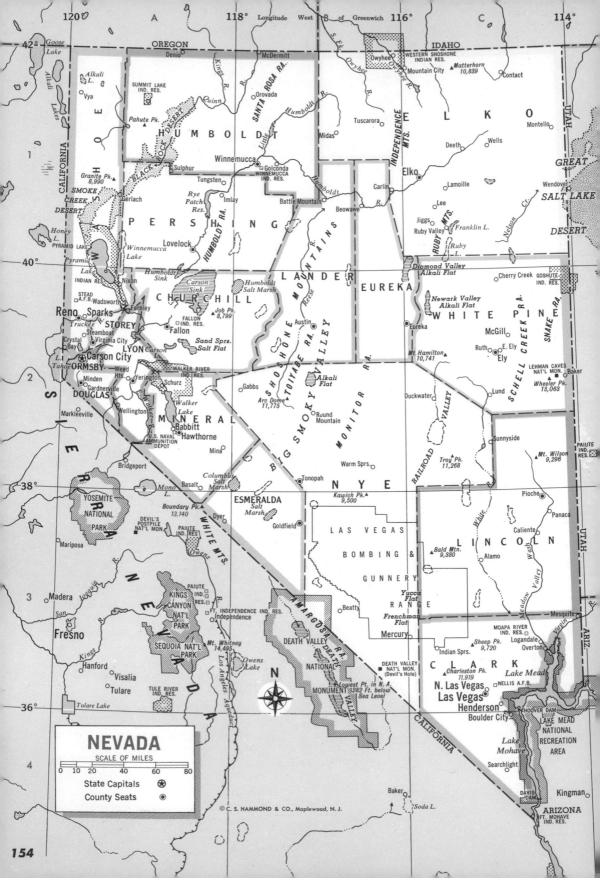

NEVADA

SCALE OF MILES

0 10 20 40 60 80

⊛ State Capitals

⊙ County Seats

© C. S. HAMMOND & CO., Maplewood, N. J.

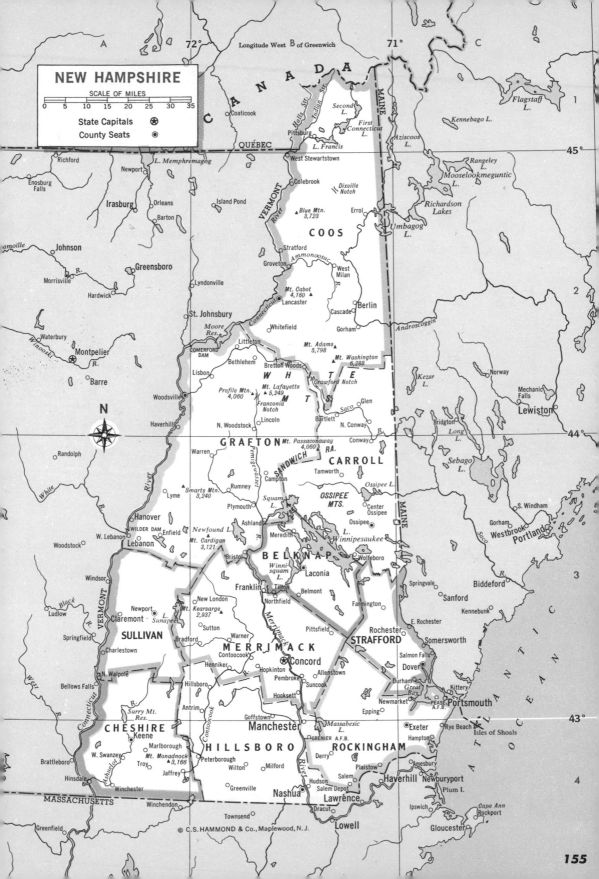

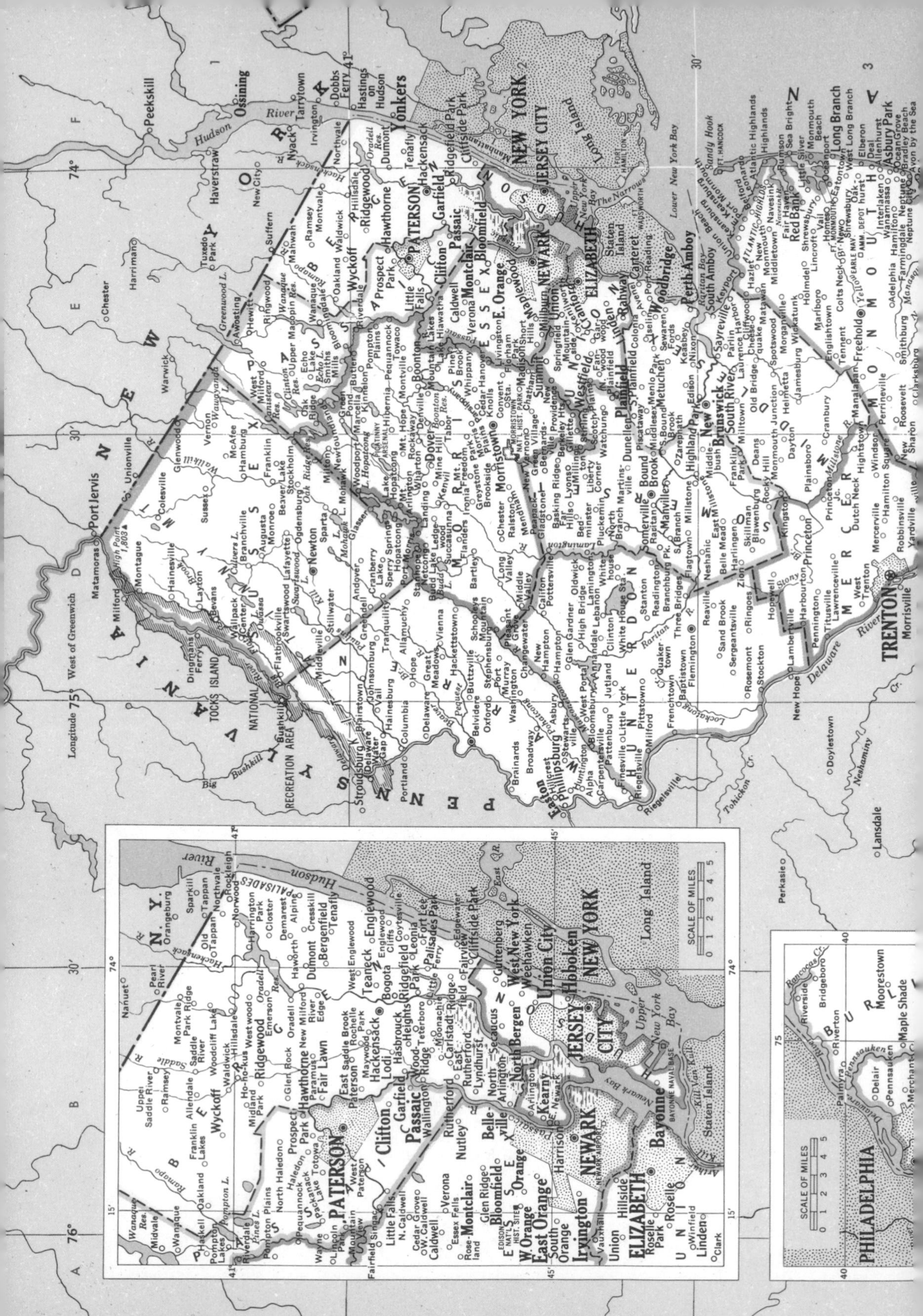
NEW YORK
PENNSYLVANIA
Longitude 75° West of Greenwich
TOCKS ISLAND NATIONAL RECREATION AREA
SUSSEX
PASSAIC
BERGEN
MORRIS
ESSEX
WARREN
HUNTERDON
SOMERSET
UNION
MIDDLESEX
MONMOUTH
MERCER
HUDSON
TRENTON
NEWARK
PATERSON
ELIZABETH
JERSEY CITY
NEW YORK
Long Island
Staten Island
Perth Amboy
New Brunswick
Princeton
Morristown
Plainfield
Phillipsburg
Easton
Port Jervis
Yonkers
Ossining
Peekskill
Red Bank
Long Branch
Asbury Park
Freehold
Hackensack
Passaic
Clifton
Montclair
Bloomfield
E. Orange
Bayonne
Hoboken
Union City
Kearny
Irvington
PHILADELPHIA
Lower New York Bay
Sandy Hook
High Point 1,803
Delaware River
Hudson River
N.Y.
SCALE OF MILES

NEW JERSEY

SCALE OF MILES

State Capitals ⊛ Canals

County Seats ⊙

Copyright by C. S. HAMMOND & CO., N.Y.

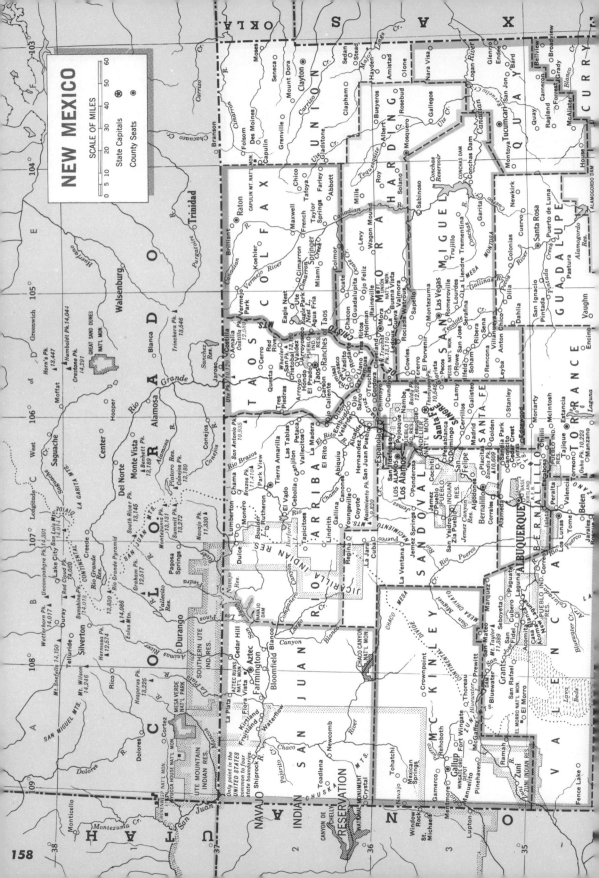

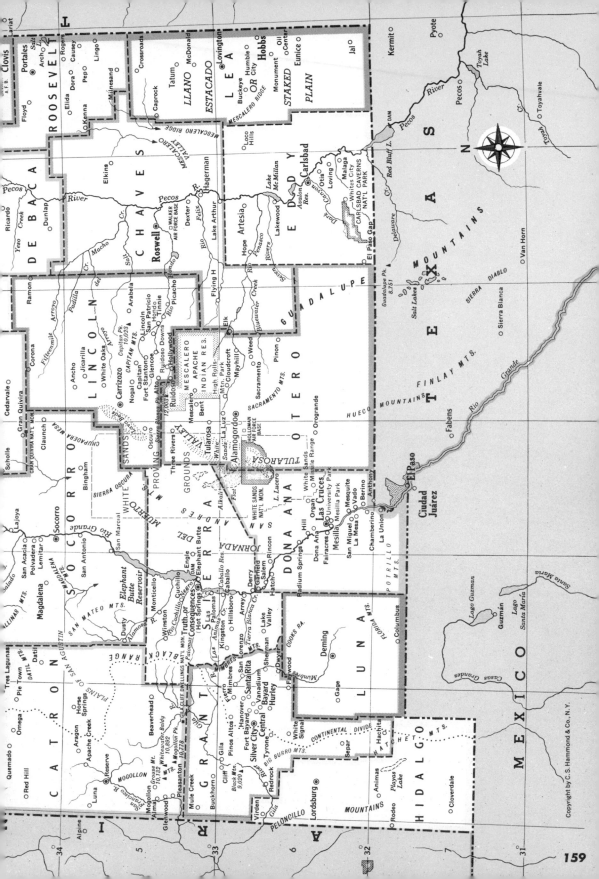

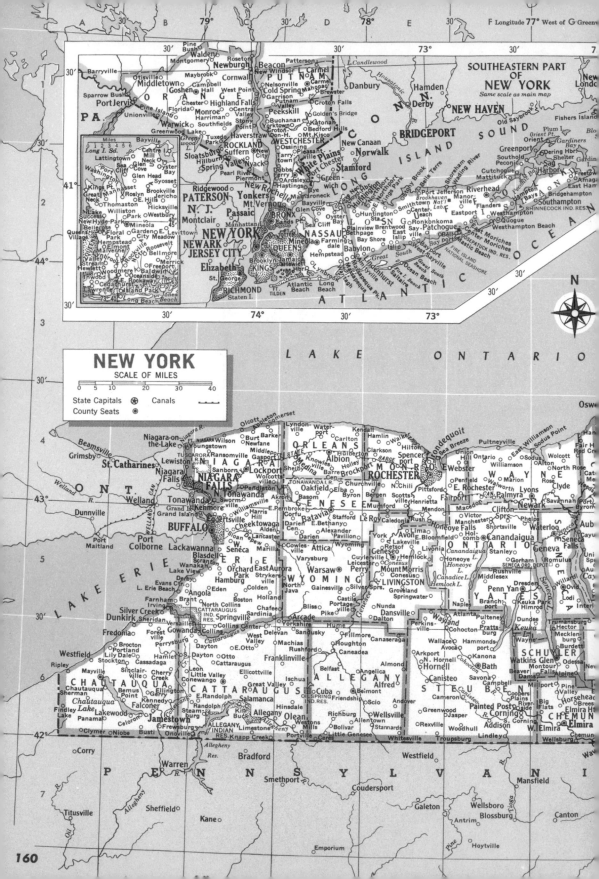

TENN.

VIRGINIA

SOUTH CAROLINA

GEORGIA

County and place names across the map include:

Bristol, Mountain City, Bluff City, Elizabethton, Roan Mt., TENN., WATAUGA, AVERY, MITCHELL, Bakersville, Spruce Pine, Marion, MC DOWELL, Old Fort, BURKE, Morganton, Hickory, CALDWELL, Lenoir, ALEXANDER, Statesville, IREDELL, CATAWBA, Newton, LINCOLN, Lincolnton, RUTHERFORD, POLK, CLEVELAND, Shelby, GASTON, Gastonia, Belmont, MECKLENBURG, CHARLOTTE, Pineville, UNION, Monroe, ANSON, Wadesboro, CABARRUS, Concord, Kannapolis, Albemarle, STANLY, MONTGOMERY, Troy, ROWAN, Salisbury, DAVIDSON, Lexington, Thomasville, High Point, GUILFORD, GREENSBORO, WINSTON-SALEM, FORSYTH, DAVIE, YADKIN, WILKES, N. Wilkesboro, ASHE, ALLEGHANY, Sparta, SURRY, Mt. Airy, STOKES, ROCKINGHAM, Reidsville, CASWELL, PERSON, ORANGE, ALAMANCE, Burlington, Graham, CHATHAM, Siler City, RANDOLPH, Asheboro, MOORE, Carthage, Southern Pines, Aberdeen, RICHMOND, Rockingham, Hamlet, SCOTLAND, Laurinburg, HOKE, Raeford, ROBESON, Lumberton, Spartanburg, Gaffney, York, Rock Hill, Pageland, Bennettsville, Dillon, Darlington, Florence, Marion, Georgetown, Conway

ASHEVILLE, BUNCOMBE, HAYWOOD, Waynesville, HENDERSON, Hendersonville, TRANSYLVANIA, Brevard, JACKSON, Sylva, MACON, Franklin, SWAIN, Bryson City, GRAHAM, Robbinsville, CHEROKEE, Murphy, CLAY, Hayesville, MADISON, Marshall, YANCEY, Burnsville, Johnson City, Elizabethton, Boone, WATAUGA, AVERY, Newland, MITCHELL, Bakersville, Spruce Pine

APPALACHIAN MTS., UNAKA MTS., GREAT SMOKY MTS., BLUE RIDGE MTS., STONE MTS., Roan Mt., Mt. Mitchell 6,684, Clingmans Dome 6,642, Mt. Guyot 6,621, Craggy Dome 6,105, Grandfather Mt., Mt. Pisgah

WESTERN PART OF
NORTH CAROLINA
Same scale as main map.

SCALE OF MILES
0 5 10 15 20 25

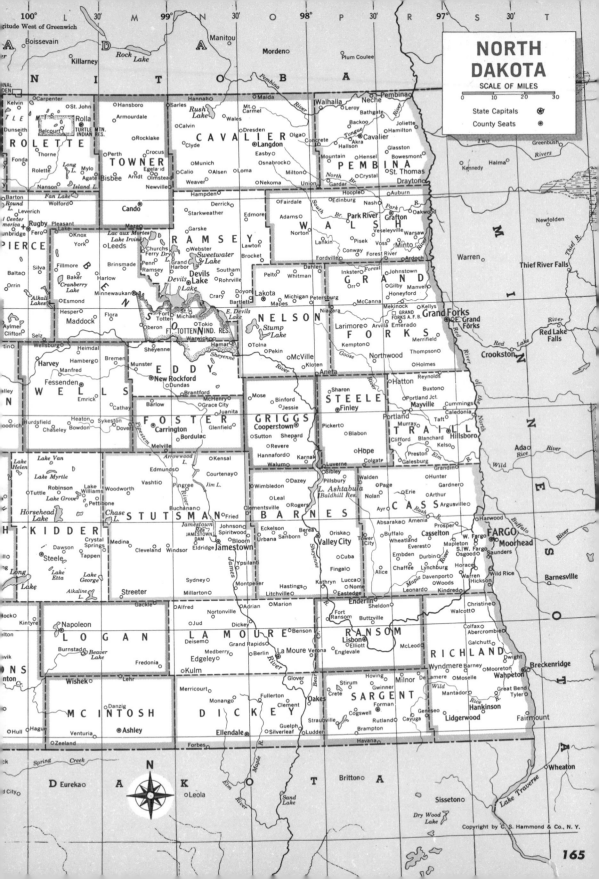

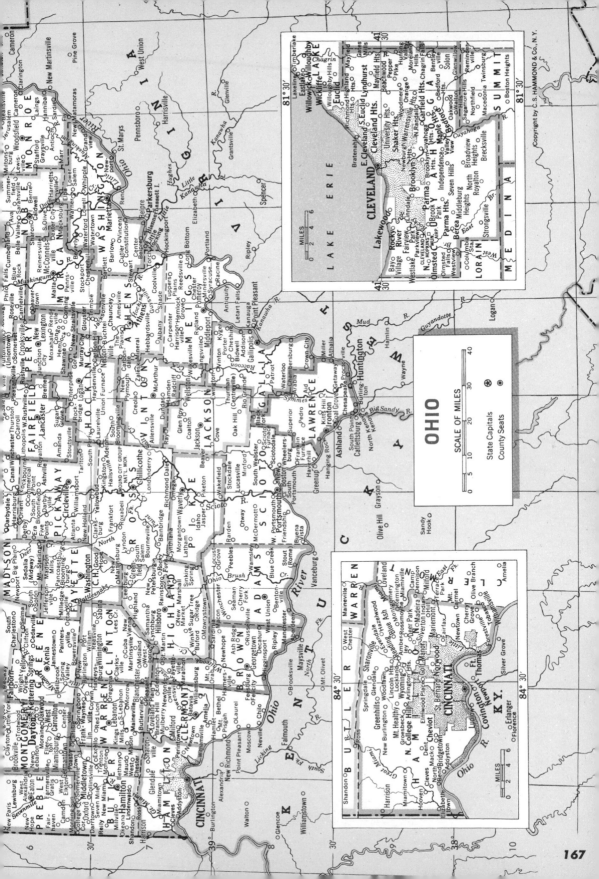

OHIO

SCALE OF MILES

State Capitals ⊛
County Seats ⊙

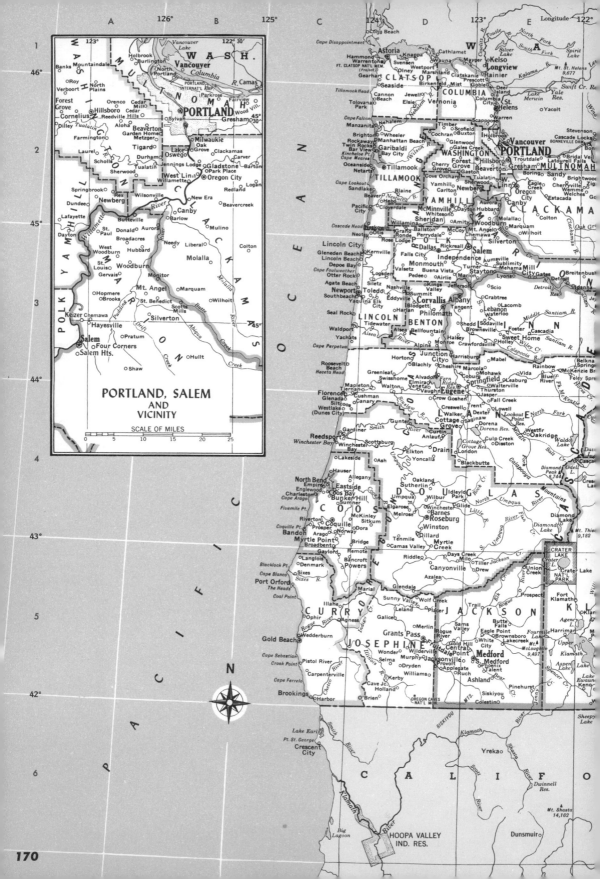

PORTLAND, SALEM
AND
VICINITY

SCALE OF MILES

0   5   10   15   20   25

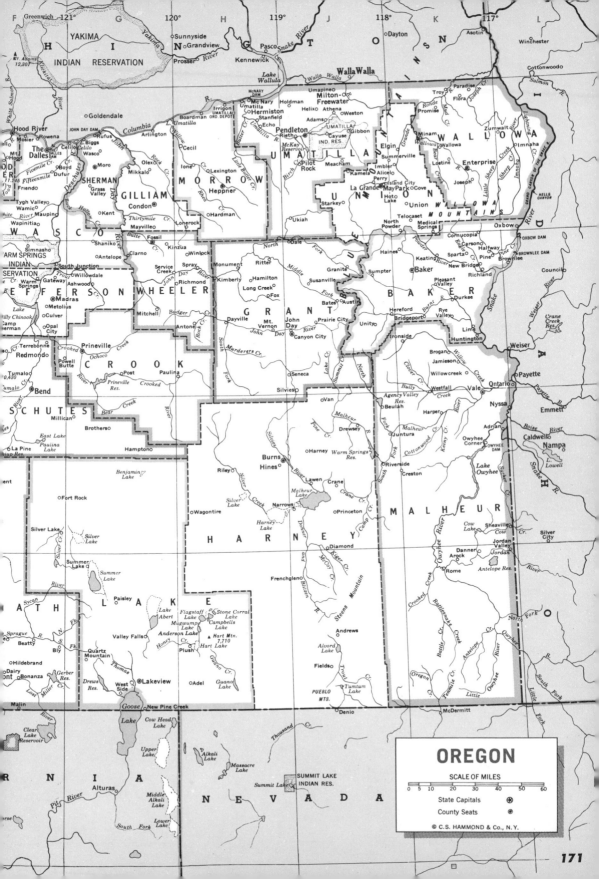

OREGON

SCALE OF MILES

0 5 10   20   30   40   50   60

⊛ State Capitals

⊙ County Seats

Ⓗ C.S. HAMMOND & Co., N.Y.

LAKE ERIE

ERIE — CRAWFORD — WARREN — McKEAN — POTTER — CAMERON — ELK — FOREST — VENANGO — MERCER — CLARION — JEFFERSON — CLEARFIELD — LAWRENCE — BUTLER — ARMSTRONG — INDIANA — CAMBRIA — BLAIR — BEAVER — ALLEGHENY — WESTMORELAND — SOMERSET — BEDFORD — FULTON — WASHINGTON — FAYETTE — GREENE — HUNTINGDON

PITTSBURGH

W. VA. — MARYLAND — WEST VIRGINIA — VIRGINIA

PITTSBURGH (inset)

MILES

SOUTH PK. MIL. RES.

PENNSYLVANIA

SCALE OF MILES

0 5 10 20 30 40

State Capitals ⊛
County Seats ⊙
Canals ━━━

© C.S. HAMMOND & Co., N.Y.

SOUTH CAROLINA

SCALE OF MILES

0 5 10   20   30   40

State Capitals   ⊛
County Seats   ⊙
Canals   ╌╌╌

SOUTH DAKOTA

SCALE OF MILES

0 5 10 20   40   60

⊛ State Capitals
⊛ County Seats

© C.S. HAMMOND & Co., N.Y.

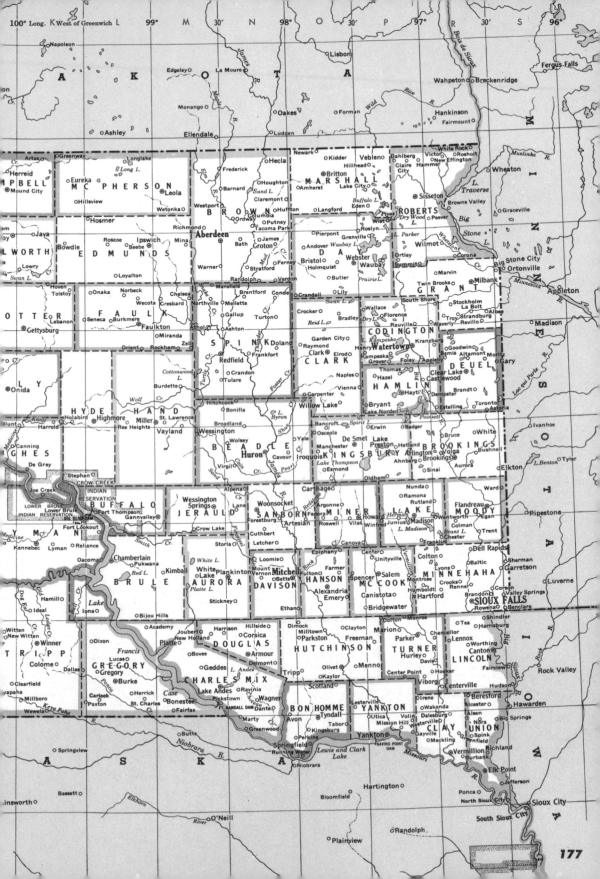

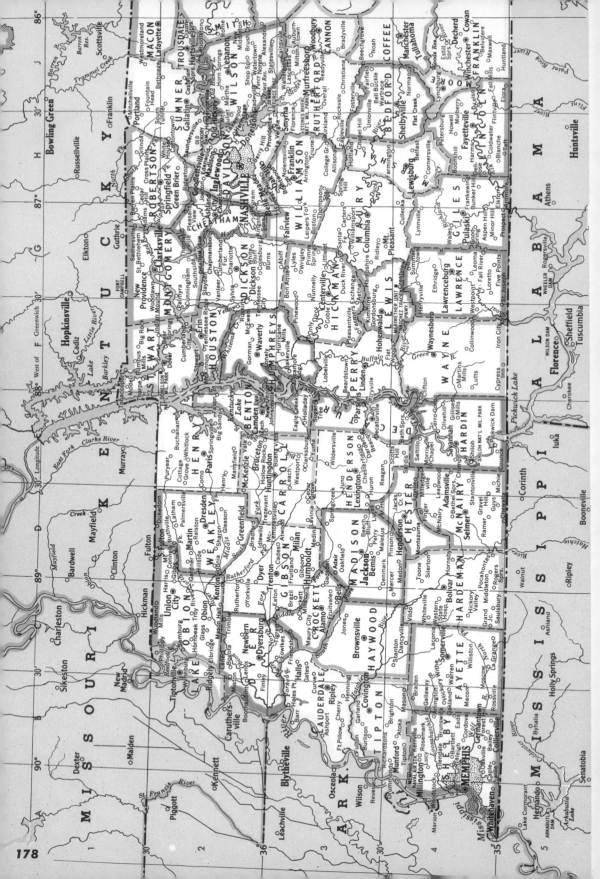

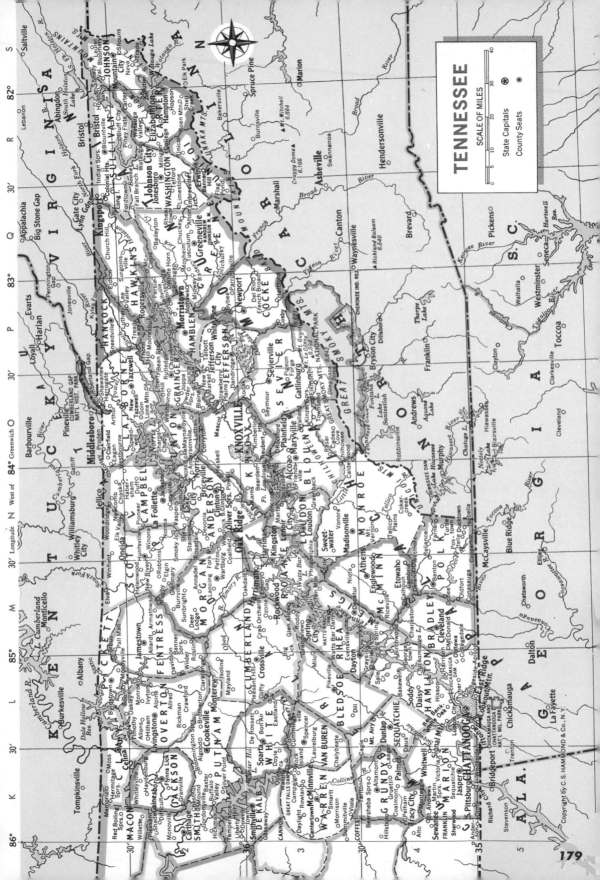

TENNESSEE

SCALE OF MILES

State Capitals
County Seats

179

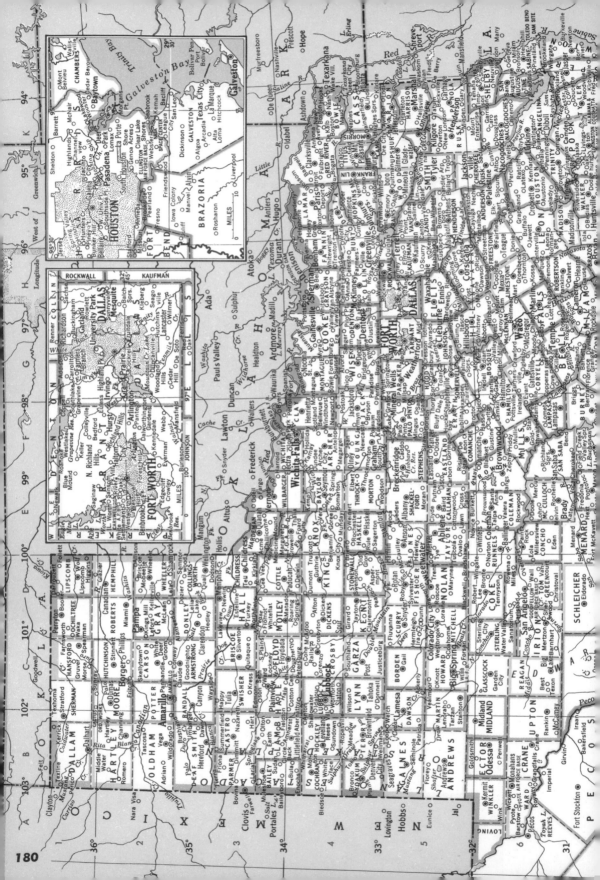

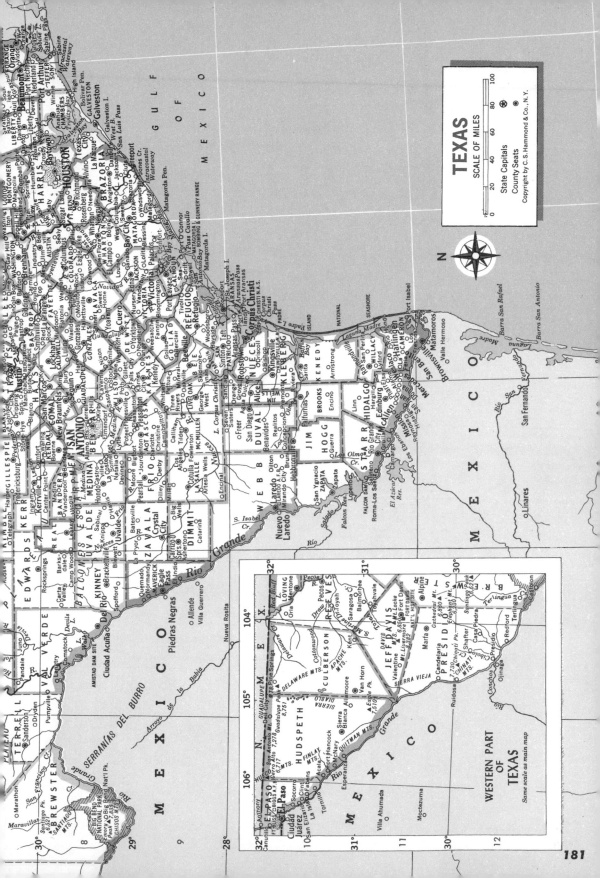

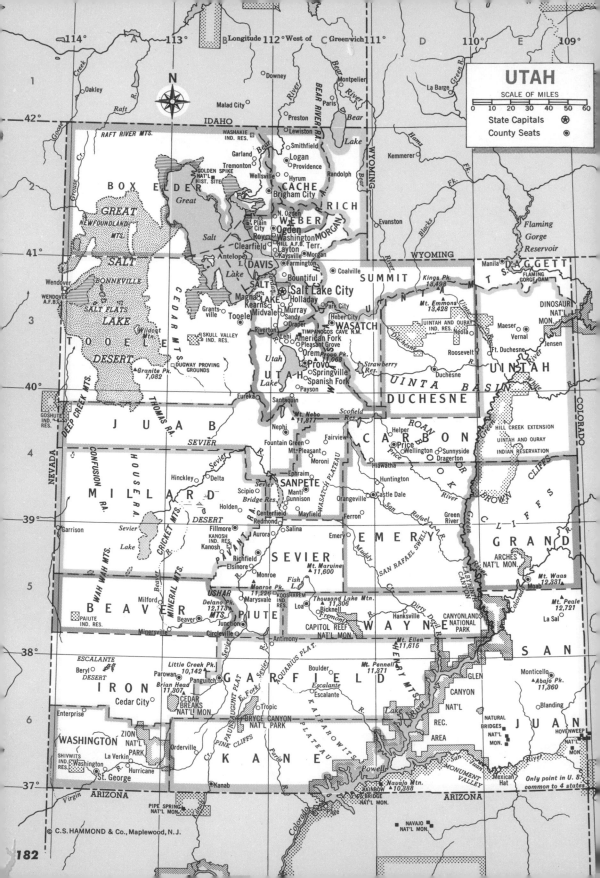

UTAH

SCALE OF MILES

0 10 20 30 40 50 60

State Capitals ✪
County Seats ◉

© C.S. HAMMOND & Co., Maplewood, N.J.

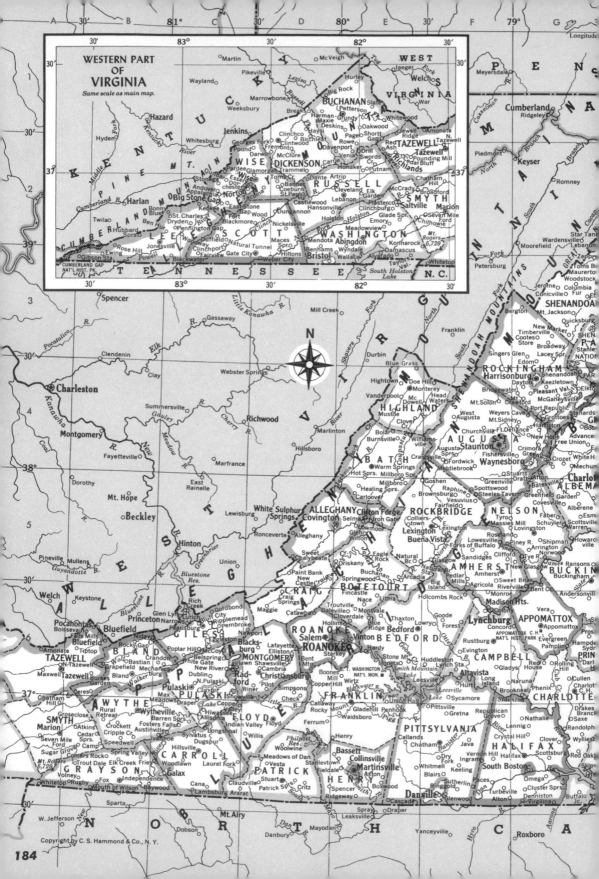

WASHINGTON
SCALE OF MILES

State Capitals ⊛
County Seats ◉

186

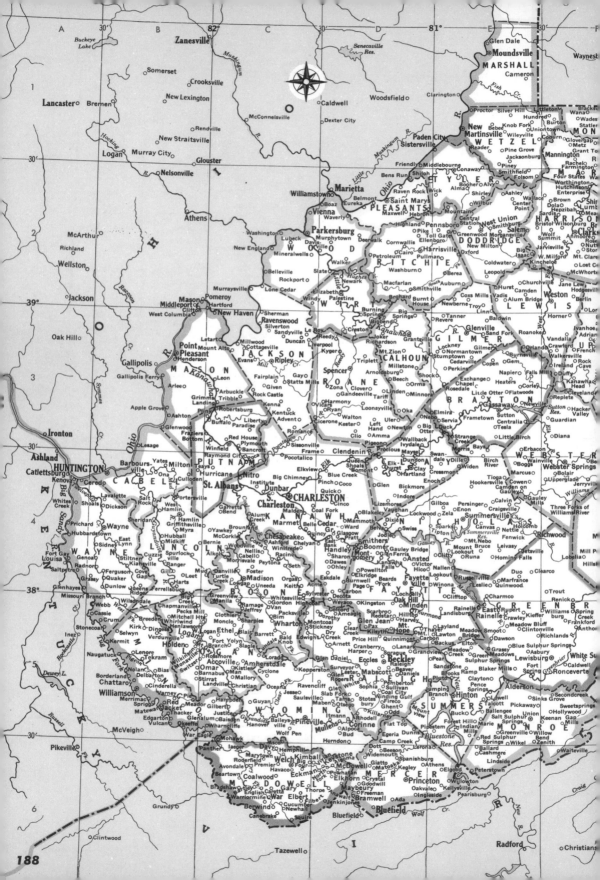

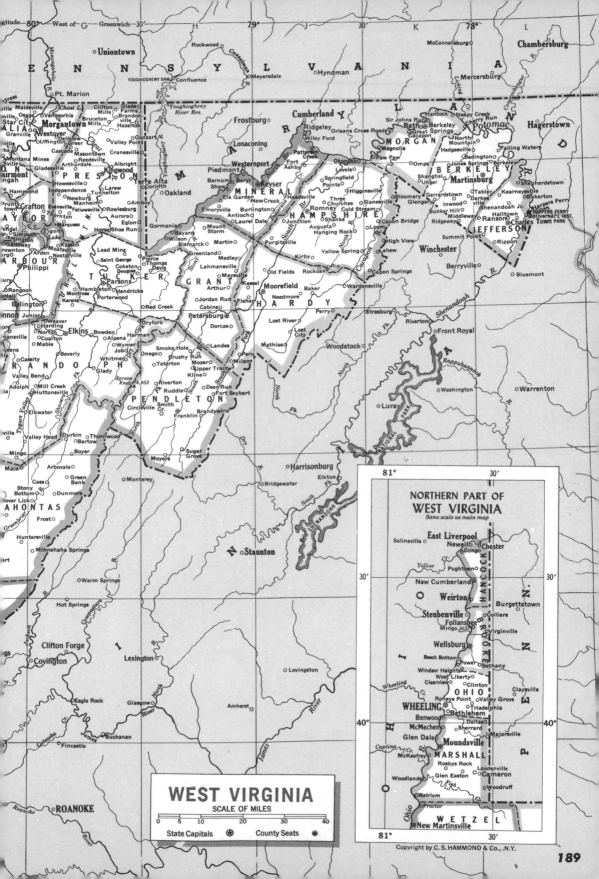

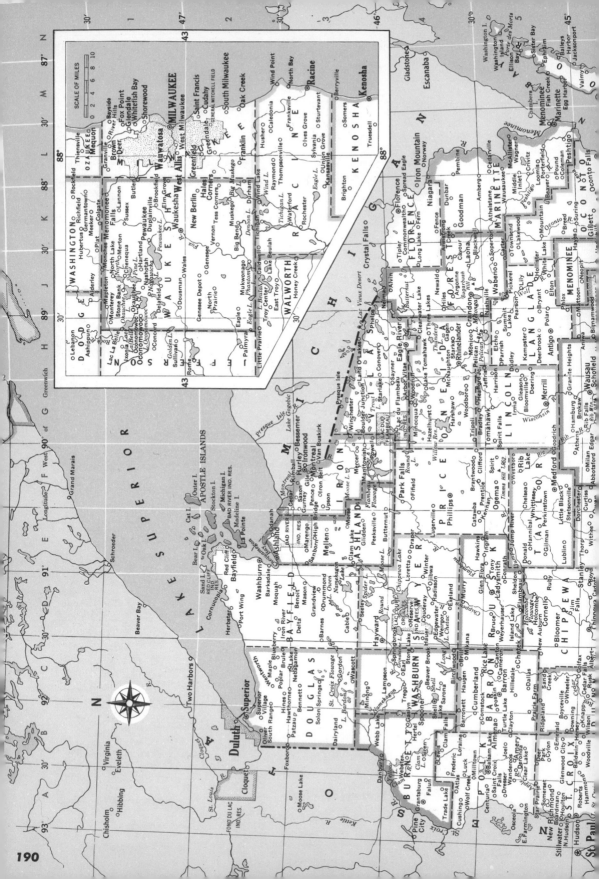

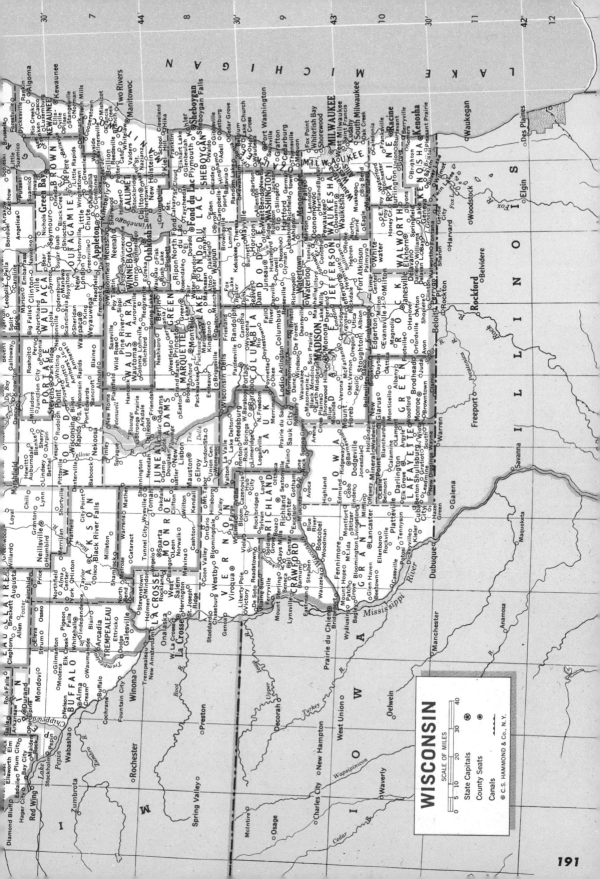

WISCONSIN

SCALE OF MILES

State Capitals ⊛
County Seats ⊙
Canals ⊙

© C.S. HAMMOND & CO., N.Y.

191

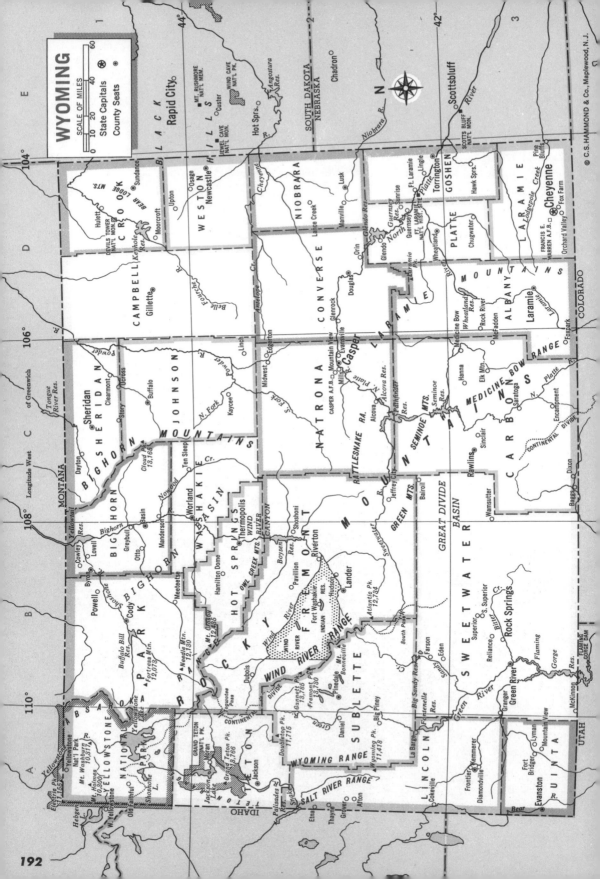

WYOMING

SCALE OF MILES
0 10 20 30 40 50 60

⊛ State Capitals
⊙ County Seats

© C.S. HAMMOND & Co., Maplewood, N.J.

GLOSSARY OF GEOGRAPHICAL TERMS

A. = Arabic Camb. = Cambodian Ch. = Chinese Dan. = Danish Du. = Dutch
Finn. = Finnish Fr. = French Ger. = German Ice. = Icelandic It. = Italian
Jap. = Japanese Mong. = Mongol Nor. = Norwegian Per. = Persian
Port.=Portuguese Russ.=Russian Sp.=Spanish Sw.=Swedish Turk. =Turkish

Å	Nor., Sw.	Stream
Abajo	Sp.	Lower
Ada, Adasi	Turk.	Island
Altiplano	Sp.	Plateau
Älv, Alf, Elf	Sw.	River
Arrecife	Sp.	Reef
Baai	Du.	Bay
Bahía	Sp.	Bay
Bahr	Arabic	Marsh, Lake, Sea, River
Baia	Port.	Bay
Baie	Fr.	Bay, Gulf
Bañados	Sp.	Marshes
Barra	Sp.	Reef
Belt	Ger.	Strait
Ben	Gaelic	Mountain
Berg	Ger., Du.	Mountain
Bir	Arabic	Well
Boca	Sp.	Gulf, Inlet
Bolshoi, Bolshaya	Russ.	Big
Bolsón	Sp.	Depression
Bong	Korean	Mountain
Bucht	Ger.	Bay
Bugt	Dan.	Bay
Bukhta	Russ.	Bay
Burnu, Burun	Turk.	Cape, Point
By	Dan., Nor., Sw.	Town
Cabo	Port., Sp.	Cape
Campos	Port.	Plains
Canal	Port., Sp.	Channel
Cap, Capo	Fr., It.	Cape
Catarátas	Sp.	Falls
Central, Centrale	Fr., It.	Middle
Cerrito, Cerro	Sp.	Hill
Ciénaga	Sp.	Swamp
Ciudad	Sp.	City
Col	Fr.	Pass
Cordillera	Sp.	Mt. Range
Côte	Fr.	Coast
Cuchilla	Sp.	Mt. Range
Dağ, Dagh	Turk.	Mountain
Dağlari	Turk.	Mt. Range
Dal	Nor., Sw.	Valley
Darya	Per.	Salt Lake
Dasht	Per.	Desert, Plain
Deniz, Denizi	Turk.	Sea, Lake
Desierto	Sp.	Desert
Eiland	Du.	Island
Elv	Dan., Nor.	River
Emi	Berber	Mountain
Erg	Arabic	Dune, Desert
Est, Este	Fr., Port., Sp.	East
Estrecho, Estreito	Sp., Port.	Strait
Étang	Fr.	Pond, Lagoon, Lake
Fjørd	Dan., Nor.	Fiord
Fleuve	Fr.	River
Gebel	Arabic	Mountain
Gebirge	Ger.	Mt. Range
Gobi	Mongol	Desert
Gol	Mongol, Turk.	Lake, Stream
Golf	Ger., Du.	Gulf
Golfe	Fr.	Gulf
Golfo	Sp., It., Port.	Gulf
Gölü	Turk.	Lake
Gora	Russ.	Mountain
Grand, Grande	Fr., Sp.	Big
Groot	Du.	Big
Gross	Ger.	Big
Grosso	It., Port.	Big
Guba	Russ.	Bay, Gulf
Gunto	Jap.	Archipelago
Gunung	Malay	Mountain
Higashi, Higasi	Jap.	East
Ho	Ch.	River
Hoek	Du.	Cape
Holm	Dan., Nor., Sw.	Island
Hu	Ch.	Lake
Hwang	Ch.	Yellow
Île	Fr.	Island
Insel	Ger.	Island
Irmak	Turk.	River
Isla	Sp.	Island
Isola	Sp.	Island
Jabal, Jebel	Arabic	Mountains
Järvi	Finn.	Lake
Jaure	Sw.	Lake
Jezira	Arabic	Island
Jima	Jap.	Island
Joki	Finn.	River
Kaap	Du.	Cape
Kabir, Kebir	Arabic	Big
Kanal	Russ., Ger.	Canal, Channel
Kap, Kapp	Nor., Sw., Ice.	Cape
Kawa	Jap.	River
Khrebet	Russ.	Mt. Range
Kiang	Ch.	River
Kita	Jap.	North
Klein	Du., Ger.	Small
Kô	Jap.	Lake
Ko	Thai.	Island
Koh	Camb., Khmer	Island
Köping	Sw.	Borough
Körfez, Körfezi	Turk.	Gulf
Kuh	Per.	Mountain

Kul	Sinkiang Turki	Lake
Kum	Turk.	Desert
Lac	Fr.	Lake
Lago	Port., Sp., It.	Lake
Lagôa	Port.	Lagoon
Laguna	Sp.	Lagoon
Lagune	Fr.	Lagoon
Llanos	Sp.	Plains
Mar	Sp., Port.	Sea
Mare	It.	Sea
Meer	Du.	Lake
Meer	Ger.	Sea
Mer	Fr.	Sea
Meseta	Sp.	Plateau
Minami	Jap.	Southern
Misaki	Jap.	Cape
Mittel	Ger.	Middle
Mont	Fr.	Mountain
Montagne	Fr.	Mountain
Montaña	Sp.	Mountains
Monte	Sp., It., Port.	Mountain
More	Russ.	Sea
Muong	Siamese	Town
Mys	Russ.	Cape
Nam	Burm., Lao	River
Nevado	Sp.	Snow covered peak
Nieder	Ger.	Lower
Nishi, Nisi	Jap.	West
Nizhni, Nizhnyaya	Russ.	Lower
Nor	Mong.	Lake
Nord	Fr., Ger.	North
Norte	Sp., It., Port.	North
Nos	Russ.	Cape
Novi, Novaya	Russ.	New
Nusa	Malay	Island
O	Jap.	Big
Ö	Nor., Sw	Island
Ober	Ger.	Upper
Occidental, Occidentale	Sp., It.	Western
Oeste	Port.	West
Oriental	Sp., Fr.	Eastern
Orientale	It.	Eastern
Ost	Ger.	East
Ostrov	Russ.	Island
Ouest	Fr.	West
öy	Nor.	Island
Ozero	Russ.	Lake
Pampa	Sp.	Plain
Paso	Sp.	Pass
Passo	It., Port.	Pass
Pequeño	Sp.	Small
Peski	Russ.	Desert
Petit	Fr.	Small
Pic	Fr.	Mountain
Pico	Port., Sp.	Mountain, Peak
Pik	Russ.	Peak
Pointe	Fr.	Point
Poluostrov	Russ.	Peninsula
Ponta	Port.	Point
Presa	Sp.	Reservoir
Proliv	Russ.	Strait
Pulou, Pulo	Malay	Island
Punta	Sp., It., Port.	Point
Ras	Arabic	Cape
Ría	Sp.	Estuary
Río	Sp.	River
Rivier, Rivière	Du., Fr.	River
Rud	Per.	River
Saki	Jap.	Cape
Salto	Sp., Port.	Falls
San	Ch., Jap., Korean	Hill
See	Ger.	Sea, Lake
Selvas	Sp., Port.	Forest
Serra	Port.	Mts.
Serranía	Sp.	Mts.
Severni, Servernaya	Russ.	North
Shan	Ch., Jap.	Hill, Mts.
Shima	Jap.	Island
Shoto	Jap.	Islands
Sierra	Sp.	Mountains
Sjö	Nor., Sw.	Lake, Sea
Spitze	Ger.	Mt. Peak
Sredni, Srednyaya	Russ.	Middle
Stad	Dan., Nor., Sw.	City
Stari, Staraya	Russ.	Old
Su	Turk.	River
Sud, Süd	Sp., Fr., Ger.	South
Sul	Port.	South
Sungei	Malay	River
Sur	Sp.	South
Tagh	Turk.	Mt. Range
Tal	Ger.	Valley
Tandjong, Tanjung	Malay	Cape, Point
Tso	Tibetan	Lake
Val	Fr.	Valley
Velho	Port.	Old
Verkhni	Russ.	Upper
Vesi	Finn.	Lake
Vishni, Vishnyaya	Russ.	High
Vostochni, Vostochnaya	Russ.	East, Eastern
Wadi	Arabic	Dry River
Wald	Ger.	Forest
Wan	Jap.	Bay
Yama	Jap.	Mountain
Yug, Yuzhni, Yuzhnaya	Russ.	South, Southern
Zaliv	Russ.	Bay, Gulf
Zapadni, Zapadnaya	Russ.	Western
Zee	Du.	Sea
Zemlya	Russ.	Land
Zuid	Du.	South

WORLD
STATISTICAL TABLES
and
DISTRIBUTION MAPS

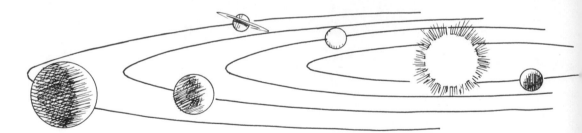

Elements of the Solar System

PLANETS	DISTANCE FROM SUN IN MILES		PERIOD OF REVOLUTION AROUND SUN IN DAYS	DIAMETER IN MILES	DENSITY (EARTH=1)
	MAXIMUM	MINIMUM			
Sun . . .	......	......	......	865,390	0.26
Mercury . .	43,404,000	28,599,000	87.87	3,009	0.68
Venus . . .	67,730,000	66,814,000	224.70	7,575	0.94
Earth . . .	94,560,000	91,446,000	365.26	7,927	1.00
Mars . . .	154,936,000	128,476,000	686.98	4,216	0.71
Jupiter . .	507,289,000	460,465,000	4,332.59	88,698	0.24
Saturn . .	936,637,000	837,655,000	10,759.20	75,060	0.12
Uranus . .	1,868,930,000	1,700,745,000	30,685.93	30,878	0.25
Neptune . .	2,820,610,000	2,773,510,000	60,187.64	27,700	0.41
Pluto . . .	4,585,000,000	2,753,000,000	90,470.23	3,600 approx.	0.7

Dimensions of the Earth

Superficial area	196,950,000	sq. miles
Land surface	57,510,000	" "
North America	8,500,000	" "
South America	6,814,000	" "
Europe	3,872,000	" "
Asia	16,990,000	" "
Africa	11,500,000	" "
Australia	2,974,581	" "
Water surface	139,440,000	" "
Atlantic Ocean	31,830,000	" "
Pacific Ocean	63,801,000	" "
Indian Ocean	28,356,000	" "
Arctic Ocean	5,440,000	" "
Equatorial circumference	24,902	miles
Meridional circumference	24,860	"
Equatorial diameter	7,926.677	"
Polar diameter	7,899.988	"
Equatorial radius	3,963.34	"
Polar radius	3,949.99	"
Volume of the Earth	260,000,000,000	cubic miles
Mass, or weight	6,592,000,000,000,000,000,000	tons
Mean distance from the Sun	92,897,416	miles

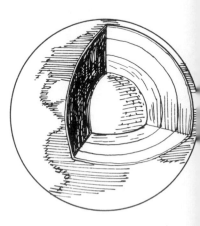

The Moon, the only satellite of the Earth, from which her mean distance is 238,857 miles, occupies an average period, in her revolution round the earth, of 29 days, 12 hours, 44 minutes, 3 seconds; her diameter is 2,160 miles, and her mean density 0.60.

Principal Lakes and Inland Seas

	AREA IN SQ. MILES		AREA IN SQ. MILES
Caspian Sea	163,800	Lake Bangweulu . . . . . Approx.	1,000
Lake Superior	31,820	Vättern	733
Lake Victoria	26,828	Dead Sea	405
Lake Aral	24,900	Lake Balaton	266
Lake Huron	23,010	Lake Geneva	225
Lake Michigan	22,400	Lake of Constance	208
Lake Tanganyika	12,700	Lough Neagh	153
Lake Baikal	12,150	Lake Garda	143
Great Bear Lake	12,000	Lake Neuchâtel	83
Great Slave Lake	11,170	Lake Maggiore	82
Lake Nyasa	11,000	Lough Corrib	71
Lake Erie	9,940	Lake Como	56
Lake Winnipeg	9,398	Lake of Lucerne	44.5
Lake Ontario	7,540	Lake of Zürich	34
Lake Ladoga	7,100		
Lake Balkhash	6,700		
Lake Chad	6,500		
Lake Onega	3,765		
Lake Titicaca	3,200		
Lake Nicaragua	3,100		
Lake Athabasca	3,058		
Reindeer Lake	2,444		
Issyk-Kul	2,276		
Vänern	2,149		
Lake Urmia	1,795		
Great Salt Lake	1,700		
Lake Albert	1,640		
Lake Van	1,453		
Lake Peipus	1,400		
Lake Tana	1,219		

Oceans and Seas of the World

	AREA IN SQ. MILES	GREATEST DEPTH IN FEET	VOLUME IN CUBIC MILES
Pacific Ocean	63,801,000	35,400	162,870,600
Atlantic Ocean	31,830,000	30,246	75,533,900
Indian Ocean	28,356,000	22,968	69,225,200
Arctic Ocean	5,440,000	17,850	4,029,400
Mediterranean Sea	1,145,000	15,197	1,019,400
Bering Sea	876,000	13,422	788,500
Caribbean Sea	750,000	23,748	2,298,400
Sea of Okhotsk	590,000	11,070	454,700
East China Sea	482,000	10,500	52,700
Hudson Bay	475,000	1,500	37,590
Japan Sea	389,000	13,242	383,200
North Sea	222,000	2,654	12,890
Red Sea	169,000	7,254	53,700
Black Sea	165,000	7,200	....
Baltic Sea	163,000	1,506	5,360

Longest Rivers of the World

	LENGTH IN MILES
Nile, Africa	4,149
Amazon, S.A.	3,900
Mississippi-Missouri, U.S.A.	3,710
Yangtze, China	3,400
Ob-Irtysh, U.S.S.R.	3,200
Congo, Africa	2,900
Amur, Asia	2,704
Hwang (Yellow), China	2,700

	LENGTH IN MILES
Lena, U.S.S.R.	2,648
Mackenzie, Canada	2,635
Mekong, Asia	2,600
Niger, Africa	2,600
Paraná, S.A.	2,450
Yenisey, U.S.S.R.	2,364
Murray-Darling, Australia	2,310
Volga, U.S.S.R.	2,290
Madeira, S.A.	2,000
Yukon, Alaska-Canada	1,979
St. Lawrence, Canada-U.S.A.	1,900
Rio Grande, U.S.A.-Mexico	1,885
São Francisco, S.A.	1,800
Salween, Asia	1,750

	LENGTH IN MILES
Danube, Europe	1,725
Euphrates, Asia	1,700
Indus, Asia	1,700
Brahmaputra, Asia	1,680
Syr-Dar'ya, U.S.S.R.	1,680
Ganges, India	1,650
Orinoco, S.A.	1,600
Zambezi, Africa	1,600
Ural, US.S.R.	1,574
Amu-Dar'ya, U.S.S.R.	1,550
Paraguay, S.A.	1,500
Arkansas, U.S.A.	1,450
Colorado, U.S.A.-Mexico	1,450
Dnieper, U.S.S.R.	1,418
Rio Negro, S.A.	1,400
Orange, Africa	1,350
Irrawaddy, Burma	1,325
Ohio, U.S.A.	1,306
Don, U.S.S.R.	1,222
Columbia, U.S.A.-Canada	1,214
Saskatchewan, Canada	1,205
Tigris, Asia	1,150
Snake, U.S.A.	1,038
Red, Texas, U.S.A.	1,018
Uruguay, S.A.	1,000
Magdalena, Colombia	1,000
Platte-N. Platte, U.S.A.	990
Canadian, U.S.A.	906
Tennessee, U.S.A.	862
Dniester, U.S.S.R.	852
Fraser, Canada	850
Colorado, Texas, U.S.A.	840

Great Ship Canals

	LENGTH IN MILES	DEPTH IN FEET
Baltic-White Sea, U.S.S.R.	141	....
Suez, Egypt	100.76	34
Albert, Belgium	81	16.5
Moscow-Volga, U.S.S.R.	80	18
Kiel, Germany	61	37
Göta, Sweden	54	10
Panama, Canal Zone, U.S.A.	50.72	41
Houston, U.S.A.	50	36
Amsterdam-Rhine, Netherlands	45	41
Beaumont-Port Arthur, U.S.A.	40	32
Manchester, England	35.5	28
Chicago Sanitary and Ship, U.S.A.	30	22
Welland, Canada	27.6	25
Juliana, Netherlands	21	11.8
Chesapeake-Delaware, U.S.A.	19	27
Cape Cod, U.S.A.	13	25
Lake Washington, U.S.A.	8	30
Corinth, Greece	4	26.25
Sault Ste. Marie, U.S.A.	1.6	24.5
Sault Ste. Marie, Canada	1.4	18.25

Principal Mountains of the World

	FEET
Mt. Everest, Nepal-Tibet . .	29,028
Mt. Godwin Austen (K2), India	28,250
Kanchenjunga, Nepal-India .	28,168
Dhaulagiri, Nepal	26,810
Nunga Parbat, India . . .	26,620
Annapurna, Nepal	26,504
Nanda Devi, India	25,645
Mt. Kamet, India	25,447
Gurla Mandhata, Tibet . . .	25,355
Tirich Mir, Pakistan	25,263
Minya Konka, China . . .	24,900
Mt. Communism, U.S.S.R. . .	24,590
Pobeda Peak, U.S.S.R. . . .	24,406
Muztagh Ata, China . . .	24,388
Chomo Lhari, India-Tibet . .	23,997
Muztagh, China	23,890
Aconcagua, Argentina . . .	22,834
Ojos del Salado, Argentina-	
Chile	22,539
Cerro Mercedario, Argentina .	22,211
Huascarán, Peru	22,205
Llullaillaco Volcano, Chile .	22,057
Tupungato, Chile-Argentina .	21,489
Sajama Volcano, Bolivia . .	21,391
Illampu, Bolivia	21,276
Vilcanota, Peru	20,664
Chimborazo, Ecuador . . .	20,561
Mt. McKinley, Alaska . . .	20,320
Mt. Logan, Yukon	19,850
Kilimanjaro, Tanzania . . .	19,565
Cotopaxi, Ecuador	19,347
El Misti, Peru	19,199
Mt. Demavend, Iran	18,934
Citlaltépetl, Mexico	18,700
Mt. Elbrus, U.S.S.R.	18,481
Mt. St. Elias, Alaska-Yukon .	18,008
Popocatépetl, Mexico . . .	17,887
Dikh-Tau, U.S.S.R.	17,085
Mt. Kenya, Kenya	17,058

	FEET
Mt. Ararat, Turkey	16,945
Ruwenzori, Africa	16,795
Cartensz, W. Irian	16,400
Klyuchevskaya Sopka, U.S.S.R.	15,912
Mont Blanc, France	15,781
Kazbek, U.S.S.R.	15,558
Monte Rosa, Italy-Switzerland	15,217
Ras Dashan, Ethiopia . . .	15,157
Mt. Markham, Antarctica . .	15,100
Matterhorn, Switzerland . .	14,780
Mt. Whitney, California . . .	14,495
Mt. Elbert, Colorado	14,431
Mt. Rainier, Washington . .	14,410
Mt. Shasta, California . . .	14,162
Pikes Peak, Colorado . . .	14,110
Finsteraarhorn, Switzerland .	14,026
Mauna Kea, Hawaii	13,796
Mauna Loa, Hawaii	13,680
Jungfrau, Switzerland . . .	13,667
Cameroon, Cameroon . . .	13,350
Gran Paradiso, Italy	13,323
Mt. Robson, British Columbia .	12,972
Grossglockner, Austria . . .	12,461
Fuji, Japan	12,389
Mt. Cook, New Zealand . .	12,349
Mulhacén, Spain	11,417
Mt. Etna, Italy	10,741
Irazú, Costa Rica	10,525
Lassen Peak, California . . .	10,466
Mt. Kosciusko, Australia . .	7,316
Mt. Mitchell, No. Carolina . .	6,684

Principal Islands of the World

	AREA IN SQ. MILES		AREA IN SQ. MILES		AREA IN SQ. MILES
Greenland	839,999	Prince of Wales	12,830	Tahiti	600
New Guinea	345,054	Vancouver	12,408	Oahu	589
Borneo	289,859	Sicily	9,926	Guadeloupe	583
Madagascar	241,094	Somerset	9,370	Ahvenanmaa (Åland Is.)	564
Baffin	183,810	Sardinia	9,301	Kauai	551
Sumatra	164,148	New Caledonia	7,201	Shetland Islands	550
Philippines	115,600	Fiji Islands	7,015	Rhodes	542
New Zealand: North and South Islands	103,934	New Hebrides	5,700	Caroline Islands	525
		Kuril Islands	5,700	Martinique	425
England-Scotland-Wales	88,745	Falkland Islands	4,618	Pemba	380
Honshu	87,426	Jamaica	4,411	Orkney Islands	376
Ellesmere	82,119	Bahama Islands	4,404	Madeira Islands	308
Victoria	81,930	Hawaii	4,021	Dominica	290
Celebes	72,986	Cape Breton	3,970	Tonga or Friendly Islands	269
Java	48,842	New Ireland	3,800		
Cuba	42,857	Cyprus	3,572	Molokai	261
Newfoundland	42,734	Puerto Rico	3,421	St. Lucia	238
Luzon	40,420	Corsica	3,367	Corfu	229
Iceland	39,709	Crete	3,232	Bornholm	227
Mindanao	36,537	Galápagos Islands	3,042	Isle of Man	227
Sakhalin	35,400	Hebrides	3,000	Singapore	225
Novaya Zemlya	35,000	Canary Islands	2,894	Guam	212
Ireland	32,060	Wrangel	2,819	Isle Royale	209
Molucca Islands	30,168	Kerguélen	2,700	Virgin Islands	191
Hispaniola	29,843	Prince Edward	2,184	Curaçao	173
Hokkaido	29,600	Balearic Islands	1,936	Barbados	166
Tasmania	26,215	Trinidad and Tobago	1,864	Seychelles	155
Ceylon	25,332	Madura	1,752	St. Vincent	150
Timor	24,450	South Georgia	1,600	Isle of Wight	147
Svalbard (Spitsbergen)	24,294	Cape Verde Islands	1,557	Lanai	141
Banks	23,230	Long I., New York	1,401	Grenada	133
Devon	20,861	Socotra	1,400	Malta	122
Bismarck Arch.	19,660	Gotland	1,225	Tobago	116
Solomon Islands	18,670	Samoa	1,209	Martha's Vineyard	106
Tierra del Fuego	18,500	Isle of Pines	1,180	Channel Islands	75
Melville	16,369	Réunion	970	Nantucket	60
Southampton	15,700	Azores	890	St. Helena	47
New Britain	14,600	Fernando Po	785	Ascension	34
Taiwan (Formosa)	13,885	Tenerife	785	Hong Kong	29
Kyushu	13,770	Maui	728	Manhattan, New York	22
Hainan	13,000	Mauritius	720	Bermudas	21
		Zanzibar	640		

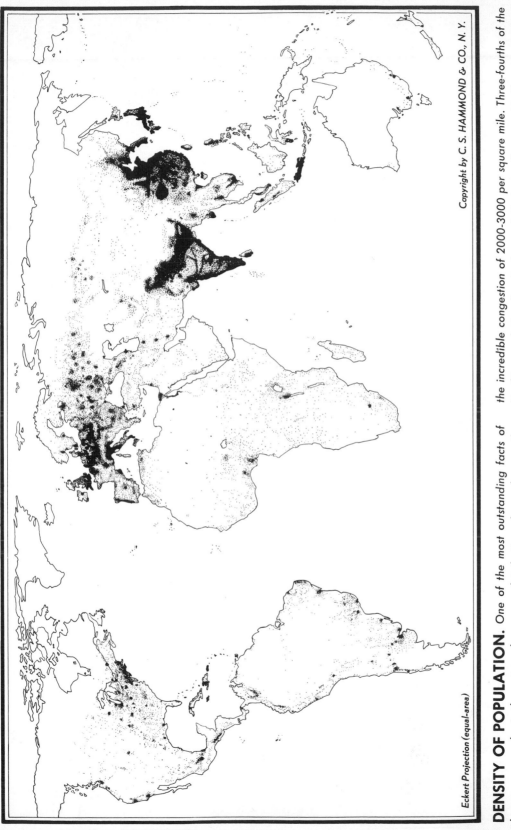

Eckert Projection (equal-area)

DENSITY OF POPULATION. One of the most outstanding facts of human geography is the extremely uneven distribution of people over the Earth. One-half of the Earth's surface has less than 3 people per square mile, while in the lowlands of India, China, Java and Japan rural density reaches the incredible congestion of 2000-3000 per square mile. Three-fourths of the Earth's population live in four relatively small areas; Northeastern United States, North-Central Europe, India and the Far East.

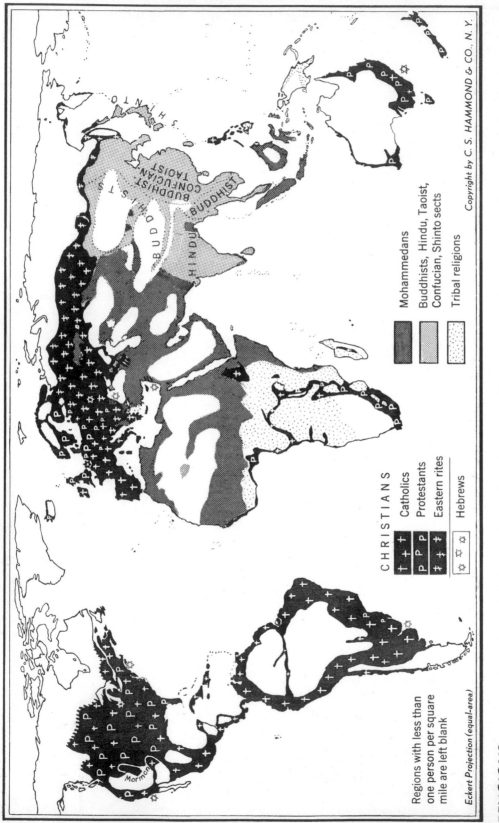

Eckert Projection (equal-area)

Regions with less than
one person per square
mile are left blank

C H R I S T I A N S
Catholics   +   ✝ ✝
Protestants   P   P
Eastern rites   ✝   ✝
Hebrews   ✡   ✡

Mohammedans

Buddhists, Hindu, Taoist,
Confucian, Shinto sects

Tribal religions

Copyright by C. S. HAMMOND & CO., N. Y.

RELIGIONS. Most people of the Earth belong to four major religions: Christians, Mohammedans, Brahmans, Buddhists and derivatives. The Eastern rites of the Christians include the Greek Orthodox, Greek Catholic, Armenian, Syrian, Coptic and more minor churches. The lamaism of Tibet and Mongolia differs a great deal from Buddhism in Burma and Thailand. In the religion of China the teachings of Buddha, Confucius and Tao are mixed, while in Shinto a great deal of ancestor and emperor worship is added. About 11 million Hebrews live scattered over the globe, chiefly in cities and in the state of Israel.

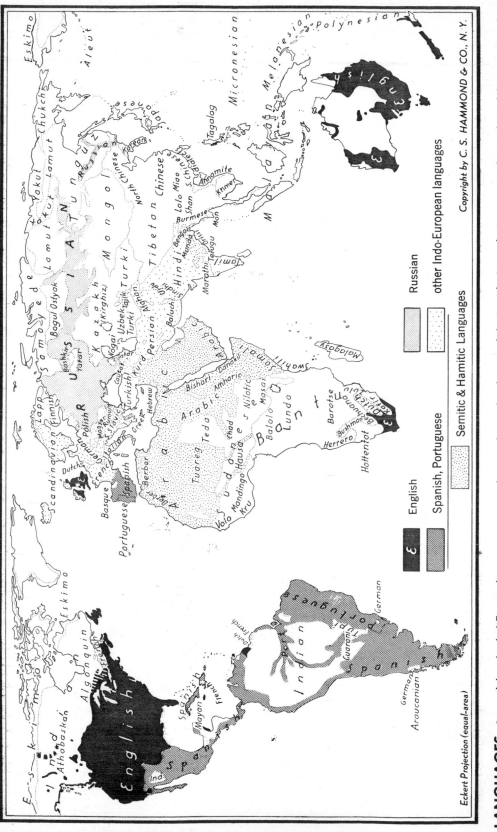

Eckert Projection (equal-area)

LANGUAGES. Several hundred different languages are spoken in the World, and in many places two or more languages are spoken, sometimes by the same people. The map above shows the dominant languages in each locality. English, French, Spanish, Russian, Arabic and Swahili are spoken by many people as a second language for commerce or travel.

Copyright by C. S. HAMMOND & CO., N. Y.

English

Spanish, Portuguese

Russian

other Indo-European languages

Semitic & Hamitic Languages

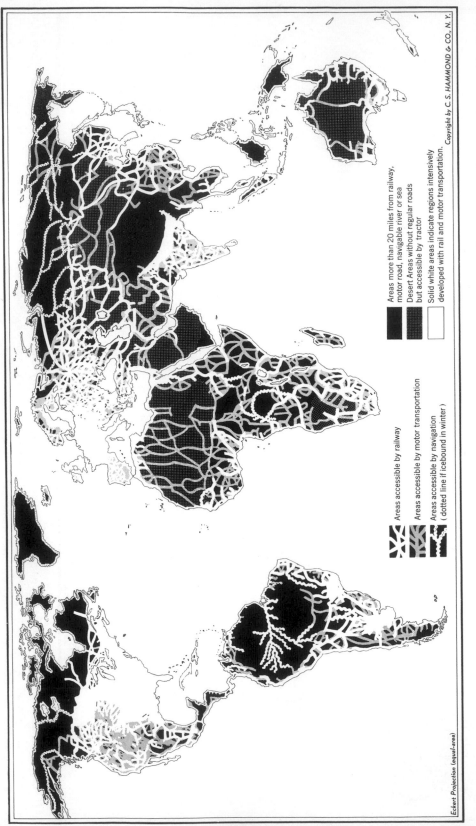

Eckert Projection (equal-area)

Copyright by C. S. HAMMOND & CO., N. Y.

Areas accessible by railway

Areas accessible by motor transportation

Areas accessible by navigation
(dotted line if icebound in winter)

Areas more than 20 miles from railway,
motor road, navigable river or sea

Desert Areas without regular roads
but accessible by tractor

Solid white areas indicate regions intensively
developed with rail and motor transportation.

ACCESSIBILITY. Many regions in the world are far from railways, roads, navigable rivers or the seas. Their economic development is retarded because their products can be brought to the world's markets only at great expense. Such areas are in the tundra (alpine), the boreal forest and in the equatorial rain forest regions. Desert areas, if not too mountainous, can be crossed by tractors. The largest inaccessible area is in Tibet, on account of high mountains, the alpine climate and isolationist attitude of the people. Airplane transportation is helping to bring these inaccessible areas into the orbit of civilization.

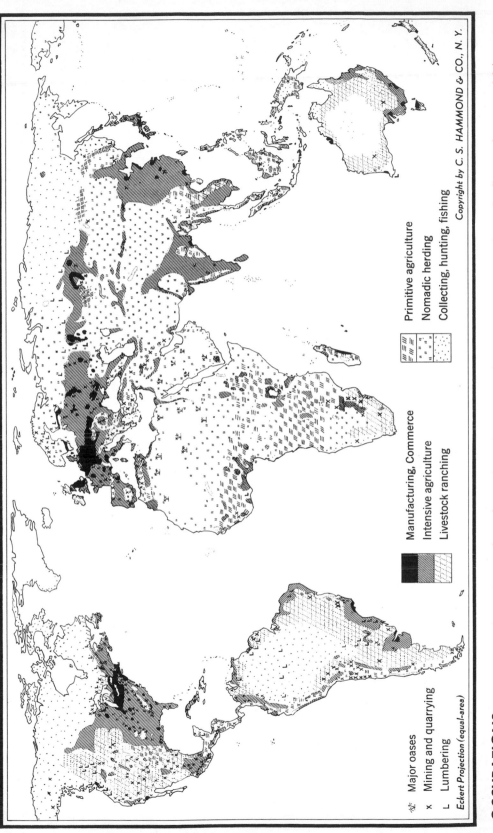

OCCUPATIONS. Correlation with the density of population shows that the most densely populated areas fall into the regions of manufacturing and intensive farming. All other economies require considerable space. The most sparsely inhabited areas are those of collecting, hunting and fishing. Areas with practically no habitation are left blank.

Manufacturing, Commerce

Intensive agriculture

Livestock ranching

Primitive agriculture

Nomadic herding

Collecting, hunting, fishing

Copyright by C. S. HAMMOND & CO., N. Y.

✳ Major oases

× Mining and quarrying

L Lumbering

Eckert Projection (equal-area)

205

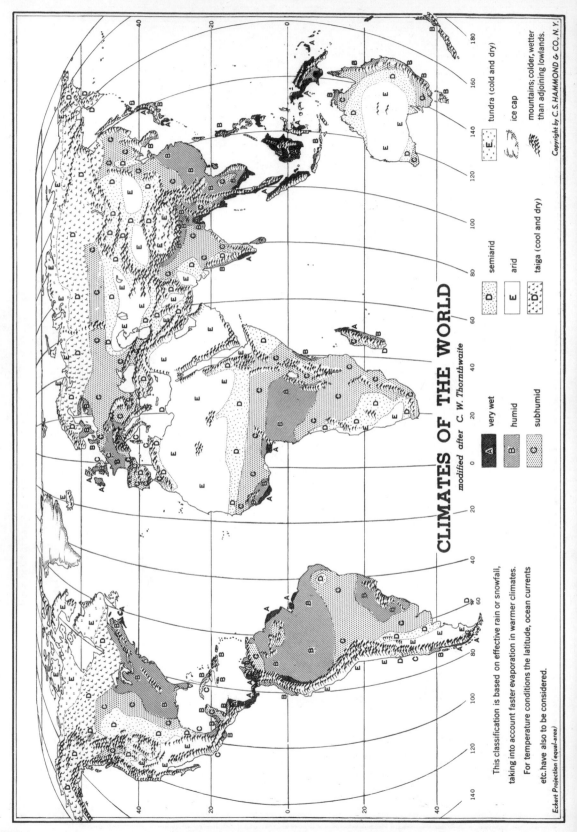

CLIMATES OF THE WORLD

modified after C. W. Thornthwaite

	very wet		tundra (cold and dry)
	humid		ice cap
	subhumid		mountains; colder, wetter than adjoining lowlands.
	semiarid	
	arid	
	taiga (cool and dry)	

This classification is based on effective rain or snowfall, taking into account faster evaporation in warmer climates.

For temperature conditions the latitude, ocean currents etc. have also to be considered.

Eckert Projection (equal-area)

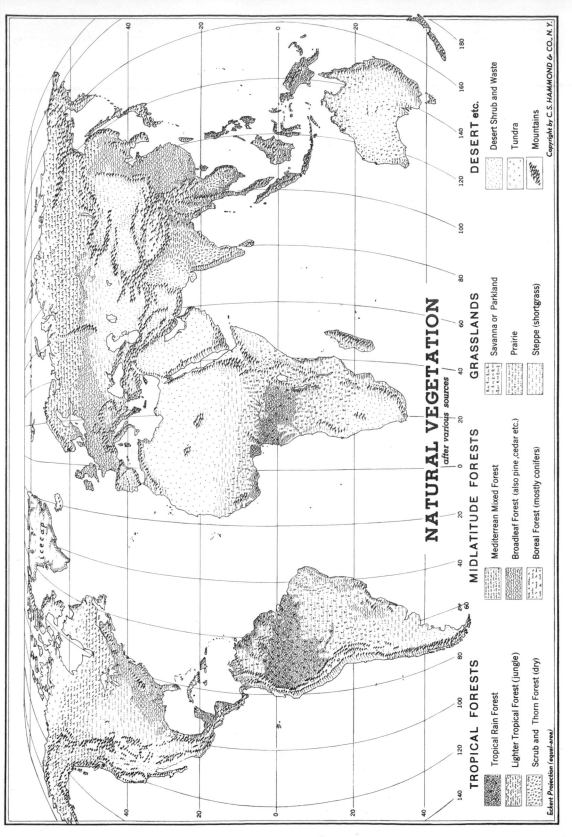

NATURAL VEGETATION
after various sources

TROPICAL FORESTS

Tropical Rain Forest

Lighter Tropical Forest (jungle)

Scrub and Thorn Forest (dry)

MIDLATITUDE FORESTS

Mediterrean Mixed Forest

Broadleaf Forest (also pine, cedar etc.)

Boreal Forest (mostly conifers)

GRASSLANDS

Savanna or Parkland

Prairie

Steppe (shortgrass)

DESERT etc.

Desert Shrub and Waste

Tundra

Mountains

Eckert Projection (equal-area)

Copyright by C.S. HAMMOND & CO., N.Y.

207

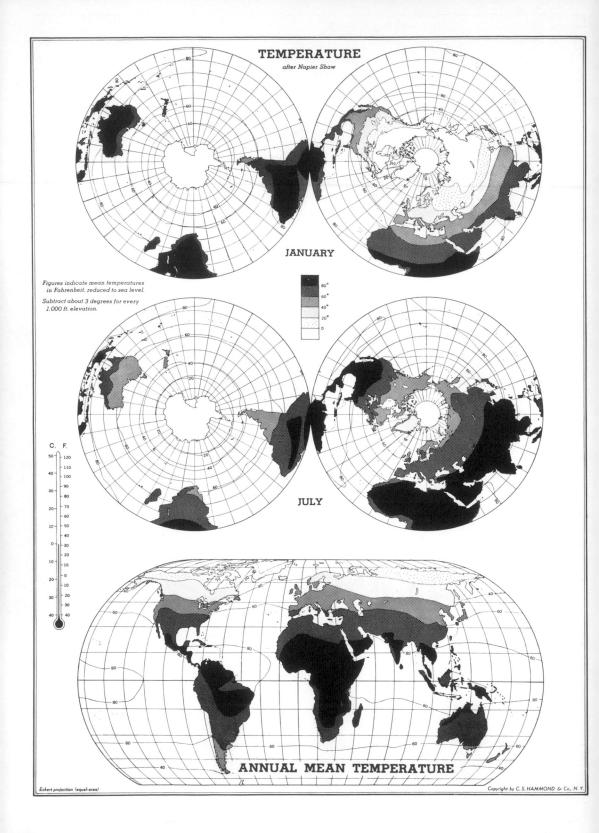

TEMPERATURE
after Napier Shaw

JANUARY

Figures indicate mean temperatures in Fahrenheit, reduced to sea level.

Subtract about 3 degrees for every 1,000 ft. elevation.

80°
60°
40°
20°
0

JULY

ANNUAL MEAN TEMPERATURE

Eckert projection (equal-area)

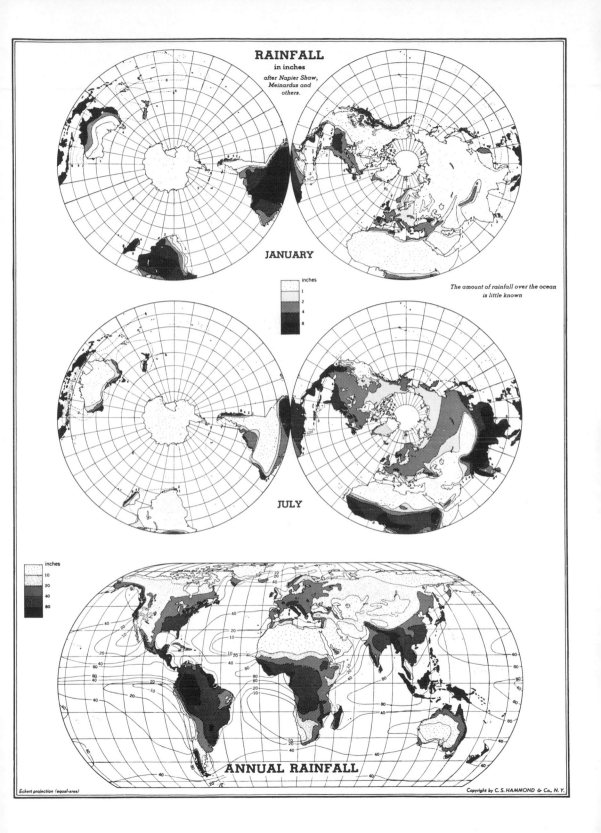

RAINFALL
in inches
*after Napier Shaw,
Meinardus and
others.*

JANUARY

inches
1
2
4
8

*The amount of rainfall over the ocean
is little known*

JULY

inches
10
20
40
80

ANNUAL RAINFALL

Eckert projection (equal-area)

Copyright by C. S. HAMMOND & Co., N. Y.

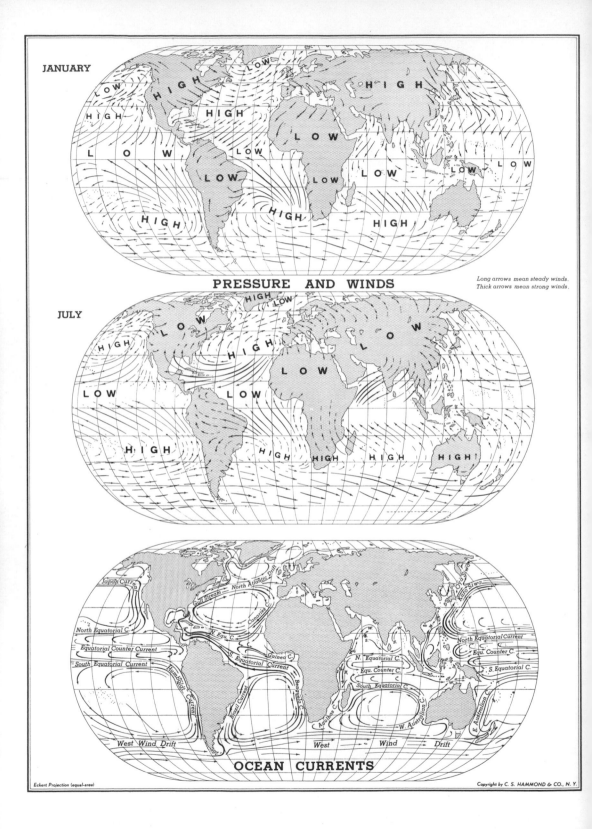

JANUARY

LOW HIGH LOW LOW HIGH

HIGH HIGH HIGH

L O W LOW L O W LOW LOW LOW

LOW LOW

HIGH HIGH HIGH

PRESSURE AND WINDS

Long arrows mean steady winds.
Thick arrows mean strong winds.

JULY

HIGH LOW LOW

HIGH HIGH L O W

LOW LOW

HIGH HIGH HIGH HIGH HIGH

Japan Current   North Atlantic Drift   Kuro Siwa
Gulf Stream   Canaries C.
North Equatorial C.   N. Equ. C.   North Equatorial Current
Equatorial Counter Current   Guinea C.   Equ. Counter C.
South Equatorial Current   S. Equatorial Current   N. Equatorial C.   S. Equatorial C.
Equ. Counter C.
Humboldt Current   Benguela C.   South Equatorial C.
Brazil Current   Agulhas C.   W. Australian C.   E. Australian C.
West Wind Drift   West   Wind   Drift

OCEAN CURRENTS

Eckert Projection (equal-area)

Copyright by C. S. HAMMOND & CO., N. Y.

Illustrated
Social and Economic Tables
of the World

The headline events of the last half-century have made the average person acutely curious of the vast world beyond his country's borders. This new national concern for the external world and its problems is one of the hopeful signs pointing to a better future for mankind. However, no matter how well-intentioned our concern for international relations may be, it is of no value unless it is grounded on an intelligent appreciation of the great diversity of social, economic and political forms extant throughout the globe.

On the following pages the editors have presented information on the world's nations, products, peoples and governments arranged in easily-found tabular form. This arrangement by tables makes comparison between political units a simpler task. These data, used with the maps in this atlas, complete the story of the nations of the world.

Social and Economic Tables

POLITICAL DIVISION	GOVERNMENT	MONETARY UNIT	LANGUAGE	RELIGION
AFARS & ISSAS, TERR. OF THE	French overseas territory with a governor and elected executive council and territorial assembly.	Djibouti franc	Hamitic languages Arabic; French	Mohammedan
AFGHANISTAN	Constitutional monarchy, with an appointed prime minister, cabinet, and a partly elected bicameral legislature.	afghani	Pushtu (Afghan) Farsi (Persian)	Mohammedan
ALBANIA	Soviet-type republic with a head of state, cabinet and unicameral legislature, actually controlled by the Communist party politburo.	lek	Albanian (Gheg, Tosk)	Moslem Orthodox Roman Catholic
ALGERIA	Republic at present under a president, council of ministers, and a revolutionary council.	Algerian dinar	Arabic French Berber	Mohammedan Roman Catholic Judaist
AMERICAN SAMOA	U.S. territory with a governor and a bicameral legislature.	American dollar	English Samoan	Protestant
ANDORRA	A republic under the joint suzerainty of the French State and the Bishop of Urgel, with a council general of 24 elective members. Executive authority is vested in the First Syndic.	French franc and Spanish peseta	Catalan	Roman Catholic
ANGOLA	Portuguese overseas province with a governor-general.	Portuguese escudo	Bantu languages Portuguese	Tribal religions Roman Catholic
ANTIGUA	Self-governing state associated with the United Kingdom, with a governor, chief minister, and executive and legislative councils.	B.W.I. dollar	English	Protestant
ARGENTINA	A republic with a president, vice-president, appointive cabinet, elective senate and house of deputies.	Argentine peso	Spanish	Roman Catholic
AUSTRALIA	Independent British Commonwealth member with a governor-general, prime minister, cabinet, and a bicameral parliament, composed of a senate and a house of commons.	Australian dollar	English	Protestant Roman Catholic
AUSTRIA	Republic with a president, chancellor and vice-chancellor, cabinet of ministers, and two-house assembly.	schilling	German	Roman Catholic
BAHAMA ISLANDS	A Counstitutional self-governing British State, with a governor, prime minister, a cabinet and a bicameral legislature.	Bahaman dollar	English	Roman Catholic Protestant
BAHREIN	British protected sheikhdom, advised by a political agent.	Bahrein dinar	Arabic	Mohammedan
BARBADOS	Independent British Commonwealth member, with a governor, prime minister, privy council and a bicameral legislature.	B.W.I. dollar	English	Protestant

of the World

MAJOR PRODUCTS

Boats, sheep; hides; salt.

Wheat, barley, millet, corn, rice, lentils, vegetables, fruits, nuts, cotton, tobacco, fat-tailed sheep (karakul), camels, wool, skins; sheepskin, textiles, leather, carpets; gold, iron, lapis lazuli, coal, copper, lead, silver, natural gas, talc.

Corn, tobacco, wheat, oats, barley, rye, rice, cotton, sugar beets, olives, fruit; cattle, sheep; fish; wool, hides; dairy products, furs; bitumen, salt, lignite, petroleum, copper, iron, chromite, flour, olive oil, cheese, cement, timber.

Wheat, barley, oats, corn, grapes, olives, tobacco, dates, figs, citrus fruits, vegetables, potatoes; sheep, goats, cattle, mules, horses, pigs, camels; hides and skins; fish; timber; iron, phosphates, zinc, natural gas, salt, lead, petroleum; wine, olive oil, carpets, cotton weaving, tobacco products, wool, cork, cement, chemicals, machinery.

Copra, taro, breadfruit, yams, bananas, arrowroot, pineapples, oranges; mats.

Tobacco, potatoes, rye, barley; sheep, cattle; lumber; dairy products.

ALGERIA: A native letter writer in the streets of Constantine, the country's third largest city.
TWA–Trans World Airlines

Coffee, corn, sugar, palm products, cotton, wheat, sisal, wax, tobacco; iron ore, diamonds; fish products, sugar.

Sugar cane, cotton, tropical fruits and vegetables, fish; barite; sugar, rum.

Wheat, corn, oats, barley, linseed, rye, grapes, cotton, sugar cane, potatoes, tobacco, vegetables; yerba maté; cattle, sheep; quebracho, lumber; petroleum, zinc, manganese, gold, lead, iron, tungsten; oils, wines, hides, wool, meats, textiles, metal products, vehicles and machinery, chemicals, wood and paper products, leather, flour, dairy products, cement.

Wheat, oats, rice, barley, fruits, vegetables, sugar; sheep, cattle; gold, coal, copper, iron, lead, silver, tin, zinc; timber, iron and steel, wool, textiles, electrical and radio equipment, appliances, drugs, chemicals, paints, optical instruments, agricultural implements, machinery, clothing, leather, furniture, airplanes, engines, ships, processed fruit and vegetables, dairy products, building materials, confectionery, automobiles.

Rye, wheat, oats, barley, corn, potatoes, sugar beets, hops, grapes, flax, hemp, tobacco; iron, copper, lead, magnesite, graphite, coal, aluminum, petroleum, lignite, salt; timber, pulp, poultry and livestock; steel, machinery, machine tools, chemicals, textiles, paper, processed foods, leather.

Tomatoes, pineapples, okra, vegetables, citrus fruits, bananas, sisal; crawfish, shells; lumber; salt; handcraft products, cement, pulpwood.

Pearl fishing, petroleum, boat building, fishing; reed mats, dates, lucerne; donkeys; textiles, building materials.

Sugar cane, cotton; flying fish; manjak (asphalt); sugar, molasses, rum, edible oil, margarine.

AUSTRALIA: The country's first oil field at Moonie, Queensland, is in a sheep herding region.
Australian Government

Social and Economic Tables

POLITICAL DIVISION	GOVERNMENT	MONETARY UNIT	LANGUAGE	RELIGION
BELGIUM	Constitutional, hereditary monarchy. King appoints a cabinet of ministers. Parliament consists of a senate and chamber of deputies.	Belgian franc	French (Walloon) and Flemish	Roman Catholic
BERMUDA	Constitutional British colony with a governor, executive and legislative councils, and an elected house of assembly.	Bermuda pound	English	Protestant
BOLIVIA	Constitutional republic, with a president, cabinet and bicameral legislature.	Bolivian peso	Spanish Indian languages	Roman Catholic
BOTSWANA	Constitutional republic, with a president, a unicameral legislature and an advisory House of Chiefs.	South African rand	Tswana; English Afrikaans Bushman	Tribal religions Protestant
BRAZIL	Federal republic with a president, vice-president, appointive secretaries of state and a bicameral legislature.	cruzeiro	Portuguese	Roman Catholic
BRITISH HONDURAS	Self-governing British colony with governor, prime minister, cabinet and bicameral legislature.	Br. Honduras dollar	English Spanish	Protestant Roman Catholic
BRUNEI	British protected sultanate, with a chief minister, privy council, and executive and legislative councils.	Malayan dollar	Malay English	Mohammedan
BULGARIA	Soviet-type republic with a one-house legislature, which elects a presidium whose president is the nominal chief of state. Actual power is Communist politburo.	lev	Bulgarian	Eastern Orthodox Mohammedan
BURMA, UNION OF	One party republic, at present under a revolutionary council of ministers.	kyat	Burmese Karen Shan	Buddhist Tribal religions
BURUNDI	Republic with a president, a cabinet, and a revolutionary committee.	Burundi franc	Kirundi French	Tribal religions Roman Catholic
CAMBODIA	Constitutional monarchy, with a head of state, prime minister, and a national assembly.	riel	Khmer Lao French	Buddhist
CAMEROON	One party federal state of the French Community, with a president, cabinet, and unicameral legislature.	CFA franc	Sudanese and Bantu languages French; English	Tribal religions Mohammedan Christian
CANADA	Independent British Commonwealth member, with a governor-general, prime minister, cabinet, and a bicameral parliament, composed of a senate and a house of commons.	Canadian dollar	English French	Protestant Roman Catholic
CAPE VERDE ISLANDS	Portuguese overseas province, ruled by a governor.	Portuguese escudo	Portuguese	Roman Catholic

of the World

MAJOR PRODUCTS

Wheat, rye, oats, barley, potatoes, sugar beets, flax, tobacco, vegetables, fruit, hops, hemp, bulbs, livestock, fish; coal, iron, zinc, lead, copper, tin, silver; coke, steel, machinery, textiles, lace, glass, chemicals, uranium refining, sugar, margarine, cheese, vinegar, alcohol, beer, matches, paper, foods, beverages, wool, cut diamonds, dairy products.

Lily bulbs, onions, bananas, cabbage, tomatoes, beans; coral; fish; perfume, pharmaceuticals.

Potatoes, corn, wheat, rice, sugar, fruits, vanilla, rubber, quinine; tin, zinc, lead, copper, silver, antimony, tungsten, gold, sulphur, petroleum; cattle; textiles, flour, cement, tobacco products, hides, beer, earthenware.

Kaffir, cotton, peanuts, beans, fruit, wheat and wheatmeal; cattle, sheep, goats, pigs; hides, gold, asbestos, manganese; meat products.

Coffee, corn, rice, cotton, cacao, sugar cane, cassava, beans, carnauba wax, medicinal plants, tropical fruits, balata, tobacco, fibers, castor oil; livestock; nuts; iron, manganese, gold, zirconium, diamonds, mica, bauxite, quartz, beryllium, chrome, tungsten, silver; foods, textiles, chemicals, pharmaceuticals, metallurgical products, paper and wood products, hides, vegetable oils, machinery.

Rice, maize, beans, bananas, coconuts, citrus fruits, sugar cane; mahogany, chicle, pine, cedar; fish; rum, food products.

Rice, sago, rubber, jelutong, cutch, sugar cane, tapioca, bananas, pineapples; timber; domestic birds, buffalo, pigs, cattle; petroleum, natural gas; boat building, cloth, brass and silverware.

Wheat, corn, barley, oats, rye, tobacco, fruit, cotton, sugar beets, potatoes; livestock, silkworm cocoons; fish; coal, salt, bauxite, copper, iron, lead, manganese, silver, zinc, kaolin; tobacco products, attar of roses, sugar, flour, textiles, leather goods, shoes, lead concentrates, wines and spirits.

Rice, sesame, peanuts, corn, cotton, millet, tobacco, sugar, beans, fruit, vegetables, pulses, rubber; teak wood, lumber; cattle, buffalo, pigs; petroleum, silver, lead, zinc, tin, copper, tungsten, rubies, sapphires, amber, jade, nickel, gold, cobalt, salt; textiles, hides, matches, lacquer ware.

Agricultural products, coffee, tea, cotton; cattle; hides.

Rice, tobacco, kapok, cotton, pepper, corn, sugar, rubber; timber; cattle; fish; silk, cotton, textiles, pottery, rush mats; precious stones, phosphates, petroleum.

Cocoa, palm kernels, bananas, caoutchouc, coconuts, coffee, cacao, palm oil; timber; cattle, sheep, pigs, horses, asses; aluminum; rubber, tobacco, cotton products.

Wheat, oats, barley, flax, rye, potatoes, turnips, vegetables, sugar beets, tobacco, fruits, dairy products, livestock; fish; forestry products; furs; gold, copper, nickel, zinc, lead, silver, platinum, iron ore, titanium, cobalt, radium, uranium, petroleum, natural gas, coal, asbestos, salt, gypsum, quartz, sulphur, cement, clay; hydro-electric power; foods, beverages, transportation equipment, iron and steel products, aluminum, metal products, pulp, paper and wood products, textiles, electrical apparatus, chemicals.

Coffee, castor beans, corn, fruit, tobacco; goats, oxen, pigs, asses; hides, skins; preserved fish, salt, lime, sugar.

BELGIUM: The Grand' Place in Brussels, with its flower market surrounded by Gothic and Renaissance architecture.

Belgian Gov't Info. Ctr.

BRAZIL: Baling cotton for export by rail and sea in the state of São Paulo.

Pan American Union

Social and Economic Tables

POLITICAL DIVISION	GOVERNMENT	MONETARY UNIT	LANGUAGE	RELIGION
CENTRAL AFRICAN REPUBLIC	One party republic of the French Community, at present under a president and a revolutionary council.	CFA franc	Sudanese and Bantu languages French	Mohammedan Tribal religions Roman Catholic
CEYLON	Independent member of the British Commonwealth ruled by a governor-general, a prime minister, a cabinet and a bicameral legislature.	Celanese rupee	Sinhala Tamil English	Buddhist Hindu Christian Mohammedan
CHAD	One party republic of the French Community, with a president and a national assembly.	CFA franc	Bantu and Sudanese languages Arabic, French	Tribal religions Mohammedan Roman Catholic
CHILE	Republic with a president, cabinet and a bicameral legislature.	Chilean escudo	Spanish	Roman Catholic
CHINA: MAINLAND (COMMUNIST)	In theory, governmental power resides in the National People's Congress and the State Council. In practice, power resides in the Communist Party's Central Committee.	Chinese (People's Bank) dollar (yuan)	Chinese Mongol Turki	Confucianist Buddhist Taoist Mohammedan
CHINA: TAIWAN (NATIONALIST)	A republic with a popularly elected National Assembly, which elects the president and vice-president. Legislative powers reside with the Legislative Yuan.	New Taiwan dollar (yuan)	Chinese	Confucianist Buddhist Taoist Christian Tribal religions
COLOMBIA	A centralized federal republic with a president, vice-president, appointive cabinet, elective senate and house of representatives.	Colombian peso	Spanish	Roman Catholic
COMORO ISLANDS	Internally self-governing French overseas territory, with a high commissioner, council, and an elected chamber of deputies.	CFA franc	Arabic French	Mohammedan
CONGO, REPUBLIC OF	Republic of the French Community, with a president and a legislative assembly.	CFA franc	Sudanese and Bantu languages French	Mohammedan Tribal religions Roman Catholic
CONGO, DEM. REPUBLIC OF THE	Constitutional republic, with a president, prime minister and a national assembly.	zaire	Bantu languages French	Tribal religions Roman Catholic
COOK ISLANDS	Internally self-governing state in association with New Zealand with a commissioner, prime minister and a cabinet.	New Zealand dollar	Polynesian dialects English	Protestant
COSTA RICA	Republic with president, cabinet and one-house legislature.	colón	Spanish	Roman Catholic
CUBA	Nominal republic with a president and appointed cabinet, dictatorial powers being held by the prime minister.	Cuban peso	Spanish	Roman Catholic

of the World

CHILE: Bathers and cabanas on the Pacific sands of Las Salinas, a popular beach at Viña del Mar.

Hamilton Wright

MAJOR PRODUCTS

Coffee, cotton, sisal, groundnuts, millet, sorghum; timber; gold, diamonds; rubber; palm products, beeswax.

Tea, coconuts, rubber, rice, millet, tobacco, cacao, cinnamon, citronella, cloves, fruits, palmyra, fish; cattle, buffalo, goats, swine; graphite, plumbago, mica, ilmenite, monazite; salt, pearls, zircon, copra, plywood, leather, shoes, glass, steel, acetic acid, ceramics, quinine, strychnine, shark-liver oil, coconut oil, textiles.

Millet, sesame, groundnuts, vegetables; livestock, hides; ivory, ostrich feathers; cotton, dates.

Wheat, potatoes, oats, rice, barley, corn, kidney beans, lentils, fruits; fish; livestock; copper, silver, nitrates, iodine, iron ore, gold, manganese, coal; foods, textiles, leather, wood products, cement, chemicals and pharmaceuticals, wines and beer, wool, iron and steel, petroleum, paper and pulp.

Rice, wheat, potatoes, corn, barley, millet, kaoliang, soybeans, cotton, tea, sugar cane, tobacco, peanuts, peas, beans, opium, tung, silk; pigs, cattle, sheep, goats, buffalo, donkeys, horses, mules, poultry; timber; fish; iron, coal, tungsten, tin, antimony, mercury, copper, lead, zinc, silver, bauxite, manganese, gold, petroleum, molybdenum; foodstuffs, textiles, chemicals, machinery, metal work, metallurgical products, cement, clothing, embroideries, ceramics.

Rice, tea, sugar, sweet potatoes, ramie, jute, turmeric, pineapples, bananas, camphor; pigs; buffalo, cattle, goats, horses; canned foods, metal products, machinery, textiles, wood products.

Coffee, sugar cane, corn, rice, potatoes, cotton, bananas, cacao, wheat, tobacco, cinchona; cattle; rubber, fibers; petroleum, gold, silver, platinum, emeralds, salt; textiles, beer, sugar, cement, flour, tobacco products, iron and steel.

Sugar cane, vanilla, rice, sweet potatoes, yams, copra, sisal, cloves, cacao, perfume plants; rum distilling.

Palm oil and kernels, hardwoods, kola nuts, coffee, cocoa, copal, rubber, tobacco; lead, gold, petroleum, diamonds, livestock; rice.

Palm oil and kernels, cotton, coffee, oil cakes, tea, cocoa, rice, groundnuts; rubber, manioc, fibers; cattle, sheep, goats; copper, coal, silver, tin, diamonds, gold, cobalt, radium, uranium, tantulum, zinc, manganese.

Citrus fruits, coconuts, copra, tomatoes, arrowroot, pineapples, breadfruit, taro, kumaras, plantains, yams; mother-of-pearl.

Coffee, bananas, cocoa, abacá, sugar cane, maize, rice, tobacco; cattle; tuna; gold, silver; cigars and cigarettes, textiles, furniture and woodwork, sugar, electric goods.

Sugar cane, tobacco, coffee, pineapples, citrus fruits, bananas, henequen; cattle; timber; fish; chromite, iron, manganese, copper, nickel; sugar, textiles, alcohol, molasses, chemicals, tobacco products, electrical goods, clothing, steel.

COLOMBIA: One of the country's principal products, coffee, drying under the tropical sun.

Pan American Union

Social and Economic Tables

POLITICAL DIVISION	GOVERNMENT	MONETARY UNIT	LANGUAGE	RELIGION
CYPRUS	British Commonwealth republic, with a president (Greek), vice-president (Turkish), cabinet, and Greek and Turkish communal chambers.	Cypriot pound	Greek Turkish	Greek Orthodox Mohammedan
CZECHOSLOVAKIA	Soviet-type republic with a president, a National Assembly and a Slovak National Council, with actual power residing in the Communist party presidium.	koruna (crown)	Czech and Slovak	Roman Catholic
DAHOMEY	Republic of the French Community, at present under a president and a revolutionary committee.	CFA franc	Sudanese languages French	Tribal religions Mohammedan
DENMARK	Constitutional, hereditary monarchy with a two-house, elective legislature and an appointive council of ministers.	krone (crown)	Danish	Protestant
DOMINICAN REPUBLIC	Nominal republic with a bicameral legislature.	Dominican peso	Spanish	Roman Catholic
ECUADOR	Constitutional republic with a bicameral legislature and a president.	sucre	Spanish Indian languages (Quechua, etc.)	Roman Catholic
EGYPT	See: United Arab Republic.			
EL SALVADOR	Republic with a president, cabinet, and unicameral legislature.	colón	Spanish	Roman Catholic
ENGLAND AND WALES	Integral part of the United Kingdom, with executive power nominally residing in the Crown, but actually exercised by the prime minister, cabinet and bicameral parliament, composed of a house of lords and a house of commons.	pound sterling	English and Welsh (Celtic)	Protestant
EQUATORIAL GUINEA	Former Spanish overseas provinces. Independent republic established in 1968.	Spanish peseta	Bantu languages Spanish	Tribal religions Roman Catholic
ETHIOPIA	Constitutional monarchy with an emperor, a council of ministers and a bicameral legislature.	Ethiopian dollar	Amharic Hamitic languages English; French	Coptic Christian Mohammedan
FALKLAND ISLANDS	British colony with a governor and an executive and a legislative council.	pound sterling	English	Protestant Roman Catholic
FIJI	Partly self-governing British colony with a governor, chief minister and cabinet; Fijian Administration is advised by a council of chiefs.	Fiji pound (dollar-1969)	English Fijian Hindustani Chinese	Protestant Roman Catholic Hindu Moslem
FINLAND	A republic with a president, a one-house elective diet and appointive council of state.	markka (mark)	Finnish and Swedish	Protestant

of the World

MAJOR PRODUCTS

Wheat, barley, oats, grapes, raisins, olives, potatoes, carobs, cotton, tobacco, hemp, flax, citrus fruits, beans, corn, melons; sponges, fish; sheep, goats, cattle, pigs; copper and iron pyrites, asbestos, chromite, gypsum, copper concentrates; tobacco products, buttons, wines, false teeth, lace, gum, boots and shoes, dried fruits, cheese.

Wheat, rye, barley, oats, corn, hops, sugar beets, grapes, potatoes; poultry, livestock; timber; coal, lignite, iron, graphite, garnets, silver, copper, lead, salt, manganese, zinc; beer, spirits, malt, metals, munitions, machinery, iron and steel, porcelain, shoes, textiles, wood products, pulp and paper, sugar, leather, foods, chemicals, rubber products.

Palm products, tobacco, groundnuts, cotton, corn, copra, coffee, castor oil, kapok, millet; gold, diamonds, bauxite, iron ore.

Barley, oats, rye, wheat, potatoes, sugar beets; livestock, fish; clay; ships and transportation equipment, butter, bacon, eggs, cheese, milk, footwear, textiles, machines, chemicals, tobacco products, metal goods, leather goods, beverages; stone, earthenware, glassware, electrical goods.

Sugar cane, cacao, coffee, tobacco, bananas, rice, corn; cattle; lumber; gold, bauxite, starch, alcohol, molasses, chocolate, sugar, meats, cigars, cigarettes, leather.

Rice, cacao, coffee, bananas, rubber, kapok, cotton, nuts, cinchona; livestock; gold, petroleum, silver, salt, balsa wood; textiles, toquilla (panama) hats, buttons, sugar, flour, shoes, chemicals, pharmaceuticals, cement, soap, candles.

Coffee, cotton, corn, tobacco, henequen, sugar cane, rice; fish, livestock; balsa and other woods, gold, silver; cotton textiles, bags, sugar, pharmaceuticals.

Potatoes, turnips, beets, oats, wheat, barley, rye, hay, beans, peas, cabbage, vetches, hops, fruits; sheep, cattle, pigs, horses, poultry; fish; coal, coke, gas, iron, copper, lead, nickel, tin, clay; dairy products, wool, cotton and linen textiles; electrical goods, vehicles, steel, scientific instruments, cutlery, foods and beverages, tobacco products, clothing and shoes, chemicals, pottery, china, machinery, locomotives, carpets, knitwear, lace, pharmaceuticals.

Cocoa, coffee, bananas, palm oil and kernels, copra; cabinet woods.

Coffee, teff, barley, durra, wheat, cotton, oil seeds, sugar cane; cattle, sheep, goats, horses, mules; hides, skins; wax, gold, rocksalt.

Forage crops, sheep; wool, skins, tallow, whale oil, whale-meat meal.

Sugar cane, coconuts, rice, fruits, cotton, rubber, oil seeds, root vegetables, groundnuts, pulses, corn, tobacco; cattle, pigs; tuna, bêche-de-mer, trochus shell; gold, silver; sugar, copra, coconut oil, soap, biscuits, molasses, butter, ghee, candlenut oil.

Hay, potatoes, wheat, oats, barley, rye, sugar beets; cattle, horses, sheep, pigs, poultry, reindeer; wood and timber; fish; copper; lumber, plywood, furniture, pulp and paper, cardboard, textiles, butter, cheese, eggs, flour, leather, chemicals, china and glass, foodstuffs, machinery, ships.

DENMARK: Amalienborg Palace in Copenhagen, the king's residence, and the statue of King Frederik V.

Danish Nat'l Travel Office

FRANCE: Fresh fruits and vegetables occupy part of Les Halles, the central market of Paris, near the right bank of the Seine.

TWA–Trans World Airlines

Social and Economic Tables

POLITICAL DIVISION	GOVERNMENT	MONETARY UNIT	LANGUAGE	RELIGION
FRANCE	A republic with a president, a two-house elective parliament and an appointive council of ministers.	franc	French	Roman Catholic
FRENCH GUIANA	Overseas department of France governed by a prefect, with an elective council-general.	French franc	French	Roman Catholic
FRENCH POLYNESIA	Overseas territory of France, with a governor, government council, and an elected territorial assembly.	CFP franc	Polynesian dialects French	Protestant Roman Catholic
GABON	Equatorial African republic within the French Community with a president and a national assembly.	CFA franc	Bantu languages French	Tribal religions Roman Catholic
GAMBIA	Republic of the British Commonwealth, with a prime minister and a unicameral legislature.	Gambian pound	Sudanese languages English	Mohammedan Tribal religions Protestant
GERMANY	Country is divided between two governments — a democratic **Federal Republic of Germany** in the west and a Soviet-dominated **German "Democratic" Republic** in the east. **Federal Republic** has an elected federal diet and council who jointly elect the president. **German "Democratic" Republic** has a communist-controlled legislative branch which selects the president, cabinet and prime minister.	East German and West German Deutsch mark	German	Protestant Roman Catholic
GHANA	Republic of the British Commonwealth, at present under a military council.	cedi	Sudanese languages English	Mohammedan Tribal religions Protestant
GIBRALTAR	Partly self-governing British colony, with a governor, cabinet, and executive and legislative councils.	pound sterling	English and Spanish	Roman Catholic
GILBERT AND ELLICE ISLS.	British colony with a commissioner, governing council and house of representatives.	Australian dollar	English Gilbertese Samoan	Protestant Roman Catholic
GREAT BRITAIN	See: England and Wales, Northern Ireland, Scotland.			
GREECE	A constitutional hereditary monarchy with a prime minister, cabinet of ministers and an elective assembly, presently ruled by a junta.	drachma	Greek	Greek Orthodox
GREENLAND	Integral part of the Danish kingdom, with representation in Parliament and a provincial council.	Danish krone	Danish and Greenlandic	Protestant
GUADELOUPE	Overseas department of France with a prefect and elective general council.	French franc	French French Patois	Roman Catholic
GUAM	U.S. territory with a governor, advisory staff, and an elected, unicameral legislature.	American dollar	English Chamorro Spanish	Roman Catholic
GUATEMALA	Republic with a president, cabinet and one-house legislature.	quetzal	Spanish	Roman Catholic

of the World

MAJOR PRODUCTS

Sugar beets, potatoes, wheat, oats, barley, rye; corn, turnips, fruits, nuts, grapes, buckwheat; cattle, sheep, pigs, horses; fish; coal, iron ore, lignite, salt, bauxite, pyrites, potash salts, sulphur, natural gas, iron and steel, chemicals; silk, cotton, rayon, wool and linen, textiles; clothing, lace, perfumes and cosmetics, automobiles, machinery, dairy products, beet sugar, wines, porcelain, aluminum, foods, leather, lumber, spirits.

Rice, cacao, bananas, sugar cane, corn, cassava, woods; gold; hides, rosewood essence, shoes, rum, fish glue.

Coconuts, tropical fruits, vanilla, sugar cane, coffee, bamboo, pearls; phosphates; mother-of-pearl, sugar, rum, copra.

Tropical woods; gold, manganese, petroleum, natural gas, uranium; fish; cocoa; rubber, coffee, kapok, waxes, kola nuts; manioc, sweet potatoes, corn, plantains.

Groundnuts, rice, palm kernels; hides and skins; fish; beeswax.

Wheat, rye, barley, oats, potatoes, sugar beets, fruits, hops; pigs, cattle, poultry, horses; fish; forest products; coal, lignite, iron, copper, potash, sulphur, salt, uranium, lead, zinc, fluorspar, gypsum, vanadium, aluminum; automobiles, steel, cement, diesel oil, gasoline, cotton yarn, woolen yarn, rayon fiber, beet sugar, beer, wines, optical instruments, sulphuric acid, sodium bicarbonate, chemicals, machinery, electrical equipment, aircraft.

Cocoa, palm oil and kernels, sorghum, millet, corn, yams, cassava, groundnuts, cotton; timber; gold, diamonds, manganese, bauxite, silver; cocoa products.

Fish for export and processing of commodities for local consumption.

Coconuts, copra, phosphate of lime; pearl shell, fish; hats, mats.

Wheat, barley, corn, oats, rye, tobacco, currants, citrus fruits, olives, figs, grapes, cottonseed, sesame seed; sheep, goats, cattle, pigs, horses, mules; fish; iron ore, sulphur, emery, magnesite, zinc, lead, lignite, marble, silver, bauxite; textiles, olive oil, foods, wines, chemicals, leather, wood and paper, metal products, machinery.

Grass for fodder; cod and other fish; sheep, furs; cryolite; processed fish, hides.

Sugar cane, bananas, coffee, cocoa, vanilla, cassava; fish; alcohol, rum.

Coconut products, corn, taro, bananas, citrus fruits, mangoes, papayas, breadfruit, sweet potatoes, cocoa, cassava, sugar cane, pineapples; cattle, pigs, poultry, buffalo.

Coffee, bananas, sugar cane, rubber, cotton, wheat, corn, rice, chicle, cacao, abacá, cattle; mahogany, and dye woods; essential oils; gold; textiles, chemicals, drugs, wood and leather goods.

GREECE: An "evzone," one of the uniquely, uniformed guards at the Royal Palace in Athens.

J. Walter Thompson

GUATEMALA: Removing the nuts from the pods at a cacao "finca," or plantation, is the first stage of processing chocolate.

I.I.A.A.

Social and Economic Tables

POLITICAL DIVISION	GOVERNMENT	MONETARY UNIT	LANGUAGE	RELIGION
GUINEA	One party republic with a president, cabinet, and national assembly.	Guinea franc	Sudanese languages French	Tribal religions Mohammedan
GUYANA	Independent member of the British Commonwealth, with prime minister, cabinet, and unicameral legislature.	Guyana dollar	English	Protestant
HAITI	Republic with a president, cabinet, and a unicameral legislature.	gourde	Creole, French	Roman Catholic
HONDURAS	Republic with a president, council of ministers and a one-house legislature.	lempira	Spanish	Roman Catholic
HONG KONG	British colony ruled by a governor assisted by executive and legislative councils.	Hong Kong dollar	Chinese English	Confucianist Buddhist Christian
HUNGARY	Soviet-type republic with a president and council selected by the national assembly. Actual power in hands of politburo, highest organ of Communist party.	forint	Hungarian	Catholic Protestant
ICELAND	A republic with a president, an elective, two-house legislature and an appointive cabinet of ministers.	króna (crown)	Icelandic	Protestant
IFNI	Overseas province of Spain, ruled by a governor.	Spanish peseta	Berber Arabic Spanish	Mohammedan
INDIA	An independent republic within the British Commonwealth with a president, cabinet and a bicameral legislature.	Indian rupee	Hindi; English Assamese, Bengali, Gujarati, Kannada, Kashmiri, Malayalam, Marathi, Oriya, Punjabi, Sanskrit, Tamil, Teluga, Urdu; Bhutia, Lepcha	Hindu Mohammedan Buddhist Animist Christian Sikh Jain Parsi Lamaist
INDONESIA	Nominal republic headed by a military cabinet, with a "people's consultative congress."	rupiah	Indonesian (Malay, Javanese, etc.)	Mohammedan Christian Hindu Buddhist Tribal religions
IRAN	Constitutional monarchy governed by a shah, prime minister, cabinet and a bicameral legislature.	rial	Persian Arabic Kurdish	Mohammedan Zoroastrian Parsi
IRAQ	Republic with a president, prime minister, cabinet, and unicameral legislature, actually controlled by a revolutionary council.	Iraqi dinar	Arabic Turkish Kurdish	Mohammedan Christian
IRELAND	A republic with a president, premier and an elective, two-house parliament.	Irish pound	Irish (Gaelic) English	Roman Catholic Protestant

MAJOR PRODUCTS

Rice, groundnuts, palm oil and nuts, wax, honey, bananas, indigo, kola, orange products, coffee; cattle, sheep, goats; hides and skins; bauxite, iron ore, diamonds.

Sugar cane, rice, coconuts, coffee, citrus fruits, cacao; balata, rubber, green heart and other timber; livestock; bauxite, diamonds, gold; textiles, milled rice, beer and rum, lime rum and oil, sugar, woods, molasses, charcoal, matches.

Coffee, sugar, fig bananas, sisal, cotton, rice, cocoa, logwood; bauxite, copper; molasses, sisal products.

Bananas, coffee, coconuts, tobacco, cotton, grapefruit, rice, henequen; mahogany; cattle; gold, silver.

Rice, sugar, ginger; fish; poultry, pigs; kaolin, lead, iron, wolfram, granite, silver, cement; shipbuilding; enameled hollow ware, textiles, wood and plastic products, jewelry.

Wheat, corn, rye, barley, oats, potatoes, sugar beets, tobacco, grapes and other fruits, peppers, hemp, flax; pigs, cattle, sheep, horses, poultry; fish; coal, lignite, petroleum, natural gas, iron ore, bauxite, manganese; flour, sugar, distilling, brewing, iron and steel, wines, textiles, paprika, chemicals, leather, metal products, wood and paper products.

Hay, potatoes, turnips, hothouse fruits and vegetables; sheep, poultry, horses, cattle; fish; dairy products, meats, animal and vegetable oils, hides, skins, leather, clothing, textiles, frozen fish, herring oil, herring meal.

Barley, alfalfa, corn, tomatoes, argan oil, wheat; fish.

Rice, wheat, legumes, groundnuts, oilseeds, tea, tobacco, jute, cotton, rubber, coffee, sugar cane, barley, millet, corn; cattle, goats, buffalo, sheep, pigs; fish; coal, manganese, gold, petroleum, salt, mica, iron, copper, chromite, ilmenite, diamonds, silver, bauxite; textiles, shawls, carpets, jute manufactures, wood-carving and metal work, leather, chemicals, shipbuilding, petroleum refining, sugar refining, cotton ginning, iron and steel mills, glass, soap, matches.

Rice, sugar cane, rubber, palm oil, tobacco, corn, coconuts, copra, spices, sweet potatoes, groundnuts, tea, beans, cotton, kapok, coffee, cinchona, cocoa, pepper, fruits, vegetables; cattle, buffalo; tin, coal, petroleum, bauxite, nickel, copper, manganese; rubber goods, chemicals, shipyards, textiles, paper.

Wheat, cotton, gums, opium, fruit, rice, barley, sugar beets, tobacco, tea, corn, millet, legumes, vegetables, nuts; sheep, goats, cattle, asses, horses, mules; fish; petroleum oil, red oxide, copper, sulphur, arsenic, coal, salt, marble, nickel, manganese, lead, cobalt, turquoise, iron ore; carpets, textiles, leather, glass, matches, chemicals, jute, tobacco products, oil refining, casings, wood, oils.

Dates, other fruits, barley, wheat, rice, tobacco, cotton, beans, corn, sorghum, sesame; sheep, goats, asses, camels, horses, buffalo; petroleum; salt, wool, textiles, cigarettes, distilling, hides.

Hay, potatoes, turnips, beets, sugar beets, oats, wheat, barley, rye, flax; cattle, sheep, pigs; fish; coal, peat, gypsum; tobacco, dairy products, foodstuffs, beer, malt, machinery, meats, textiles, boots and shoes, wood and paper products.

INDIA: A typical scene in one of the busy streets of the native section in Bombay.

TWA—Trans World Airlines

INDONESIA: Educational progress—a mother and daughter attending school together.

Indonesian Info. Office

Social and Economic Tables

POLITICAL DIVISION	GOVERNMENT	MONETARY UNIT	LANGUAGE	RELIGION
ISRAEL	Republic with president, prime minister, cabinet and elective unicameral legislature.	Israeli pound	Hebrew Arabic	Judaist Mohammedan Christian
ITALY	A republic with a president, a two-house, elective legislature and an appointive cabinet.	lira	Italian	Roman Catholic
IVORY COAST	One party republic of the French Community, with a president, cabinet, and a unicameral legislature.	CFA franc	Sudanese languages French	Tribal religions Mohammedan Christian
JAMAICA	Independent member of the British Commonwealth, with a governor-general, prime minister, cabinet, and bicameral legislature.	Jamaican pound (dollar-1969)	English	Protestant Roman Catholic
JAPAN	Constitutional monarchy with the executive power vested in prime minister and cabinet, the legislative power residing in a two-house parliament. The duties of the emperor are merely ceremonial.	yen	Japanese	Buddhist Shinto
JORDAN	Constitutional monarchy with cabinet and bicameral legislature.	Jordan dinar	Arabic	Mohammedan
KENYA	One party republic of the British Commonwealth, with a president, cabinet, and national assembly.	Kenya shilling	Bantu, Hamitic and Sudanese languages English; Swahili	Tribal religions Mohammedan Christian
KOREA	Divided by Armistice Line of August 1953: North Korea — a Communist "people's republic" ruled by the politburo; South Korea — a republic, with a president, cabinet, and a unicameral legislature.	won	Korean	Confucianist Buddhist Christian
KUWAIT	Constitutional sheikhdom, with a Sheikh, a cabinet and a unicameral national assembly.	Kuwaiti dinar	Arabic	Mohammedan
LAOS	Constitutional monarchy with a cabinet and a national assembly.	kip	Lao (Thai) French	Buddhist
LEBANON	Republic with a president, an appointed prime minister and cabinet, and an elected unicameral legislature.	Lebanese pound	Arabic French	Christian Mohammedan
LESOTHO	Kingdom with a king, prime minister, and a bicameral legislature.	South African rand	Sesotho English	Roman Catholic Protestant Tribal religions
LIBERIA	One party republic, with a president, cabinet, and a bicameral legislature.	Liberian dollar	English Sudanese languages	Christian Tribal religions Mohammedan
LIBYA	A kingdom with a prime minister, a cabinet and a bicameral legislature.	Libyan pound	Arabic	Mohammedan

of the World

MAJOR PRODUCTS

Dairy products, vegetables, eggs, fruits, wheat, hay, barley, corn, durra; goats, sheep, cattle, camels; fish; textiles, clothing, beverages, tobacco, diamond polishing, shoes, metal and woodwork, furniture, leather, dairy products, electrical products, paper, printing, false teeth, pharmaceuticals, chemicals, dyes, soap, radios, oil refining, wines.

Wheat, corn, oats, sugar beets, potatoes, tomatoes, rice, olives, grapes, lemons and other fruits, hemp, tobacco, nuts; fish; sheep and goats, cattle, pigs; iron ore, sulphur, zinc, bauxite, lead, mercury, marble, manganese; textiles, chemicals, wines, automobiles and machinery, electrical goods, beet sugar, olive oil, cheese, clothing, processed foods.

Coffee, cocoa, bananas, pineapples, corn, rice, kola, coconuts, palm oil, groundnuts, cotton, millet, tobacco; mahogany, caoutchouc; sheep, cattle, goats; diamonds; manganese.

Sugar cane, bananas, tobacco, coconuts, cacao, pimentoes, coffee, ginger; bauxite; honey; logwood; rum, textiles, cigars.

Rice, wheat, barley, mulberry trees, potatoes, sweet potatoes, fruits, rape, vegetables, oats, tobacco, soy beans, tea, flax, hemp, camphor; timber; bamboo; horses, cattle, sheep, goats, pigs, rabbits; fish, agar, pearl oysters; silkworms; coal, pyrites, gold, copper, pyrethrum, manganese, silver, sulphur, chromite, zinc, salt, tin, lead, iron, petroleum; textiles, steel, paper, porcelain, earthenware, lacquer ware, vegetable oil, toys, shoes, machinery, vehicles, electric goods, instruments.

Wheat, barley, legumes, vegetables, fruits, olives; sheep, goats, camels; salt, phosphate, potash; wool, tobacco products, flour milling, building materials, olive oil, leather goods.

Sisal, wheat, tea, coffee, pyrethrum, cotton, corn, sugar cane, sesame, groundnuts, wattle; hides and skins; timber; sodium carbonate, gold, kyanite, salt, silver, lime, bags, butter, sugar, sisal products, petroleum products.

Rice, barley, millet, wheat, soya beans, cotton, tobacco, hemp, ginseng, fruit; timber; draft cattle, pigs, sheep, fish; gold, iron ore, coal, tungsten, copper, silver, graphite, salt, kaolin, bismuth, fluorite, minerals (N. Korea), textiles, fertilizer, chemicals, cement, heavy industries (N. Korea); textiles, cement, silkworms, chemicals, machinery, metal, rubber, wood, paper and tobacco products (S. Korea).

Petroleum, shipbuilding (dhows), pearls, skins, wool, fish.

Rice, coffee, tea, citrus fruits, corn, cinchona, gum, benzoin, tobacco, cardamon; stick-lac; teak; tin; wool products.

Wheat, barley, corn, potatoes, fruits, onions, olives, tobacco; goats, asses, cattle, buffalo, sheep, horses, mules; iron, lignite; textiles, cement, olive oil, tobacco products, soap, matches, petroleum refining, gasoline, leather.

Corn, wheat, sorghum, barley, oats, beans, peas; cattle, sheep, goats, horses, donkeys, pigs, mules; diamonds; wool, mohair.

Rubber, rice, coffee, cassava, sugar cane, cacao, palm oil and kernels, piassava, groundnuts; rum; iron ore, diamonds.

Barley, wheat, olives, grapes, dates, almonds, figs, peanuts, citrus fruits, tobacco, esparto; goats, sheep, camels; sponge and tuna fishing; hides and skins; petroleum; matting, carpets, leather articles, embroidered fabrics, olive oil.

ITALY: A gondolier and his craft on one of the many waterways in Venice.

TWA—Trans World Airlines

LUXEMBOURG: La Place Guillaume, in the heart of the grand duchy's picturesque capital city.

Office Nat'l du Tourisme

Social and Economic Tables

POLITICAL DIVISION	GOVERNMENT	MONETARY UNIT	LANGUAGE	RELIGION
LIECHTENSTEIN	Principality, with an elected unicameral legislature.	Swiss franc	German	Roman Catholic
LUXEMBOURG	Constitutional grand duchy, with a minister of state, cabinet, council of state, and a unicameral legislature.	Luxembourg franc	Letzeburgisch (German dialect) French	Roman Catholic
MACAO	Portuguese overseas province ruled by a governor.	pataca	Chinese Portuguese	Confucianist Buddhist Taoist Christian
MALAGASY REPUBLIC	Republic of the French Community, with a president, cabinet, and a bicameral legislature.	Malagasy franc	French Malagasy and Bantu languages	Tribal religions Roman Catholic Protestant
MALAWI	Republic of the British Commonwealth, with president, cabinet, and a unicameral legislature.	Malawi pound	Bantu languages English	Tribal religions Protestant Roman Catholic
MALAYSIA	Independent federation of the British Commonwealth, with a head and a deputy head of state, a council of rulers, cabinet, and bicameral legislature.	Malaysian dollar	Malay English Chinese Indonesian languages Hindi, Tamil	Mohammedan Confucianist Tribal religions Buddhist Hindu Taoist
MALDIVE ISLANDS	Independent sultanate, with a prime minister and a unicameral legislature.	Celanese rupee	Maldivian English	Mohammedan
MALI	One party republic at present under a revolutionary committee and a consultative group. The president rules by decree.	Mali franc	Sudanese and Hamitic languages French	Mohammedan Tribal religions
MALTA	An independent member of the British Commonwealth, with a prime minister, a cabinet and a unicameral legislature.	Maltese pound	Maltese and English	Roman Catholic
MARTINIQUE	Overseas department of France with a prefect and elective general council.	French franc	Creole, French	Roman Catholic
MAURITANIA	One party republic of the French Community, with a president, cabinet, and a unicameral legislature.	CFA franc	French Arabic	Mohammedan
MAURITIUS	Independent member of the British Commonwealth, with a governor, premier, cabinet, and unicameral legislature.	Mauritius rupee	English Hindustani French	Roman Catholic Hindu Mohammedan
MEXICO	Federative republic with a president, council of ministers and a two-house legislature.	Mexican peso	Spanish	Roman Catholic
MONACO	Principality with elected national and communal councils.	French franc	French	Roman Catholic
MONGOLIA	Communist republic, ruled by chairman of the presidium of a unicameral legislature.	tughrik	Mongolian Kazakh	Lamaist Tribal religions
MOROCCO	Constitutional monarchy, with appointed prime minister and cabinet, and a bicameral legislature.	dirham	Arabic Berber French Spanish	Mohammedan Roman Catholic Jewish

of the World

MAJOR PRODUCTS

Grain, fruit, grapes, wood; cattle, pigs, chickens; cotton textiles, wine, leather, false teeth, pottery, wood-carving.

Oats, potatoes, wheat, rye, grapes; livestock; iron ore, slate, gypsum, sand and gravel; iron, steel and metal working; chemicals, non-metallic minerals, beverages, tobacco, leather, wines, dairy products, quarrying.

Fish; preserves, firecrackers, vegetable oil, cement, metal work, lumber, tobacco (processed), matches, wine.

Cassava, rice, corn, potatoes, vanilla, cloves, coffee, sugar cane, beans, groundnuts, sisal, castor oil, tobacco, raffia; timber; cattle, pigs, goats, sheep; graphite, mica, phosphates; textiles, sugar and rice factories, tapioca.

Tobacco, tea, cotton, pulses, tung oil, sisal, corn, sugar cane, cassava, wheat, rice, millet, groundnuts, rubber, beeswax, timber; goats, cattle, pigs, sheep; hides, skins, meat, ghee, soap; gold, mica, corundum.

Rubber, rice, coconuts, coffee, pineapples, pepper, sugar, tobacco, fibers, vegetables, tea; timber, buffalo, swine, oxen, goats; fish; tin, iron ore, bauxite, petroleum, antimony, manganese; copra, palm oil, timber, gold, rubber products, canning, shipping, milling, gasoline, wood products, textiles.

Coconuts, copra, coir, fruits, nuts; fish, cowries; cloth, mats, boats.

Millet, rice, sorghum, groundnuts, corn, sweet potatoes, gum arabic, cotton, manioc, tobacco, nuts, sisal; cattle, goats, sheep, horses, asses, camels; hides and skins; pottery, bricks, jewelry, weaving, leather, rice mills, soap.

Wheat, barley, potatoes, onions, grapes and other fruits, cumin seed, cotton; goats, sheep, pigs, cattle; fish; lace, filigree, wine, footwear, beer, cigarettes, buttons, pipes, gloves.

Sugar cane, cocoa, mangoes, avocados, pineapples, bananas, coffee; rum, sugar.

Millet, gum, dates, corn, watermelons, wheat, henna; sheep and goats, cattle, camels, asses, horses; hides and skins; fish; salt, iron ore.

Sugar, aloe fiber, rice, vanilla beans, hemp, sisal, groundnuts, tea, yams, manioc, pineapples, tobacco, coconuts; alcohol, molasses, rum, copra.

Corn, wheat, sugar, bananas, barley, cotton, coffee, vegetables; cattle; henequen; fish; silver, petroleum, lead, gold, zinc, copper; textiles, sugar, alcohol, foundry products, oil refining.

Principal revenue derived from Monte Carlo gambling casino. Tobacco, postage stamps, perfume, liqueurs, olive oil, oranges.

Stock raising (sheep, goats, cattle, horses, camels); milk, butter, cheese; wool, hides, skins, horns, bricks, machinery; coal, lead, gold.

Wheat, barley, olives, almonds, citrus fruits, dates, beans, grapes, vegetables, linseed; cork, cedar; hides & skins; timber; sheep, goats, cattle, asses, camels, horses; fish; phosphates, iron ore, anthracite, manganese, zinc, cobalt, antimony; leather, carpets, olive oil, wine, wool.

MEXICO: The Pyramid of the Sun at San Juan Teotihuacan, not far from Mexico City.

J. Walter Thompson

MOROCCO: Downtown Casablanca, the chief port, with the Place Lyautey in the foreground.

French Gov't Tourist Office

Social and Economic Tables

POLITICAL DIVISION	GOVERNMENT	MONETARY UNIT	LANGUAGE	RELIGION
MOZAMBIQUE	Portuguese overseas province ruled by a governor and a government council.	Portuguese escudo	Bantu languages Portuguese	Tribal religions Roman Catholic
MUSCAT AND OMAN	An independent sultanate.	Persian Gulf Indian rupee Maria Theresa dollar	Arabic Hindi	Mohammedan Hindu
NAURU	Republic with a president, cabinet, and legislative assembly.	Australian dollar	English Nauruan	Protestant
NEPAL	Constitutional monarchy, with cabinet, privy council, and a unicameral legislature.	Nepalese rupee	Nepali Hindi Tibetan	Hindu Buddhist Lamaist
NETHERLANDS	A constitutional, hereditary monarchy governed by the queen, her ministers and a two-house legislature, partly elective and partly chosen by provincial councils.	guilder	Dutch	Roman Catholic Protestant
NETHERLANDS ANTILLES	Self-governing part of Netherlands Union with governor, executive council and one-house legislature.	Dutch guilder	Dutch and Papiamento	Roman Catholic Protestant
NEW CALEDONIA	French overseas territory with a governor, a government council and a territorial assembly.	CFP franc	Melanesian dialects French	Roman Catholic Tribal religions
NEW GUINEA, TERR. OF	Australian U.N. trusteeship, governed jointly with Papua by an administrator, an administrative council and a house of assembly.	Australian dollar	Papuan Pidgin English English	Tribal religions Roman Catholic Protestant
NEW HEBRIDES	British and French condominium administered by British and French resident commissioners, with a partly elected advisory council.	Australian dollar New Hebrides franc	Melanesian dialects Pidgin English English French	Tribal religions Protestant Roman Catholic
NEW ZEALAND	An independent member of the British Commonwealth governed by a governor-general, a prime minister, a cabinet and a unicameral assembly.	New Zealand pound	English Maori	Protestant
NICARAGUA	Republic with a president, cabinet and a two-house legislature.	córdoba	Spanish	Roman Catholic
NIGER	One party republic of the French Community, with a president, cabinet, and unicameral legislature.	CFA franc	Sudanese Hamitic Arabic French	Mohammedan Tribal religions
NIGERIA	Federal republic of the British Commonwealth, at present under military rule, with a president, a supreme military council and a federal executive council.	Nigerian pound	Sudanese languages English	Mohammedan Christian Tribal religions
NIUE	New Zealand dependency, with a resident commissioner and a legislative assembly.	New Zealand dollar	Melanesian and Polynesian dialects; English	Protestant

of the World

MAJOR PRODUCTS

Sugar, corn, cotton, copra, sisal, cashew nuts, bananas, coffee, kapok, sorghum, manioc, tea, tobacco, vegetable oils; mangrove bark, timber; oxen, goats, pigs, sheep; gold, silver, asbestos, uranium, bauxite, samerskite.

Dates, pomegranates, limes and other fruits, tobacco, sugar cane; dried fish; petroleum.

Phosphates.

Rice, grains, jute, sugar cane, tea, vegetables, tobacco, cotton, potatoes, medicinal herbs; timber; cattle, hides, skins, ghee; iron, coal, copper, lead, zinc; cotton cloth, pottery, paper.

Potatoes, sugar beets, rye, wheat, oats, barley, flax, legumes, flower bulbs, seeds, vegetables, fruit; cattle, pigs, sheep, horses, poultry; fish; coal, petroleum, natural gas, salt; leather, rubber, footwear; metal products, textiles, paper, building materials, chemicals, foods and beverages, clothing, shipbuilding, cheese, fertilizers, ceramics, cement, tobacco products, petroleum products, machinery.

Fish; dividivi (tannin), crude salt, phosphates; refined petroleum.

Coconuts, copra, coffee, cotton, manioc, corn, tobacco, bananas, pineapples, wheat, rice, kauri logs; cattle, pigs, horses, goats, sheep, hides; guano, trochus shell; nickel, chrome, manganese, iron, cobalt, copper, lead, platinum; canned meat.

Coconuts, copra, cocoa, dairying, timber; gold, silver, platinum; boat making.

Coconuts, copra, cocoa, coffee, yams, taro, manioc, fruits; kauri pine; cattle, pigs; trochus shells.

Wheat, oats, barley, seeds, kauri, gum; sheep, cattle, pigs, horses; hides, skins; fish; gold, silver, coal, copper, limestone, manganese, iron, tungsten; dairy products, meats, wool, clothing, lumber, woodwork, furniture, electrical and radio goods, motor assembly, printing, publishing, biscuits, confections, footwear, rubber products, chemical fertilizers, tobacco products, brewing.

Coffee, sugar cane, sesame, corn, bananas, rice, cacao, cotton, beans; cattle; hardwoods; gold, copper, silver; sugar, wood products.

Millet, manioc, groundnuts, rice, wheat, cotton, gum arabic, kapok, kidney beans, corn, onions, sorghum, dates, sugar cane; goats, sheep, cattle, asses, camels, horses; hides and skins, leather; natron, sodium sulphate, salt, tin.

Palm oil and kernels, cacao, groundnuts, cotton, rubber, bananas, seeds, nuts, cassava, corn, rice, fruits, millet, coffee; cattle, sheep, goats; hides and skins; timber; tin, coal, columbite, gold, petroleum, zinc; cigarettes, soap, sugar.

Copra, sweet potatoes, bananas; hats, baskets.

NEW ZEALAND: Mt. Cook, the country's highest peak, and the Southern Alps are seen across Lake Matheson, on the South Island.

Nat'l Publicity Studios

NORWAY: The popular resort of Balestrand, on the Sogne Fjord in western Norway.

Scandinavian Travel Comm'n

Social and Economic Tables

POLITICAL DIVISION	GOVERNMENT	MONETARY UNIT	LANGUAGE	RELIGION
NORTHERN IRELAND	Executive power vested in appointed governor and cabinet responsible to legislative two-house parliament.	pound sterling	English	Protestant Roman Catholic
NORWAY	A constitutional, hereditary monarchy headed by the king, his council of state and a two-house, elective legislature.	krone (crown)	Norwegian	Protestant
PACIFIC ISLANDS, TRUST TERR.	United States U.N. trusteeship, with a high commissioner and a bicameral Congress of Micronesia.	American dollar	English Micronesian dialects	Roman Catholic Protestant
PAKISTAN	Independent republic within the British Commonwealth ruled by a president, cabinet and unicameral legislature.	Pakistani rupee	Urdu, Bengali, Pujabi, Pushtu, Sindhi, Baluchi English	Mohammedan Hindu
PANAMA	Republic with a president, two vice-presidents, a cabinet and a unicameral legislature.	balboa	Spanish	Roman Catholic
PAPUA	(For Government, see New Guinea, Terr. of)	Australian dollar	Papuan Pidgin English English	Tribal religions Protestant Roman Catholic
PARAGUAY	A centralized republic with a president, an appointed cabinet and a bicameral legislature.	guaraní	Spanish Indian (Guaraní)	Roman Catholic
PERU	A republic with a president, two vice-presidents, appointive cabinet and a two-house legislature.	sol	Spanish Indian (Quechua, Aymará)	Roman Catholic
PHILIPPINES	Republic governed by a president, cabinet and a bicameral legislature.	Philippine peso	Tagalog (Pilipino) English Spanish	Roman Catholic Mohammedan Tribal religions
PITCAIRN ISLANDS	British colony, with a chief magistrate under the governor of Fiji.	New Zealand dollar	English Tahitian	Seventh Day Adventist
POLAND	A Soviet-type "People's Republic" headed by a one-party legislative Sejm which elects an executive Council of Ministers. Actual power in the hands of politburo, highest organ of Communist party.	zloty	Polish	Roman Catholic
PORTUGAL	A "unitary corporative republic" with a president, premier, and a one-house elective legislature.	escudo	Portuguese	Roman Catholic
PORTUGUESE GUINEA	Portuguese overseas province ruled by a governor.	Portuguese escudo	Sudanese languages Portuguese	Tribal religions Roman Catholic
PORTUGUESE TIMOR	Portuguese overseas province ruled by a governor.	Portuguese escudo	Malay Portuguese	Mohammedan Tribal religions Roman Catholic

of the World

MAJOR PRODUCTS

Potatoes, oats, flax, turnips, hay; cattle, sheep, pigs; basalt and igneous rocks, sand and gravel; linen, rayon, woolen goods, carpets, hosiery, cotton goods, shirts, collars, shipbuilding, aircraft, machinery, rope, tobacco, whiskey.

Hay, potatoes, oats, barley, wheat, rye, fruits, vegetables; dairy products, livestock; fish; iron, copper, zinc, nickel, molybdenum; timber; pulp, cellulose, paper, canned foods, electro-chemical products, transportation equipment, salted, dried and canned fish, leather, textiles, fertilizers, shipbuilding, aluminum.

Copra, vegetables, fish, tropical fruits, coconuts, trochus shell; poultry, livestock.

Rice, wheat, corn, jute, cotton, sugar cane, fruit, oilseeds, tobacco, tea, fibers; timber; cattle, goats, sheep, horses, camels; hides, skins, wool; fish; salt, copper, petroleum, chromite, gypsum, limestone, natural gas, antimony; textiles, flour, cement, iron and steel, sugar, leather, chemicals, glass, sportsgoods, handicrafts, surgical instruments.

Bananas, cacao, abacá, coconuts, rice, sugar cane, coffee, pineapples; fish, shellfish, cattle; hardwoods; gold; hides, sugar, wood products, textiles, leather products.

Coconuts, rubber, sweet potatoes, yams, taro, sago, rice, bananas, coffee, kapok, bamboo, sisal hemp, copra; shells, sponges; cattle, goats, poultry; gold, copper, manganese.

Cotton, tobacco, sugar cane, rice, yerba maté, corn, coffee, citrus fruits; cattle, hides; lumber, quebracho; iron, manganese, copper; canned meats, vegetable oils, cigarettes.

Cotton, sugar, potatoes, barley, corn, rice, wheat, coca, quinoa, cacao, tobacco, coffee, quinine, flax, rubber, balata, guano; fish; livestock; petroleum, lead, zinc, copper, silver, gold, vanadium; textiles, foodstuffs, cement, leather, wool, hides, pharmaceuticals, paper products, clothing, metal.

Rice, sugar cane, copra, manila hemp (abacá), corn, tobacco, maguey, rubber, bananas, pineapples, mangoes, papaya, citrus fruits; hogs, carabaos, cattle, horses; fish; timber, gum resins, tan and dye barks; gold, iron, copper, chromite, silver, manganese, asbestos, asphalt, coal, petroleum; sugar, textiles, distilling, desiccated coconuts, tobacco products, rice milling, cocoa, coconut oil, embroideries.

Fruits, vegetables, goats, poultry; handicraft.

Potatoes, hay, rye, sugar beets, oats, barley, wheat, peas, beans, flax, hemp, rapeseed; livestock; fish; zinc, lead, coal, salt, iron ore, petroleum, natural gas, phosphates, lignite; iron and steel, coke, foods and beverages, textiles, cement, lime, bricks, electrical goods, chemicals, wood, timber, paper, cellulose, leather, leather products, glass.

Wheat, corn, oats, barley, rye, rice, beans, potatoes, grapes, olives; livestock; cork, lumber, resin; fish; copper pyrites, coal, copper, tin, kaolin, cement, wolfram, sulphur, tungsten, iron; wines, olive oil, canned sardines, textiles, porcelain, tiles, embroideries, lace, jute, machinery.

Rice, palm kernels and oil, wax, groundnuts; hides.

Coffee, copra, sandalwood, wax, cocoa; hides, shells.

PERU: The beginning of festivities in the bull ring in Lima, the capital city.

Pan American World Airways

PORTUGAL: The Praça dos Restauradores in Lisbon, with the monument dedicated to the seventeenth century restorers of Portuguese independence.

Photo "Sni-Yan"

Social and Economic Tables

POLITICAL DIVISION	GOVERNMENT	MONETARY UNIT	LANGUAGE	RELIGION
PUERTO RICO	Self-governing "free state" associated with the United States, with a governor, advisory council, and a bicameral legislature.	American dollar	Spanish, English	Roman Catholic
QATAR	British protected sheikhdom, advised by a political agent.	riyal	Arabic	Mohammedan
RÉUNION	French overseas department, with a prefect and general council.	French franc	French	Roman Catholic
RHODESIA	Self-governing British Commonwealth member, with a governor, prime minister, cabinet, and legislative assembly. Unilateral independence declared in 1965.	Rhodesian pound	Bantu languages English	Tribal religions Protestant
RUMANIA	A Soviet-type "People's Republic" with a president, a 17-member State Council, cabinet of ministers and a one-house legislature. Supreme power resides in Communist party politburo.	leu	Rumanian	Rumanian Orthodox
RWANDA	An independent republic with a president, a council of ministers and a legislative assembly.	Rwanda franc	Kinyarwanda Swahili French	Tribal religions Roman Catholic
RYUKYU IS.	U.S. administered, with a high commissioner, civil administrator and an elected local chief executive and unicameral legislature.	American dollar	Luchuan Japanese English	Shinto Animism Christian
ST. HELENA	British colony with a governor, advisory and executive councils.	pound sterling	English	Protestant
ST. PIERRE AND MIQUELON	French overseas territory with a governor, privy council and elective general council.	CFA franc	French	Roman Catholic
SAN MARINO	Republic with two regents, council of state, one-house legislature.	lira	Italian	Roman Catholic
SÃO TOMÉ AND PRÍNCIPE	Portuguese overseas province administered by a governor.	Portuguese escudo	Bantu languages Portuguese	Tribal religions Roman Catholic
SAUDI ARABIA	Absolute monarchy, with premier and cabinet responsible to the king and advisory councils.	riyal	Arabic	Mohammedan
SCOTLAND	A secretary of state for Scotland in the British cabinet has in his charge four departments for agriculture, education, health and home. Authority in other matters is exercised by other members of the British cabinet.	pound sterling	English and Gaelic	Protestant
SENEGAL	Republic in the French Community, with a president, cabinet, and unicameral legislature.	CFA franc	Sudanese languages French	Mohammedan Tribal religions Roman Catholic
SEYCHELLES	British colony with a governor and executive and legislative councils.	Mauritius rupee	English French	Roman Catholic
SIERRA LEONE	One party member of the British Commonwealth, with prime minister, cabinet and unicameral legislature, at present under a military junta.	leone	Sudanese languages English Creole	Tribal religions Mohammedan Christian

of the World

MAJOR PRODUCTS

Sugar cane, tobacco, fruits, pineapples, grapefruit, coconuts, coffee, cotton, livestock, vegetables; molasses, embroideries, rum, canned fruit and juice, alcohol, cordials, tobacco products.

Dates; pearl fishing, dried fish; camels; petroleum.

Sugar, rum, vanilla, tapioca, essences, fruit and vegetable preserves.

Corn, tobacco, groundnuts, wheat, potatoes, cotton, tea, sugar, citrus and other fruits; cattle, sheep, pigs, goats; meats, hides; copper, gold, asbestos, chromite, coal; footwear, apparel, cigarettes, flour, groundnut oil, wood products.

Wheat, barley, rye, corn, oats, potatoes, sugar beets, hemp, flax, grapes, fruits, tobacco; lumber; sheep, cattle, pigs, horses; petroleum, natural gas, salt, coal, lignite, iron and copper ores, gold, silver, bauxite, lead, manganese, zinc; flour, brewing and distilling, iron and steel, metal products, textiles, wood and paper products.

Coffee, cotton, tea, corn, groundnuts, vegetables; cattle, goats; hides; cassiterite, pyrethrum.

Sweet potatoes, sugar cane, rice, fruits, mulberries; swine, cattle, goats, horses, poultry; silkworms; fish; Panama hats, textiles, lacquer, pottery, china, glassware, tiles, plywood.

Hemp, lily bulbs, potatoes, tow, rope and twine, lace; sheep, goats, cattle, donkeys, poultry.

Fish, silver fox; dried cod and cod liver oil; sienna earth, yellow ocher.

Cattle, hides, wines, quarrying; textiles, tiles, ceramics.

Cacao, coffee, coconuts, copra, palm oil, cinchona, bananas.

Dates, sorghum, wheat, rice, henna, coffee, fruits, nuts, vegetables, gum, sesame oil; fish; camels, sheep, goats, cattle, donkeys, horses; hides, wool, butter, charcoal, pottery, salt, soap; petroleum, gold, pearls, copper, lead, silver.

Turnips, potatoes, wheat, barley, sugar beets, flax, vegetables, furits; sheep, cattle, horses; coal, iron ore, granite, sandstone, limestone, slate, lead, clay; steel, machinery, tools, locomotives, electronic equipment, linoleum, shipbuilding, watches, bagging, textiles, hosiery, thread, lace, carpet, yarn, chemicals, whiskey, paper, clay products, preserves, boots and shoes, furniture.

Millet, groundnuts, manioc, rice, corn, gum arabic, palm nuts, honey, sisal, indigo; sheep, goats, cattle; fish; titanium, phosphates; brick, pottery, weaving, jewelry, oil cakes.

Coconuts, cinnamon, patchouli, copra, vanilla, corn; guano; salted fish, tortoise shell, calipee.

Palm oil and kernels, coffee, kola nuts, ginger, piassava, groundnuts, cocoa; diamonds, iron ore, chrome ore.

PUERTO RICO: One of the island's chief products, pineapples, on their way to the cannery.

Hamilton Wright

SCOTLAND: Loch Garten, a highland lake in the eastern part of Inverness.

British Travel Ass'n

Social and Economic Tables

POLITICAL DIVISION	GOVERNMENT	MONETARY UNIT	LANGUAGE	RELIGION
SINGAPORE	Republic in the British Commonwealth, with a president, cabinet, and unicameral legislature.	Singapore dollar	Malay Chinese Tamil English	Confucianist Buddhist Taoist; Hindu Mohammedan Christian
SOLOMON ISLANDS	British protectorate, with high commissioner and executive and legislative councils.	Australian dollar	Melanesian Pidgin English English	Tribal religions Protestant Roman Catholic
SOMALI REPUBLIC	Republic with a president, prime minister, cabinet, and a unicameral legislature.	Somali shilling	Somali; Arabic Italian English	Mohammedan
SOUTH AFRICA	Republic with a state president, prime minister, executive council and bicameral legislature.	rand	Afrikaans English Bantu languages Bushman	Protestant Roman Catholic Mohammedan Hindu Buddhist
SOUTHERN YEMEN	Republic with president and cabinet.	South Arabian dinar	Arabic	Mohammedan
SOUTH-WEST AFRICA	Mandated to South Africa, now governed by an administrator and legislative assembly, with representation in the South African legislature.	South African rand	Afrikaans English; German Bantu languages Bushman	Tribal religions Protestant Roman Catholic
SPAIN	A nominal monarchy governed by a chief of state. The legislative Cortés prepares laws subject to the veto of the chief of state. A king is to be chosen by a regency council upon the death or incapacitation of the chief of state.	peseta	Spanish Catalan	Roman Catholic
SPANISH SAHARA	Overseas Spanish province, with a high commissioner, cabinet and a unicameral legislature.	Spanish peseta	Arabic Spanish	Mohammedan
SUDAN	Republic at present under a council of state, nominally aided by a premier and an assembly.	Sudanese pound	Arabic Sudanese and Hamitic languages English	Mohammedan Tribal religions Christian
SURINAM	Self-governing part of the Netherlands Union, with governor, ministerial, advisory, and legislative councils.	Netherlands Antilles guilder	Dutch	Christian Moslem Hindu
SWAZILAND	Monarchy within the British Commonwealth, with a prime minister, cabinet and bicameral legislature.	South African rand	Bantu languages English Afrikaans	Tribal religions Christian missions
SWEDEN	A constitutional hereditary monarchy with a prime minister, council of state and a two-house elective legislature.	krona (crown)	Swedish	Protestant
SWITZERLAND	A republic with a president, vice-president, an executive federal council and a two-house, elective legislature.	Swiss franc	German French Italian Romansch	Protestant Roman Catholic

of the World

MAJOR PRODUCTS

Rubber, coconuts, fruits, vegetables, rice, coffee, tapioca, tobacco, sweet potatoes, pepper, pineapples; pigs, poultry, cattle; fish; tin; tin smelting, rubber milling, coconut milling, soap, beer, pineapple canning, biscuits, brick making, shipping, textiles, palm oil, cigarettes, gasoline, kerosene.

Copra, pigs, poultry; trochus shell, turtle shell, bêche-de-mer.

Sugar, cotton, tobacco, bananas, aromatic gums, resin, kapok, grains, beans; camels, goats, sheep, cattle; skins, hides; tunny, mother-of-pearl.

Corn, wheat, potatoes, oats, kaffir-corn, barley, tobacco, sugar cane, tea, citrus fruits, rye, groundnuts, grapes, pineapples; cattle, sheep, goats, pigs, horses, donkeys, mules; gold, coal, diamonds, copper, asbestos, manganese, lime, limestone, platinum, chrome, iron, silver, tungsten, mercury, vanadium, tin, antimony, silver, uranium, talc; hides, chemicals, wool, footwear, rubber, machinery, clothing, textiles, food, vehicles, printing, furniture, building materials, steel.

Dates, gums, tobacco, salt, fish oil, butter; wheat, barley, sesame, millet, sorghum, aloes, ghee; goats, sheep, camels, cattle; dhow building, ship bunkering.

Cattle, donkeys, horses, pigs; karakul; fish; diamonds, copper, lead, zinc, salt, tin, manganese, germanium.

Wheat, barley, potatoes, oranges, olives, oats, rye, rice, corn, peas, beans, grapes, onions, sugar beets, esparto, flax, hemp, pulse, cork, nuts; livestock and poultry; fish; coal, lignite, iron ore, lead, iron pyrites, potash, zinc, mercury, sulphur, copper; textiles, wines, olive oil, paper, cement, hides, leather, chemicals, machinery, vehicles, iron and steel, furniture.

Barley, corn; goats, sheep, camels; fish.

Cotton, cotton seed, gum arabic, Senna leaves and pods, groundnuts, sesame, millet, dates, dom nuts (vegetable ivory), wheat, shea nuts; sheep, goats, cattle, camels, asses; mahogany; hides and skins, ivory, gold, salt, trochus shell, mother-of-pearl.

Rice, citrus fruits, coconuts, coffee, bananas, sugar cane, cacao, balata, corn, tobacco; lumber; gold, bauxite; sugar, rum, plywood, molasses.

Tobacco, corn, groundnuts, kaffir-corn, sugar cane, wheat, oats, rye, barley; cotton, rice, fruits; cattle, goats, sheep, pigs; timber; butter; hides, skins; asbestos, gold, tin, iron.

Hay, sugar beets, potatoes, oats, wheat, rye, barley; forest products; cattle, pigs, sheep, horses; fish; iron ore, sulphur, arsenic, zinc, copper, silver, gold, lead, manganese; wood products, machinery, textiles, iron and steel, metal goods, chemicals, dairy products, tobacco products, porcelain, glass, shipbuilding, matches.

Wheat, potatoes, sugar beets, rye, oats, barley, fruits, tobacco; livestock; salt, iron, manganese; dairy products, textiles, watches and clocks, chemicals, foods, wines, dyes, drugs, machinery.

SOUTH AFRICA: Commissioner Street, in the downtown part of Johannesburg, the country's largest city.

South African Gov't Info. Office

SWITZERLAND: Milk still being delivered by dog cart in a rural section of the republic.

TWA–Trans World Airlines

Social and Economic Tables

POLITICAL DIVISION	GOVERNMENT	MONETARY UNIT	LANGUAGE	RELIGION
SYRIA	Officially the Syrian Arab Republic, with a president and cabinet, under a revolutionary council.	Syrian pound	Arabic Turkish Kurdish	Mohammedan Christian
TANZANIA	United republic within the British Commonwealth, with a president, two vice-presidents, cabinet, and two national assemblies (Tanganyika and Zanzibar).	Tanzanian shilling	Bantu languages English Arabic Swahili Gujarati	Tribal religions Mohammedan Christian missions
THAILAND (SIAM)	Constitutional monarchy, with a prime minister, council and a bicameral legislature.	baht	Thai Khmer	Buddhist Mohammedan Confucianist
TOGO	Republic of the French Community, with a president and a council of ministers.	CFA franc	Sudanese languages French	Tribal religions Mohammedan Roman Catholic
TOKELAU ISLANDS	An island territory of New Zealand with a high commissioner.	New Zealand dollar	Samoan	Protestant Roman Catholic
TONGA	British protected autonomous constitutional monarchy, with a privy council, cabinet and unicameral legislature. Independence sought.	pa'anga	Tongan English	Protestant Roman Catholic
TRINIDAD AND TOBAGO	Independent British Commonwealth member, with prime minister, cabinet, and a bicameral legislature.	Trinidad and Tobago dollar	English	Roman Catholic Protestant Hindu; Moslem
TRUCIAL OMAN	Seven sheikhdoms under British protection with a British agent.	riyal	Arabic	Mohammedan
TUNISIA	A republic with a president, a cabinet of secretaries of state, and an assembly.	Tunisian dinar	Arabic French Berber	Mohammedan Roman Catholic
TURKEY	Republic with a president, prime minister, cabinet, and a bicameral legislature.	Turkish pound (lira)	Turkish Kurdish Arabic	Mohammedan
UGANDA	Republic of the British Commonwealth, with a president, vice-president, cabinet and assembly.	Uganda shilling	Sudanese, Bantu, Hamitic languages English	Tribal religions Christian
U.S.S.R.	A federation of 15 socialist republics with a two-chamber legislative assembly (Supreme Soviet) which elects the executive presidium and council of ministers. The policy of the state is largely defined by the Central Committee of the Communist party, the only legal party.	ruble	Russian, Ukrainian, White Russian, Uzbek, Tatar, Azerbaidzhani, Georgian, Lithuanian, Armenian, Yiddish, Latvian, Mordvinian, Chuvash, Tadzhik, Estonian, Kazakh, etc.	Russian Orthodox Moslem
UNITED ARAB REP. (EGYPT)	Republic with a president (with supreme powers), cabinet, and elected unicameral legislature.	Egyptian pound	Arabic	Mohammedan Christian minorities
UNITED KINGDOM	See: England and Wales, Northern Ireland, Scotland.			

of the World

Wheat, barley, sorghum, corn, cotton, vegetables, olives, grapes, tobacco; sheep, goats, cattle, camels, horses; wool, hides, skins; gypsum; leather, textiles, cement, wine, flour.

Sisal, cotton, cloves, coffee, bananas, tobacco, papain, vegetables, nuts, tea, oil seeds, beeswax, grains, sugar; cattle, goats, sheep; hides, skins; wood, timber, wax, gum arabic; diamonds, gold, mica, salt, camphor, tungsten, lead, silver; cement, textiles, petroleum products.

Rice, rubber, coconuts, sugar cane, tobacco, cotton, corn, beans; teak and other woods; bullocks, buffalo, horses, elephants; fish; tin, wolfram; lac, jute.

Palm oil and kernels, tapioca, cocoa, yams, coffee, plantains, corn, groundnuts, cotton, copra, kola, cassava, rubber; sheep, goats, pigs, cattle, asses, horses; phosphates.

Coconuts, fiber, taro, copra; pigs, chickens; fish; hats, mats.

Copra, bananas, fungus, candlenuts; pigs, cattle, goats.

THAILAND: The heroine and hero in costume for a classical dance in the Asian kingdom.

Gov't of Thailand

Coffee, cocoa, sugar cane, citrus fruits; cattle; petroleum, asphalt; rum, canned grapefruit juice, sugar, chemicals, textiles, plastic products.

Dates, grains, vegetables; fishing, pearl fishing.

Wheat, barley, oats, corn, sorghum, beans, grapes, olives, nuts, citrus fruits, dates, oranges, cork; sheep, goats, cattle, horses, asses, camels; fish, sponges; flour milling, oil refining, wine, olive oil, wool spinning, pottery, leather, silk weaving; phosphates, iron ore, lead, silver.

Tobacco, cereals, olives, cotton, figs, nuts, fruits; cattle, livestock; fish; chromium, iron ore, copper, coal, lignite, meerschaum, manganese; textiles, iron and steel, paper, rugs, olive oil, cement, petroleum products.

Cotton, coffee, tea, plantains, sisal, groundnuts, millet, cotton seed, tobacco, chilies, sugar cane, rubber; cattle, sheep, goats; hides, skins; copper, gold, phosphates, tin; cigarettes.

Wheat, rye, oats, barley, corn, sugar beets, sunflower seeds, cotton, forage crops, flax, hemp, potatoes, tobacco; cattle, sheep, goats, pigs, horses; lumber, furs; fish; coal, peat, petroleum, iron, lignite, copper, lead, zinc, nickel, aluminum, phosphates, manganese, gold, sulphur, potash, asbestos, platinum, salt, chromite; steel, machinery, textiles, sugar, flour, meats, automobilcs, paper, synthetic rubber, foods, wines, chemicals.

TURKEY: The Galata Bridge, spanning the Golden Horn in Istanbul, one of the most heavily traveled bridges in the world.

Turkish Info. Office

Cotton, barley, wheat, rice, sugar cane, onions, oil seeds, corn, millet, fruits, vegetables; sheep, goats, cattle, buffalo, camels; fish; petroleum, cement, phosphates, salt, manganese, asbestos, chromite; cotton ginning, milling, pottery, perfume, soap, iron and steel.

Social and Economic Tables

POLITICAL DIVISION	GOVERNMENT	MONETARY UNIT	LANGUAGE	RELIGION
UNITED STATES	Federal republic with a president, vice-president and two-house legislature (senate and house of representatives), and an appointed cabinet. It consists of 50 states, each with a governor and state legislature.	American dollar	English	Protestant Roman Catholic Judaist
UPPER VOLTA	One party republic of the French Community, at present under a president ruling by decree, and a military dominated council.	CFA franc	Sudanese languages French	Tribal religions Mohammedan
URUGUAY	A republic governed by a National Council, an appointed cabinet and a two-house elective legislature.	Uruguayan peso	Spanish	Roman Catholic
VATICAN CITY	The Pope, elected for life by cardinals of the Roman Catholic Church, exercises absolute legislative, executive and judicial power. He appoints a governor of the state.	Italian lira	Italian Latin	Roman Catholic
VENEZUELA	A republic with a president, appointive cabinet, and elective two-house legislature.	bolívar	Spanish	Roman Catholic
VIETNAM	Divided in two parts by Armistice Line Sept. 1954. North of 17th parallel is Communist controlled "republic." South is a republic with a president and a bicameral legislature.	South: piastre North: dong	Vietnamese Khmer Lao French	Taoist Buddhist Confucianist Roman Catholic
VIRGIN ISLANDS (BR.)	British colony with an administrator, an executive and a legislative council.	B.W.I. dollar	English Creole	Protestant
VIRGIN ISLANDS (U.S.)	U.S. territory with an appointed governor, local executive departments and a local unicameral legislature.	American dollar	English Creole	Roman Catholic Protestant
WESTERN SAMOA	Independent state, with a head of state, prime minister, cabinet and unicameral legislature.	Western Samoa pound	Samoan English	Protestant Tribal religions
WEST IRIAN	Indonesian administered with independence due before 1969, ruled by a governor and a legislative assembly.	West Irian rupiah	Indonesian Papuan	Tribal religions
YEMEN	Under interim rule with rival royal and republican factions in control of parts of the country.	riyal	Arabic	Mohammedan
YUGOSLAVIA	A Soviet-type republic combining six republics under a central government with a president, fed. executive council and two-house elective legislature. Actually ruled by Communist League.	Yugoslav dinar	Serbian-Croatian Slovenian Macedonian	Eastern Orthodox Roman Catholic Mohammedan
ZAMBIA	Independent republic within the British Commonwealth, with a president, a cabinet and a unicameral legislature.	kwacha	Bantu languages English	Tribal religions

MAJOR PRODUCTS

Corn, hay, tobacco, wheat, cotton, oats, soy beans, potatoes, barley, sorghums, peanuts, rye, rice, citrus fruits, fruits, sugar beets, sugar cane, vegetables, tree nuts, feed grains and hay; livestock; fish; lumber; petroleum, coal, cement, iron, natural gas, copper, sand and gravel, zinc, lead, stone, gold, silver, molybdenum, bauxite, phosphates, mica, sulphur; foods, transportation equipment, machinery, primary metal products, electrical machinery, textiles, chemicals, paper and wood products, beverages, dairy products.

Millet, groundnuts, corn, karite nuts and butter (shea nut), vegetables, rice, tapes, cotton, kapok, sesame, sorghum, tea; sheep, goats, cattle, asses, pigs; gold, manganese, copper, silver, chrome, lignite, iron; hides and skins.

Wheat, corn, oats, seeds, peanuts, barley, rice, citrus fruits, peaches, grapes, vegetables, tobacco; sheep, cattle; gold; meat, hides, wool, textiles, leather, shoes, wines, chemicals.

UNITED STATES: The American Falls at Niagara Falls, New York, a major tourist attraction.
N.Y. State Dep't of Commerce

Coffee, cacao, sugar cane, corn, rice, cotton, tobacco, coconuts, beans, bananas, rubber; livestock; fish, pearls; petroleum, iron, gold, coal, copper, phosphates, nickel, asphalt, salt, diamonds; textiles, leather, sugar, cement, wood products, chemicals, vehicles, food products, meats; refined petroleum.

Rice, corn, sugar, tobacco, coffee, fruits, nuts, tea, cotton, medicinal plants, soya, rubber, copra, groundnuts, sweet potatoes, cinnamon; bamboo, silk; cattle, buffalo, pigs; lumber; gold, tin, copper, coal, zinc, iron, cement, limestone, calamine, tungsten, manganese, phosphate, lead, bauxite; paper, textiles, chemicals, cement, sugar.

Poultry and livestock, fish, fruit, vegetables.

Vegetables, citrus fruits, coconuts; cattle; fish; rum, bay rum, bay oil, molasses, handicrafts, sugar, lime juice, hides, bitters.

Copra, cocoa beans, bananas, taro; fish; pigs, poultry.

Sago, coconuts, sweet potatoes, wild nutmeg, mace, copra; bird of paradise plumes; petroleum.

Coffee, barley, wheat, millet, sesame; cattle, hides; fish.

Wheat, barley, rye, oats, corn, sugar beets, hemp, hops, opium, tobacco, flax, alfalfa, vegetables, fruits; sheep, cattle, pigs, goats, horses, poultry; coal, lignite, iron, copper, lead, salt, zinc, mercury, antimony, petroleum, bauxite, chrome, cement; lumber, textiles, foods, beverages, sugar, wood-distillates, wines, machinery, chemicals, shipbuilding.

Corn, wheat, potatoes, tobacco, sorghum, millet, groundnuts, cassava, rice, beans, cowpeas, cotton; lumber; cattle; copper, lead, manganese, zinc, cobalt, tin.

VENEZUELA: Avenida Bolívar and the thirty story office buildings of downtown Caracas.
Hamilton Wright

ECUADOR: Independence Plaza in Quito, with the Cathedral, the center of tourist activity in the country.
Hamilton Wright

ENGLAND: Trafalgar Square and the famous pillar dedicated to Lord Nelson, in London.
British Info. Services

AUSTRALIA: A view of Sydney Harbour, with the botanical gardens at Farm Cove in the foreground.
Qantas

INDIA: The Hawa Mahal at Jaipur, in the state of Rajasthan, with old and new forms of transportation.
Gov't of India Info. Bur.

TRINIDAD & TOBAGO: A typical mosque in Port of Spain.
Trinidad & Tobago Tourist Board

INDEX OF PRINCIPAL CITIES OF THE WORLD

This alphabetical list of cities and towns gives statistics of population based on the latest official census reports or most recent reliable estimates. Each line begins with the name of a place, followed by the name of the country or state, the population, the index reference and plate number. This index reference gives the location of the city or town name on the accompanying map plates. The name is found within the square formed by the two lines of latitude or longitude which enclose each of the co-ordinates—i.e. the marginal letters and numbers. In the case of maps consisting entirely of insets, the name is found near the intersection point of imaginary lines connecting the co-ordinates.

Where space on the map has not permitted giving the complete form of a name, the extended form is shown in the index. Where a place may be known under different names or by various spellings of the same name, the different forms have been included, to a large extent, in the index. Where an alternative spelling in parentheses is shown on the map itself, the first name gives the local official form, the conventional form following in parentheses.

* Capitals of countries, states and provinces. † Population figure includes suburbs or subdivision.